Square and
Folk Dancing

Square and Folk Dancing

A Complete Guide for Students, Teachers and Callers

HANK GREENE

Drawings by Manosalvas

Harper & Row, Publishers, New York
Cambridge, Philadelphia, San Francisco, London
Mexico City, São Paulo, Sydney

1817

Grateful acknowledgment is made for permission to reprint:

"Pistol Packin' Mama." Copyright © 1942 Vogue Music. Copyright renewed. (c/o The Welk Music Group, Santa Monica, CA 90401.) Used by permission.

"Alla en el Rancho Grande." Copyright © Edward B. Marks Music Corporation. Used by permission.

"Mañana" by Peggy Lee and Dave Barbour. Copyright © 1948 by Criterion Music Corp. Copyright renewed 1976 Criterion Music Corp. Used with permission. All rights reserved.

FIRST EDITION

Designer: *Sheila Lynch*

Library of Congress Cataloging in Publication Data

Greene, Hank.
   Square and folk dancing.

   Bibliography: p.
   1. Square dancing.   2. Folk dancing.   3. Square
dancing—Study and teaching.   4. Folk dancing—Study
and teaching.   I. Title.
GV1763.G69   1984   793.3'4   84-47575
ISBN 0-06-015325-3
ISBN 0-06-464088-4 (pbk.)

84 85 86 87 88 1 2 3 4 5 6 7 8 9 10
84 85 86 87 88 1 2 3 4 5 6 7 8 9 10

To Charlotte, my uncompromising wife:
a demanding dance partner and literary critic who never
permits me
to make a misstep in either field

CONTENTS

ACKNOWLEDGMENTS

First among those who must be mentioned is my wife, Charlotte, whose razor-sharp mind excised the inadvertent cliché, the redundant phrase, and the overworked commentary.

I wish to express my thanks to Manosalvas, whose charming illustrations succeeded admirably in capturing the flavor of the many square dance figures.

Special appreciation goes posthumously to my dear friend and the talented musician Vincent Maffei for his piano arrangements of the square dance music.

John Kaltenthaler, executive secretary of Callerlab, has my gratitude for providing me with important, up-to-date historical notes on the objectives and achievements of Callerlab.

I am indebted to Daniel Bial of Harper & Row, whose intuitive ability to home in on language both precise and concise and whose gift for unraveling sequential snarls helped me create a more functional text.

My gratitude also goes out to the many dancers who have responded to my calls and instructions over the years. Their enthusiasm (or occasional lack thereof) to the various dances I introduced in one-night stands or in my many classes gave me the insight necessary for the selection of the square and folk dances included in this book.

The following music publishers gave me permission to include special piano arrangements of songs protected by copyright:

Marks Music Corporation for "El Rancho Grande"
Welk Music Group for "Pistol Packin' Mama"
Criterion Music Corporation for "Mañana"

FOREWORD

I can think of no one better qualified to write a book on square and folk dancing than Hank Greene. His varied experience has given him the background to bridge the gap between the rich historical heritage inherent in this dance form and the fresh approaches needed to sustain and advance it in today's world.

Square and Folk Dancing: A Complete Guide for Students, Teachers and Callers is a book long overdue. Its innovative schematic presentations of square dance calls and folk dance instructions meet the needs of both novice and experienced leaders. Important facets of the art, such as tempo, timing and transitions are emphasized, as well as movement anticipation and cueing finesse. It also serves as a storehouse of terms and dance techniques for beginners and advanced dancers. The music and accompanying lyrics for the singing calls and the clear illustrations provide additional reinforcement for teachers and students alike.

The book gives wise, concrete advice to the caller on how to cope with problems arising from the structural shortcomings of a dance area. It also includes a fascinating treatment of the historical development of the square and folk dance movement. Of special interest is the chapter that explains how dances should be revised to meet the particular requirements of senior citizens.

Hank Greene was the Chairman of the Department of Health and Physical Education at Samuel J. Tilden High School in Brooklyn, New York, where he taught classes in folk, square, and social dancing for a number of years. At Tilden he organized and conducted many assembly dance programs and festivals. He inaugurated the first coeducational program in square and folk dancing in the New York City high schools. He not only continues to lead square and folk dance groups in New York City and other areas in the Northeast, but has also involved himself in a very particular interest: leading square and folk dances for deaf adults.

Many of the dances described in this book were included in Hank Greene's doctoral dissertation, which he completed at Teachers College, Columbia University.

This book will be a significant addition to the body of knowledge in this field and will be enjoyed by teachers and students, callers and dancers.

Gene Ezersky, Ed.D.
Former Director of Outdoor Education/Recreation Education,
New York University
District Director, NYC Programs,
Cornell University, Cooperative Extension

Square and
Folk Dancing

INTRODUCTION

Square and folk dancing has a universal appeal which encompasses all ages and levels of ability. Young children, teenagers, adults, senior citizens, even certain handicapped groups derive enormous satisfaction from this activity. The social interplay at a square dance function is unique, often allowing insecure dancers to shed their inhibitions in the homespun ambiance. I saw this happen time and time again at a large New York City high school where I taught square and folk dancing for many years. Teenagers who were shy, insecure and self-conscious blossomed into exuberant participants. Boys, unburdened by the need to take the initiative in asking a girl to dance (as is expected in a regular social dance situation), became relaxed and confident. Male and female were able to dance together unselfconsciously, realizing that no eyes were focusing on them alone, since they were members of a group. Their only responsibility was to respond to the caller.

Adults, of course, may suffer from the same insecurities. Many have discovered that square and folk dancing provide a potion that dissolves aloofness and shyness. They have learned that square and folk dance affairs have an aura of neighborly wholesomeness. Because of the informal attire and "folksy" atmosphere, the dancers can "let down their hair" and enjoy an evening of friendly banter and shared pleasure in the learning and perfecting of these dance skills.

Large numbers of senior citizens have also been drawn into the ever-widening circle of square and folk dancers. Their enjoyment is as keen as that of younger groups, but because of their age and some

1

physical limitations, they require specialized dance material. For this reason, I have included a separate chapter directed particularly to the older population. Recreation leaders in charge of senior citizen centers can consult this chapter to learn how to revise the more energetic dance steps so that they meet the special needs of this age group.

Over the years I have had my share of rewarding experiences working with teenagers, adults and senior citizens, but none was as heartwarming as my introduction to an organization called LARO ("oral" spelled backwards). The members of this group are either completely deaf or seriously hearing-impaired. They communicate by reading lips and verbalizing instead of using sign language, which means they can have conversations with hearing people as well as with their own deaf peers.

For me, the preparation for their function was as much fun as conducting it. A group of four couples came to my home one week prior to the affair to rehearse as a pilot group. I invented hand and body signals for the simpler moves such as "circle," "swing," "promenade," "do-sa-do," "star," "balance," and "sashay" and taught them to the group. The dancers were enthralled. Although they could not hear the music, they sensed the drum beat and thus were able to move in unison.

I mimeographed instructions for six square dances, together with sketches of the hand and body signals. These instructions were distributed to the general membership for study.

The function was a huge success. The pilot group demonstrated the dances in response to my signals, then the entire club performed them to live music. (They had insisted on a complete band because they wanted every aspect of the affair to have the ingredients of a dance for hearing people.)

For me, as well as for the members of the LARO club, this was a thrill of a lifetime. It proved that even the deaf or hearing-impaired can reap the rewards of this most enjoyable pastime.

What are square and folk dances? Square dances are easy to identify: they always involve four couples in a set who are led by a caller through a variety of maneuvers and formations.

Folk dances, on the other hand, may be performed by couples, by groups or in circles. They are the artistic expression, through the medium of the dance and natural rhythmic movements, of the joys, fears, hopes and sorrows shared by a group of people. They are organized national dances which are passed on from generation to generation. In this sense, a square dance should be considered one type of American folk dance. Folk dances can be instruments for enriching the cultural awareness of participants, highlighting one's own heritage as well as demonstrating the nature of other cultures.

I'm not exaggerating when I say it's patriotic to join a square dance!

Square and folk dancing in this country has become so popular that on June 1, 1982, President Reagan signed a bill designating the square dance as the national folk dance of the United States.

How to Use This Book

Students

You do not have to aspire to great heights of performance, expertise and style to make use of this book. It was designed for beginners as well as those who have had some experience in square and folk dancing.

A student has several things to learn. First you must become familiar with the terminology. To do so, consult the two glossaries in the back of the book, where every square and folk dance figure used in the descriptions is fully described.

Then you should learn the dances. This book contains descriptions of fifty-six square dances and twenty-eight folk dances. If you learn all the square and folk dance steps and patterns included in them, you can be completely confident in even the most serious dance company.

In the square dance sections, the dance descriptions have been kept as brief as possible without sacrificing clarity. Thus, in reading a square dance description for the first time you can quickly get a fairly comprehensive idea of the individual movements as well as the formation changes. If you are reading a dance description as a "refresher," you will be spared the chore of having to wade through lengthy explanations.

To encourage rapid learning of any of the square dances, all the calls are presented first. In many instances this will be all you need to understand the movements. The call explanations (with numbered lines corresponding to the call lines) follow, spelling out in detail the meaning of each call.

You may think of yourself primarily as a student, but don't let that keep you from reading the sections for teacher/callers. Someday the time may come when you'll be asked to call a few dances. People will know of your superior talent and knowledge and ask you to help them out. Be prepared! It will be worth it. I, for one, enjoy leading a dance as much as dancing one.

In the area of folk dancing, this book can also serve as a launching pad for both beginners and those with more experience. Many of the most common folk dance steps are described in detail. If you have ever been to a folk dance session led by a professional leader, you can refer to the text and/or glossary to give your memory a boost.

Square Dance Teacher/Callers

The material presented in chapters 5 and 6 includes traditional calls, several of my original calls and some new modern calls. The dances, which progress from the simple to the complex, were carefully selected for their wide range of figures and maneuvers, all of which are described in detail. To eliminate any confusion, I have included illustrations of key maneuvers.

This book takes the guesswork out of patter calls. It contains a unique visual device—my teaching "invention," if you will. Although simple, it is enormously effective and has proven to be of great assistance to callers of all levels of ability. The device is a verbal-schematic method of teaching square dance calls, and very clearly delineates word phrasing, word emphasis, timing, cueing and transitions. A number of patter call sequences are analyzed in the book using the schematic method. Study these examples carefully, and then you will be able to apply the principles of timing and cueing to any patter square dance calls.

Singing calls do not have a timing problem. Most of the singing calls here are accompanied by the sheet music and the lyrics. By studying the music you can learn precisely how the calls and dance figures coordinate with the musical line. No formal knowledge of music is necessary. You have merely to match the words of the calls visually with the musical notes above them.

The dances presented in chapters 5 and 6 will give you a sampling of the square dance figures—traditional, basic and mainstream—currently being used by leaders throughout the country. For a complete list of all of the currently used basic and mainstream movements (of which there are sixty-eight), write for the handbook *Basic and Mainstream Movements of Square Dancing*, from the American Square Dance Society, 462 North Robertson Boulevard, Los Angeles, CA 90048.

Folk Dance Leaders

I had a problem selecting the folk dances: every country in the world has an enormous number. So I chose those that have steps and patterns in common with other national dances. In many instances, then, the learning of one dance will facilitate the learning and teaching of another.

For the folk dances, as with square dances, the verbal-schematic method is employed to assist you in teaching the various steps. First, of course, you must know the dance perfectly, if need be by dint of many repetitions either at home or in a studio. Having mastered the dance, you will demonstrate the figures and then have the group perform the steps without music. When you then play the record, however, you will often discover that the dancers have forgotten the step patterns, sequence or proper timing of steps. This is where the schematic method is most important and where the folk dance leader plays a crucial role.

The schematic examples in the book stress, in addition to proper timing, the essential factors of cueing and anticipation. Once the principles of timing, cueing and anticipation are mastered, you can verbally "push" the group from step to step with succinct and properly timed cues.

HISTORY

How Square Dancing Started

Who were the first people to perform square dances? Where did these dances originate? Did the four-couples-in-a-set format evolve from some other dance structure? Definitive answers to these and related questions are somewhat elusive. Dance historians love to disagree about the facts and the many conjectures regarding the evolution of square and folk dances.

The most likely explanation of the metamorphosis of the square dance is that it evolved from the longways, or contra, dance, a dance involving two parallel lines of dancers. But whence came the contra dance? Curt Sachs, in his book *The World History of the Dance*, describes many dances of ancient tribes and shows that a number of patterns in these dances appear today in current European and American dances. One Indo-Chinese tribe, the Naga, has a double column dance with some moves that approximate figures in a seventeenth-century Spanish dance and an early English country dance (crossing of the two columns, the chain and two circles which return to the original lines). So it appears that the modern New England contra dance evolved from the English longways dance, which in turn harkens back to ancient tribal choreography.

Until the mid-seventeenth century, English country dances were passed on from one generation to the next by observation and imitation. Then, in 1650 the steps were written out for the first time, in a manual

7

printed by a London bookseller, John Playford. It was entitled *The English Dancing Master, or Plaine and Easie Rules for the Dancing of Country Dances, With the Tune to Each Dance.* The book, containing descriptions of 104 country dances, introduced these dances to the urban community and became an overnight best-seller. Practically every dancing master in England and on the continent obtained a copy and passed the colorful rustic dances on to his students. The book included circle dances, couple dances, longways dances for four couples, and a handful of square dances which had evolved from the shortened longways dances. The explanations of the maneuvers in these square dances, however, are very sketchy and there are no descriptions of the actual figures. Calls for the dances as we know them today did not exist; the movements and figures had to be memorized.

When these dances were performed, the leader was usually the fiddler. He would pick a melody that suited him, then arbitrarily select a combination of figures to be danced to the tune. Because of this, figures would seldom be danced in the same manner or sequence each time a dance was performed; but although the steps and figures varied, different fiddlers would play the tunes more or less uniformly. When Playford compiled the dances in his book, he achieved total uniformity by titling the melodies and choreographing specific sequences for each one.

It is not clear why, in the years following Playford's first publication, many of the circle dances and squares lost their popularity in favor of the longways dances. Perhaps it was due to the large numbers of new manuals published by ambitious dancing masters whose explanations differed markedly from one another, thereby discouraging their use. Perhaps it was because the demand for country dancing escalated dramatically, and the longways dances could more comfortably accommodate large numbers of dancers. Successive issues of *The Dancing Master* illustrate graphically how the popularity of the longways dance mushroomed. The first edition contained 35 longways dances out of 104. In the seventh edition, published fifty years later in 1700, better than half were longways dances. In the final edition of three volumes in 1721, there were 904 longways dances out of a total of 918. Longways dances remained the most popular in England and Europe as well as in the American colonies until the end of the eighteenth century.

Throughout this long period, certain religious groups frowned upon dancing in any form. This was particularly true of the early Pilgrims. The clergy felt that any activity which took time away from the task of surviving in the new wilderness was a creation of the devil. Daily worship and hard dawn-to-dusk toil were the order of the day. Thus dancing was considered wasteful and sinful by many of the early colonists. What is not generally known, however, is that many of the early Puritans had a great love for dancing. One finds references to the pleasures of dancing in the writings of the English Puritan authors Edmund Spenser and John Milton; and John Bunyon wrote that "all good people dance, from the angels down." At the wedding of his daughter in 1657, Oliver Cromwell, who loved music, arranged for "mixt dancing." It is believed that the dances performed at the wedding were from Playford's book.

This difference of opinion about the acceptability of dancing persisted in America: some would not tolerate dancing of any kind; others enjoyed all the dance traditions imported from England; and others were able to accept dancing so long as it did not interfere with work or religious life.

In order to get a clear picture of the history of dancing in America, one must consider the important role played by dancing masters. From the time of the early settlers until well into the nineteenth century, English dancing masters, much in the tradition of English itinerant craftsmen, traveled from town to town in New England. Their acceptance (or lack of it) usually depended on the attitude of the local preacher. If accepted, the dancing master would make it known that he was conducting classes and would rent space, usually in a home, and remain in town one night or longer.

One such well-known dancing master was John Griffin. His career has been partially traced from newspaper notices and from the dates and locations of his dance manuals. He is known to have traveled from Providence, Rhode Island, to Walpole, New Hampshire—and newspaper accounts track him as far south as Charleston, South Carolina. There were many other itinerant dancing masters like Griffin, all of whom helped foster the growth of country dances in the colonies. Typical of the manner in which they advertised their availability is the following newspaper notice, which appeared on March 20, 1789, in the *New Hampshire Spy:*

> Dancing School. Mr. Flagg begs to inform those ladies and Gentlemen who wish their children to acquire the knowledge of that polite Accomplishment that he will again open a school, at the Assembly Room on Wednesday, the first of April next, and on the Saturday following, if a sufficient number of scholars offer. He will teach the mode of the English Minuets, Cotillions and the Newest Contra Dances.

After the Revolution, when America began to choose the foreign powers with which it wished to trade, commerce with France expanded because of the military alliance between the two countries during the war. This friendship with France spawned the introduction of French culture into American society. French dancing masters poured into America and developed sophisticated versions of the English country dances. In addition they introduced variations of their own *con-tredanse,* which they eventually shortened from the old longways formations to line dances consisting of four couples. These dances in turn were transformed into *quadrilles,* the French term for a four-couple dance formation—the forerunner of the American square dance. It appears that this formation, although unusual, was not uniquely a French invention. As we have seen, squares had appeared in Playford's book in England in 1650. The enthusiasm of the French dancing masters helped promote the growth of this type of dancing in America during the eighteenth and nineteenth centuries.

Another reason for the growth of popularity of French "square" dancing was the anti-British sentiment which was generated after the War of 1812. Because of this negative feeling about England, many Americans refused to dance the English dances. In New England, however, the old English contra dances continued to flourish; in the back-country areas there was still a strong allegiance to the dances of the mother country. Even today, New England is the area in the United States where contra dancing enjoys the greatest popularity.

The dance scene in the southern Appalachian region developed somewhat differently. The mountain communities were relatively untouched by the sophisticated influences (generated by the itinerant dancing masters) that so changed the dancing in New England. They did not care for contra dances, either, but instead preferred many of the old rural country dances that had appeared in Playford's first edition of *The Dancing Master.* Many of these dances were performed in a four-couple square formation which historian Cecil Sharp called the Kentucky Running Set. They are considered to be another link between the old dances of England and modern square dancing.

The Kentucky Running Set of Appalachia eventually developed into Big Circle Dances, which are today the most popular dances in the southern mountains. Children's party games, which include singing old songs and rhymes while dancing, are still done there in Big Circle formation.

The discovery of gold in 1848 brought hordes of settlers to the West along with their dances and music. A new type of dance developed at this time called the *cotillion,* a dance done in square formation. Unlike the quadrille, whose movements were memorized, the cotillion was "called," most frequently by the fiddler, who would spontaneously create and shout out a series of directions. These directions were not preplanned but were made up on the spot; they were the forerunner of today's *prompt calls.* Cotillions were danced to traditional music, which included lively jigs and reels from Scotland and Ireland, or to the newer compositions of composers such as Stephen Foster.

This type of calling spread rapidly throughout the country, and at balls or community dances, the fiddler would call out these prompt calls, telling the dancers what to do next. The ingenious and alert caller would add to the prompt calls by devising humorous fill-in lines, called in time to the music. These fill-ins became the *patter calls* of today. Later, the call instructions were given in time and in tune with the music, and so the *singing call* developed. The calling of square dances took the initiative and influence away from the dancing masters, who had stressed formal techniques and memorized sequences; and as new people took over the chore of calling, new steps and step patterns were invented, and square dancing became a more vital and flexible dance form.

Square dancing was performed at almost all functions and gatherings in America. At huskings, raisings, sugaring-offs; after the business of the day was over, the fiddler would tune up and the weary workers would magically gain new energy as the sets went through the paces. Square dances were even performed at weddings. But a special event was not always necessary to provide the reason for a square dance. A *junket,* or impromptu square dance, might be announced by a loud-voiced citizen standing on the steps of the general store, shouting "Junket, junket!" As the people gathered, he would give the location of the dance, and before long more people than could usually be comfortably accommodated appeared in some local farmer's kitchen or barn. The furniture would be pushed back to the walls and the caller would frequently have to perch in the sink or on top of a woodbox to make room for the dancers. Sometimes, when the dancing went on in two or more rooms, the caller placed himself strategically at a doorway in order to be heard throughout the house.

Growth of Square Dancing in the Cities

Urbanization grew at a rapid rate throughout the latter half of the nineteenth century. In 1840 there were only 2 million Americans living in cities, whereas in 1890 there were more than 22 million urbanites. By 1900, one in seven Americans lived in a city with a population of 25,000 or more. Thus the stage was set for the refinement and sophistication of the old rural square dances.

In the cities during the early 1800s when quadrilles were still popular, women's dress styles reflected the demeanor of the dance. In order to achieve a delicate, touch-me-not air, they replaced the comfortable chemise gown with costumes requiring multiple crinoline petticoats. This bulky clothing did not allow body contact between partners.

Toward the latter half of the century, as urbanization expanded and the more active cotillions grew in popularity, the young people of the day, wanting dances of a more personal and even more strenuous nature, rebelled against this type of dance. The young women reverted to the loose-fitting gown. Dancers became so impatient with the slow movements and the waiting intervals at the conclusion of each cotillion maneuver that they would insert an occasional waltz step or polka at the end of each dance figure. This practice became so widespread that the Congress of the Episcopal Church in America seriously considered banning square dances, which had been thought to be a worthy substitute for the wicked couple dances. The clergy considered the waltz an indecent dance because of the very close position of the man and woman. Clergymen and dancing teachers debated this issue heatedly into the twentieth century.

It was Henry Ford who, in 1925, gave square dancing a new push forward. In his book *Good Morning* and other writings, he extolled the virtues of square dancing in an attempt to foster a dance form that would counteract what he considered to be the evils of jazz. Even though Ford was not successful in his attempt to keep the old square dances (quadrilles) as proper and elegant as they had been during the Victorian era, his efforts did stimulate the burgeoning of many square dance societies; and consequently there was a vast increase in the number of books and pamphlets published on this subject.

In the 1930s, Lloyd Shaw taught European folk and old cowboy dances to his students at the Cheyenne Mountain High School in Colorado. In 1938 his pupils exhibited these dances in Los Angeles, Boston, New York and New Orleans. At first the programs included many European dances, but soon, in response to audience enthusiasm, the presentations consisted entirely of Western square dances such as "Texas Star" and "Wagon Wheel." The calls were laced with cowboy slang and were filled with expressions that typified the popular Western scene.

In 1939 Shaw published his important book *Cowboy Dances* and subsequently established a number of summer workshops to teach the dances to educators who gathered from all over the country. These workshops served as an important spur to the development of Western square dancing throughout the nation.

About 1940, the square dance field began to emerge as a big business. Spurred by the tremendous participation of thousands of people at the New York World's Fair in 1940 (led by Ed Durlacher, a well-known caller of the day), big record companies began to publish a multitude of square dance records. Square dancing immediately began to flourish in a new location, as people started to dance in the privacy of their own living rooms.

By 1950 the square dance boom was in full stride. In every corner of the country square dance clubs and associations were formed, spawning hundreds of new callers. Although their popularity was widespread, the greatest concentration of dancers was in southern California. In July

1950, Santa Monica celebrated its seventy-fifth anniversary with what was probably the world's largest square dance: an unprecedented attendance of 15,200 dancers. Wilshire Boulevard was closed to traffic to accommodate the people who danced through the night to the calls of thirty-five callers.

The Modern Square Dance Movement: The Emergence of Callerlab

The proliferation of square dancing around the country during the years since 1950 has been phenomenal. It is estimated that there are 6 million people who square dance today with some degree of regularity, and there are countless others who have had a casual contact with the activity through one-night stands or by watching it on a movie screen or on television.

As far back as the late 1940s when the square dance clubs began to proliferate, callers came to realize that the old-fashioned routines suitable for one-night stands could and should include new variations. So they experimented with different approaches; and it became evident that major changes in style, content and delivery were becoming a part of this new breed of callers' repertoire.

The need for leadership training became apparent during the early fifties. Those in the forefront of the activity realized that for square dancing to become stabilized and increasingly popular, it would be necessary to develop a degree of standardization in the calls and movements. The old-fashioned routines in which one couple visited each of the other couples in turn and performed the same maneuvers with each one gave way in part to dances in which head couples and side couples moved simultaneously. In this way, all dancers were active at the same time. This made it possible to establish all sorts of variations in traffic patterns.

Because not too much new material was available during this period, callers began to exchange ideas and improvise new figures in which intermingling was the important consideration. Thus they began to coin new terminology and figures, such as *California twirl, square thru* and *slide thru;* these and other figures were incorporated into a host of patter calls as well as new singing calls written to current catchy tunes.

Another trend in patter calls developed during the fifties. The established set patterns of movements in many patter calls gave way to freestyle "hash" combinations, in which each movement not only stood alone but was worked in with other figures at the caller's discretion. This made it necessary for dancers to pay strict attention to the calls, and it became extremely popular, particularly for those dancers who liked to be kept on their toes.

But there was a price to pay for the flood of new calls and movements being introduced. Confusion abounded. There was no standardized manner of calling many of the new movements, and dancers could no longer be certain that their response to a call they had learned from one caller would be correct when called by another. The old basic vocabulary was no longer used universally.

In 1969, in an attempt to solve this problem, Bob Osgood, editor of the national magazine *Square Dancing*, organized a committee of experts called Sets in Order American Square Dance Society (SIOASDS). This organization had as its goal the promotion of standardization of teaching procedures, terminology and movements. It published two booklets: *The Basic Movements of Square Dancing* and *The Extended Basic Movements of Square Dancing*.

In 1974 new figures were added to the list. Stan and Cathie Burdick, editors of *American Square Dance*, published ten additional movements in a booklet called *Plus-50 Experimental Movements* written by Willard Orlich, the magazine's workshop editor. That same year, the Association of Square Dance Callers, under the name Callerlab, had its first formal convention. It was attended by 100 callers who met for three days to discuss all phases of square dancing. Three years later its membership had jumped to 600, and it is still growing.

Callerlab meets each year for a three-day convention to discuss every aspect of square dancing, including cultural exchange, caller accreditation, contracts, ethics, and standardization of all movements. The most recent list of Callerlab movements was published in 1982 by SIOASDS (see page 4 for their address).

The tremendous strides made by Callerlab in the area of standardization are directed largely to square dance clubs and organizations which meet on a regular basis to perfect their dancing skills. Regional types of square dance are still very much in evidence, and many people still gather for party dancing and one-night stands based on old-time, simple figures.

The Folk Dance Picture

Despite the fact that the square dance has been designated by law as our national folk dance, it is generally considered to be a breed apart from other types of folk dance. The square dance has its own identity, as the only dance form performed by four couples in a square set, whose steps and formations are directed by a caller. Thus we are dealing with two separate dance forms; the square dance and the folk dance. Into the folk dance category fall all the other national dances. For the purposes of this book, I have limited discussion to those folk dances which can be performed in couple, circle or other group formation, and which may be either American or foreign in origin.

Some dance historians maintain that the United States has no indigenous folk dances except those of the American Indian. They claim that our folk dances are adaptations of those brought here by settlers from European countries. I don't hold with this view. There are steps and patterns which appear in folk dances the world over, and which provide a kind of common heritage. While American folk dances may be traced in part to those of other nations, they have developed their own distinctive characteristics and should therefore be considered and recognized as truly American.

In tracing the growth of the popularity of folk dances, we must start from the time these dances were brought here by the Pilgrims. Special events of all kinds were often celebrated by the dancing of English country dances on the village greens or in farmhouses. The more fancy minuets and gavottes were danced in the drawing rooms of high society. All of these dances gradually diminished in popularity from the early 1700s until the Revolution. There was a temporary upsurge in their popularity for a decade or so following the Revolution, but the general downtrend continued until about 1870. Throughout this period of about 150 years, on the other hand, contra dancing grew in favor at a steady pace.

In the 1870s the rural frontiers began to disappear and give way to urbanization and industrialization. New England's economic base gradually shifted from agriculture to manufacturing, and as rural areas disappeared the older traditional country dances were all but swept from the scene. The contra dances, however, continued to be danced, although with diminished popularity.

During this post–Civil War period, feuds in the Southern mountains created a deadly animosity between families, and in many cases between communities. This made cultural pursuits involving intercommunity group participation all but impossible. The church created still another obstacle to the growth of dancing: many Southerners espoused fundamentalist beliefs, which for the most part forbade any type of dancing. However, rough interpretations of the old English country dances were still danced by a handful of "sinners." Their music was played by a fiddler whose melodies were given such typical frontier names as "Cumberland Gap" and "Cripples Creek."

Despite this marked attrition in New England and Southern mountain dancing by the end of the nineteenth century, the folk dance scene was quite different in the West after the discovery of gold. In the cities, the fashionable folk dances of Boston and New York were imitated; in the mountain mine areas, old country dances and cotillions flourished, a combination of which (as we discussed earlier) later became the Western square dance. But by 1900, with the dramatic decline in the rural population, country folk dances—which at one time had provided entertainment for every segment of society—had all but disappeared from the national scene.

Then folk dancing once again began to grow in popularity. In 1903 Dr. Luther Gulic, athletic director of the New York City schools, added folk dancing to the curriculum for boys and girls. His success did much to spread the dance movement to schools and colleges in other American cities. However, the movement did not catch on in adult communities, largely because it was not aimed at that age group.

During the next fifteen years, the folk dance movement gained added impetus through the efforts of three people: Louis Chalif, Elizabeth Burchenal and May Wood Hinman. Chalif, a Russian ballet dancer and choreographer, conducted numerous dance training courses for teachers at the Chalif Russian Normal School of Dancing, which he opened in 1907. In 1914 he wrote four folk dance textbooks which were recommended by the New York City Board of Education. While directing his school, Chalif also conducted numerous folk dance festivals. Burchenal, who organized the folk dance committee of the Playground and Recreation Association of America, fostered the development of folk dancing in playgrounds and schools throughout the country through her books, demonstrations and lectures. And Hinman, a teacher in Chicago, taught a wide variety of folk dances and used this experience to help organize many folk dance festivals throughout the country.

For the next twenty-five years or so, folk dances were taught, for the most part, in physical education departments in schools. They were also danced by groups of all ages in many rural areas where this significant folk art was an important part of the community's social life. In recent years, however, there has been a revival of folk dance participation in all sections of the country, including towns and large cities; dances once relegated to children are now being performed by adult groups on a regular basis in clubs that have been formed exclusively for that purpose.

The allure of folk dancing grows constantly more seductive, proving that it has a durability in marked contrast to the ephemeral quality of dances like the twist and the hustle. Folk dances, after all, reflect the personality and temper of a people—which is a great part of their lasting appeal.

2

SQUARE DANCING: FOR THE STUDENT

Construction of a Square Dance

Most square dances have four major subdivisions:

1. Introduction: This usually consists of a simple figure in which all dancers in the set are active at the same time. Most introductions are interchangeable (except for some singing calls) and may be used in any square dance.

2. Main Figure: This is the series of motions or maneuvers that make up the bulk of the square dance. There are different types of main figures: One individual or couple may perform a figure with each of the other three couples in turn; the men or the ladies may perform a figure in unison; the head or side couples may do a figure together; any lady or man may perform a figure with any other lady or man in the set; or all four couples may be called upon to perform a figure simultaneously. The main figure is usually done four times.

3. Breaks or Trimmings: These are usually inserted each time a main figure is completed and, as with the introduction, may be interchanged and used in any square dance. Their use helps avoid the monotony (especially in visiting couple dances) of repeating the same figure too many times. In more advanced dances where all dancers move simultaneously and change partners, these breaks help dancers get their bearings before the main figure is started again.

4. Terminating Movement: This is the last figure and may be used in any square dance, at the caller's discretion. It is usually a simple figure performed simultaneously by the four couples.

17

How to Use Square Dance Records

There are two types of singing call square dance records: those that have music only, and those that include calls with the music. In many instances, the records are combinations: they have the music on one side and the calls with the same music on the flip side.

Select the dances you wish to learn and obtain the music-only or combination records for these dances (see the list below). Then invite your partner and three other couples to get together to practice the dances. The interaction of the four couples is essential for mastering the figures; an individual can't get the feel of the dance patterns merely by reading the instructions.

Don't be in a hurry to play the record until the calls and instructions, as explained in this book, are thoroughly understood. Discuss the maneuvers in detail with your group, and walk through the figures several times until the transitions are smooth. Then be brave. Try your hand at calling for your small group. Play the record and read the calls directly from the book, while someone substitutes for you in the set. The whole group will find this inspires a lot of self-confidence.

After you have followed this procedure a number of times, it would be a good idea to obtain several records containing simple singing calls. These records usually include a printed sheet of calls and call explanations. Follow the same procedure: study the printed sheet, walk through the figures without playing the record, and then try the record. Your sense of achievement in responding to the calls on a record at home will be second only to that experienced when dancing in a large group to the calls of a live caller.

Here are a few records with singing calls on the flip side that you can use for this purpose:

> *Life on the Ocean Waves* (Folkraft 1251)
> *Spanish Cavaliero* (Folkraft 1280)
> *El Rancho Grande* (Grenn 12148)
> *Solomon Levi* (Lloyd Shaw 502)

The printed instructions and singing calls that accompany these records are somewhat different from my versions. If you find the call explanations a bit sparse, consult the glossary in the back of this book for more detail.

Note: I have omitted any mention of hoedown records (listed in Chapter 6). Patter calls at this stage are best left to professional callers because of their special anticipation and timing considerations (see page 38).

Styling of Square Dance Movements

As a dancer you not only want to know the movements, you also want to look good. This requires proper posture, a smooth gliding step, and a gentle touch or firm grasp, as necessary. Here are some important styling considerations to keep in mind as you go along.

• The dance step should be an easy, smooth shuffle step. It is a soft walking-sliding movement with the heels slightly raised. The foot glides forward as it advances, and at the end of each forward slide, the heel drops gently to the floor.

• When circling left or right, stand erect; do not twist the torso from one side to the other. This emphasis on erect posture applies to all dance movements.

• In honoring one's partner, the man bows slightly from the waist as his partner curtsies. The lady curtsies by pointing forward with the left toe touching the floor, right leg slightly bent. Her right hand holds her skirt.

• When a man swings a lady, the swing finishes with the lady unfolding to the right side of the man, so that both dancers stand side-by-side in couple position, facing in the same direction.

• When swinging a lady, the man supports her firmly with his right arm around her waist; and he turns smoothly, without pushing her around with undue roughness.

• Inactive dancers should adjust to the movements of the active dancers. For example, when one couple passes through another couple, the inactive couple, anticipating this movement, should move apart to allow the active couple to pass through.

• Never rush through a figure. You are not in a competition to finish a movement ahead of the other dancers, so move smoothly and unhurriedly, taking one step to each beat of the music.

• When standing in couple position, the inside hands should be joined, with the man's palm up and the lady's palm down. Where the couple consists of two people of the same sex, the left-hand dancer turns palm up and the right-hand dancer turns palm down. Arms are bent, with the hands held slightly higher than the elbow.

• In the forearm turn, each dancer holds the inside of the forearm of the other dancer. The thumb does not wrap around the other's forearm, but is held fairly close to the index finger.

• In movements such as a right and left grand, the handshake hold is used.

• When one of two dancers turns under her arm, hands are held loosely, fingers pointing up. Only slight pressure is required as the hands revolve around each other.

• In the hands-up turn, opposite dancers place palms together, fingers pointing up, thumbs closed on the back of the opposite's hand.

• When men form a star, they use the packsaddle grip: each man, with palm down, grasps the wrist of the man ahead.

• In the palm star formation, all hands are touching in the center with fingers pointing up. The thumb closes over the back of the adjacent dancer's hand.

• When ladies perform the movement known as the skirt flourish, they hold their skirt in their free hand, waist high. Skirts are moved forward on one step, back on the next step, etc.

Dancer Etiquette

You must concentrate on the calls. It is impossible to be an effective dancer while discussing your latest business venture with your corner, or the latest gossip with your opposite lady. Not only will you miss the calls or instructions, but others in the set also will not be able to hear them.

Nor do you want to correct or second-guess the caller. That means that you don't anticipate the next call or, for that matter, sing along with the music.

When a caller is organizing sets, he needs to determine which couples are available to fill vacancies. Indicate to the caller that you are filling the vacancy by raising your hand as you move forward. By the same token, if you need one or more couples to complete your square, raise your hand and indicate with one, two or three fingers the number of couples required to round out the set.

One of the worst breaches of etiquette is to disappear from your set without a word of explanation to the other couples. When you have been part of a set and have completed dancing the first dance of a "tip" (the term used to denote a series of square dances, usually three in number), never, never commit the sin of leaving the square before the tip is ended. If (for whatever reason) you *must* vacate the set, get a replacement before you leave.

You want to have a good time, so of course don't step on your partner's toes, or swing your partner too hard. The only acceptable pain in square dancing is when you find yourself smiling too much.

Additional dancer characteristics deemed desirable by the square dance community are extolled in the following delightful parody of Rudyard Kipling's "If," which appeared in *Manisquare* magazine.

IF (For Square Dancers)

> IF you can straighten out the square when all the rest are lost,
> IF you can dance with duffers and never count the cost,
> IF you can do a bend-the-line while another four square through,
> IF you can still enjoy the dance and they enjoy it too,
> IF you can always wear a smile upon your shining face,
> IF you can swing your partner with gentleness and grace,
> IF you can dance with strangers and make them glad they came,
> IF you can meet with multitudes and not forget a name,
> IF you can go to any dance and willingly pay each dollar,
> No matter the name or fame or skill of the individual caller,
> IF you can have your square break down upon a simple call,
> And yet you never get uptight and still can have a ball,
> IF you can walk a figure that you've known well for years,
> And never get frustrated or yet reduced to tears,
> IF you can listen to the calls and never lose your cool,
> IF you can guide a dancer who feels a bit unsure,
> And then can watch them make mistakes with thoughts that still are pure,
> IF you can come each nite to dance and never pack a square,
> IF you can dance with one and all, my God, but you are rare,
> IF you can do all the above, I'll tell you what to do,
> Come out each night and dance with us,
> WE NEED LOTS MORE LIKE YOU.
>
> —Doug and Dorothy McLaren
> Winnipeg, Canada

Fig. 1. Two adjacent circles

3

SQUARE DANCING:
FOR THE TEACHER/CALLER

Organizing a Square Dance Group

Time spent in organizing a group for instruction should be kept to a minimum. A quick and effective method of assigning different couples is as follows:

1. Form two large adjacent circles, one of men and one of ladies, each circle holding hands, facing into the center.

2. Women walk to their left (clockwise), and men walk to their right (counterclockwise) (Fig. 1).

3. Designate one lady and one man to break from each circle and move toward the front of the dance area, leading the rest of the circle along with them. As the first man and first lady meet, they join hands. Each succeeding man and lady in line join hands as they meet, moving toward the front of the dance area. In this manner, a line of couples will quickly be formed (Fig. 2).

At this juncture, in order to form sets of four couples, follow one of these three procedures:

1. Do a grand march. This is the most time-consuming, but it's fun and organizes sets uniformly. After the line of couples has been formed, the lead couple is directed to turn to the right and walk to the side of the

Fig. 2. Forming couples from two adjacent circles

Fig. 3. Couples peeling off for a grand march

dance area. The second couple turns left and walks to the other side of the dance area. The third couple goes to the right, the fourth couple to the left, etc. (Fig. 3). The two lead couples now continue to march around the outside perimeter of the dance area until they meet at the center rear, directly opposite the leader. The first two couples now form a line of four abreast and walk toward the leader, holding hands. Each succeeding pair of couples does the same until the entire class is organized into lines of four abreast, one line behind the other (Fig. 4).

Fig. 4. Forming lines of four for a grand march

Fig. 5. Forming lines of eight for a grand march

These lines of four now march alternately around the sides of the dance
area to meet at the rear, where each pair of fours forms a line of eight
and walks down the center of the dance area, one line behind the other,
toward the leader (Fig. 5).

Each line of eight now holds hands and forms a circle in a different
area of the dance floor, each area being quickly designated by the
leader. The circles are now ready to be formed into square sets.

2. The second procedure is to form square sets directly from the line
of couples as organized in Fig. 2. The leader quickly walks down the line

of couples, sending each group of four couples to a designated area.

3. The third and most rapid approach, which is followed after the line of couples has been formed (Fig. 2), is simply to announce, "Form your sets." This procedure should not be followed until the group understands the meaning of the term *set*, of course. The couples will then form their own sets quickly, as in any normal square dance situation.

Although square dance movements can be taught to a class after sets have been formed, with a large group it is more effective to teach with the class in a couple circle formation. From your position on a platform, overseeing one large circle rather than many individual groups will enable you to spot and correct errors more easily.

Thus, prior to forming sets of four couples, form a circle of couples: after the line of couples has been formed as in Fig. 2, direct the lead couple to walk to its left, around the perimeter of the dance area, with the other couples following, until a large circle of couples has been formed (Figs. 6, 7).

Fig. 6. Starting a circle of couples from the formation in Fig. 2

Fig. 7. Double circle of couples

Most of the basic square dance movements that involve two people at a time—such as honor, swing, do-sa-do, balance and promenade—can be taught in a couple circle formation. For movements that involve two couples—such as right and left thru and ladies chain—instruct alternative couples to face about, so that the circle of couples consists of sets of four dancers (Figs. 8, 9).

Fig. 8. Alternate couples face about

Fig. 9. Alternate couples join hands: sets of four

Introductory Teaching Suggestions

As soon as sets of four couples have been formed, prepare the group to dance its first square dance. The following instructions are suggested:

"Men, be sure your partner is standing close to you, shoulder to shoulder, at your right. Each couple stand on the side of an imaginary square, with your backs parallel to one of the four walls, as you face the center of the set. Couple number one, you have your backs to the platform. Couple number two, the couple on the right, you have your backs to this side wall [caller points to the side wall]. Couple number three, you are facing the platform. Couple number four, you have your backs to this side wall [caller points to other side wall]. You are standing in your 'home' position, which is the starting and finishing position of all square dance figures" (Fig. 10).

Make sure that everyone in the group understands the meaning of the terms *partner, corner, head* and *side couples, opposite couple, opposite lady* or *gent, right* or *left hand couple* and *right* or *left hand gent.* (See the glossary.)

During your instructions, tell the group specifically which words you will employ during the actual calling of the figure. This applies especially to beginning groups. For example, your walk-through instructions may begin by telling the set to join hands, form a circle, and walk to the left. Don't use embroidered calls until both you and the group are accustomed to the maneuvers and the timing of the simple patter and singing calls. Instead of "With your big foot up and your little foot down, circle wide around the town," it's much simpler to say, "All join hands and circle left."

With the sets now ready to dance, select a visiting couple dance (using whatever type of call you feel you can handle effectively). Give instructions briefly but clearly as the sets walk through the figures. A simple patter call I recommend for the first dance is "Birdie in the Cage," or if you prefer a singing call, try "Red River Valley."

It's a good idea to stand on a platform when you give instructions, so you can easily observe the responses of all of the sets during the preliminary instructions and walk-through.

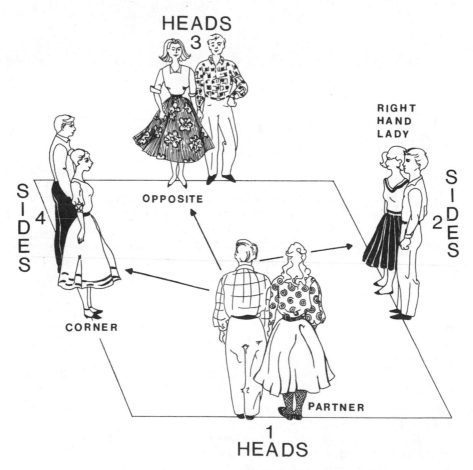

Fig. 10. Square dance formation

Beginners will usually tire very quickly. In their initial enthusiasm, they tend to move about energetically—jumping, running, hopping and skipping during the swings and promenades. Discourage this unnecessary expenditure of energy. In your early group sessions, teach students to promenade and to move through the dance figures with an easy, smooth shuffle step (described on page 19). Have the group practice this shuffle step either in a large circle or after sets have been formed. With this movement mastered, square dancers will be able to dance for long periods without tiring.

At first you should gear your instructions to the dancers with the lowest level of ability. Then after the first two or three dances, meet the level of ability of the majority of the dancers in the group. Remember, a group welcomes the challenge of new steps or formations and does not wish to be underestimated.

Be clear and brief in your description of a figure. Lengthy explanations often create restlessness and confusion. It is important to get the group dancing as quickly as possible, so don't spend too much time attempting to break down and perfect each step or step sequence. Style and "feel" of the steps can be taught if time permits. If not, style may be introduced at a later session after the group feels comfortable dancing several basic figures. Devote some time to review at each session. Repeating a dance already learned will give the group a deserved feeling of accomplishment and will help sustain interest.

If the group seems uninterested or sluggish you should at once try to determine the cause. Is the dance too difficult? too easy? Can they hear the music and your voice? Have you been tactful when errors were made? Have you injected excitement and personality into your teaching?

Although it is extremely helpful for you to have firsthand knowledge of any dance you plan to teach, it is not essential. If you read the instructions to a square dance (Chapters 5 and 6) over and over again, and close your eyes and thoroughly familiarize yourself with the dance formation or maneuver by creating a mental image of it, you should be able to teach it without difficulty. If you have trouble visualizing the dance formations, obtain eight figurines, place them on a tabletop, and slide them through the formations. You can also prepare at home by practicing the calls with the record that you will use for the group. While practicing the calls, you may find it helpful to tap your foot to the beat of the music.

Calling Techniques

Your basic goal as a caller is to cue your dancers through the various figures and floor patterns smoothly and rhythmically.

Command Calls

The simplest type of call is the "command call." Here the caller simply gives the command, then waits for the proper number of beats until the next command. Command calls should accompany hoedowns, in which the melody is relegated to the background and the beat is accentuated. (A list of hoedown records appears in Chapter 6.)

Patter Calls

You can make simple command calls more interesting by adding "patter"—clever but meaningless words that help fill the silences between calls. (Patter is never given the same vocal stress as the cue words, which give the dancers their directions.)

The four major subdivisions of the square dance were discussed on page 17. Memorize several introductory calls, break or trimming calls, promenade patter and terminating calls so you can lend variety and interest to your calling. As you gain experience, you may wish to invent some of your own. (Main figure calls, of course, are not included here; they appear in Chapters 5 and 6). Here are some examples.

Introductory Calls

Swing 'em boys, and do it right,
Swing those girls till the middle of the night.

All eight balance, all eight swing,
Now promenade around the ring.

Swing your partners, don't be late.
Now swing on the corner like swingin' on a gate.
Now your own and promenade eight.

Give your partner a swing and a whirl,
Do-sa-do the corner girl.
Now swing your darling, swing your maid,
Keep on swinging till you promenade.

Honor your partners, corners salute,
All join hands, go lick-a-de-scoot
Half way 'round in a great big ring,
Half way back then you break and swing
And promenade your pretty little thing.

Up in the air and never come down
And swing that little girl 'round and 'round.
Swing her fast and swing her slow,
Swing her till she hollers, "Whoa."

One, three, five, nine, circle left, you're doin' just fine.
Two, four, six, eight, the other way back and don't be late.

Honor your partners and corners all,
Swing your opposites across the hall,
Now gents to your corners and give 'em a whirl,
The same with your own, that pretty little girl.

Swing your honey, swing her hard,
Swing your girl in your own back yard.
The ace is high, the deuce is low,
Promenade all and away you go.

Say "Hi Ya" to your partners
And "Hi Ya" corners all,
Now all join hands and circle the hall.
Go halfway 'round, the other way back,
Make your feet go whickety whack.
Now swing your gal 'cause she's so nice,
Swing her, boy, and hug her twice.

Break or Trimming Calls

Allemande left with your left hand,
Right hand to your partner and right and left grand.
Here we go in a little red wagon,
The hind wheel's off and the axle's draggin'.
Meet your own and promenade,
Promenade eight till you come straight.

Swing on the corner like swingin' on a gate,
Now your own if you're not too late.
Now allemande left with your left hand
Right hand to your partner and right and left grand.
Hand over hand go round the ring,
Meet your partner, pretty little thing
And promenade.

Allemande left your corners all,
Grand right and left around the hall.
Meet your honey and turn right back,
Right back over the same ol' track,
Down the river and 'round the bend,
Meet your honey, turn back again,
Meet your partner and promenade.

Swing that girl across the hall,
Now go home and swing your own.
Do-sa-do your corners all,
Promenade your partner 'round the hall.

Four ladies chain across the set.
Chain right back you're not through yet.
Turn around with your left hand ·
And promenade with your ol' man.

Ring, ring, pretty little ring,
Break that ring with a corner swing.
Ring, ring, pretty little ring,
Break that ring with a corner swing.
Ring, ring, pretty little ring,
Break that ring with a corner swing.
Break that ring and swing your own,
Now promenade your honey home.

You honor your partners, your corners all,
And the little ol' gal across the hall.
The gal on your right and you've honored them all.
So allemande left with your left hand,
A right to your own go right and left grand.
Meet your honey, pat her on the head,
If she don't like biscuits, feed her corn bread
And promenade.

Promenade eight and don't slow down,
Keep on walking those gals around.
Gals roll back to the next in line,
Promenade again and keep in time.

Ladies to the center and back to the bar,
Gents in the middle with a right hand star.
A right hand star in the middle of the hall,
Come back by the left to your partners all
Then promenade around the hall.

Ladies to the center and back to the bar,
Gents to the center with a right hand star.
Back by the left in the middle of the land,
Meet your own, go right and left grand,
Hand over hand around the hall,
Meet your partners and promenade all.

Allemande left, Alamo style,
A right to your own and balance a while,
It's forward and back.
A left hand turn and catch the next
And balance in and out again.
A right hand turn, go halfway round
Rock in and out to the center now.
A left hand turn, you meet your own
And promenade around the town.

Allemande left and allemande "thar"
Right and left and form a star.
Shoot the star through the heavens whirl
And right and left to the next little girl
And star again.
Shoot the star and find your own
And promenade that lady home.

Allemande left and the ladies star,
Gents 'round the outside but not too far.
Allemande left and gentlemen star,
Ladies 'round the outside but not too far.
Allemande left with your left hand
A right to your own, go right and left grand,
Meet your partner and promenade.

Promenade Patter

Horses in the corral, cows in the stall,
Promenade now one and all.

Little bit o' heel, little bit o' toe,
Promenade as you always do.

Promenade yours, I'll promenade mine,
My, oh, my—won't that be fine.

Promenade up and promenade down,
Strut with your honey 'round the town.

Promenade eight till you come straight,
Chow's on the table so don't be late.

Terminating Calls

Honor your partner, your corners all,
Wave to that pretty girl across the hall.

Promenade, you know where,
Take your honey to a nice soft chair.

Grab your honey and promenade there,
You know where and I don't care.

That's all there is, there ain't no more,
Wave to the caller at the door.

The jug is empty, the keg is dry,
So leave your partner and say good-bye.

Promenade that girl so sweet,
Take her out and give her a treat.

Promenade your partners across the hall,
Walk 'em away to a quiet little stall.

Now swing your opposite across the hall,
You haven't swung her since last fall.
Now trot right home and swing your own
And thank your stars the bird ain't flown.
Now promenade right out of town.

First old couple you rip 'n' snort,
Go down the middle and cut 'em off short,
Gent go left and the gal go right,
Everybody else just hang on tight.
Then down the center you go once more
And promenade right off the floor.

Singing Calls

Singing calls are those in which the words of the call are substituted for the words of a well-known song. Occasionally two or more square dances are called to the same tune. Today singing calls comprise a significant part of every caller's repertoire.

The limitation of singing calls is a lack of flexibility in phrasing. Since the call words must be fitted to a specific melody, you can neither add nor cut down on the number of beats to which a figure must be performed. Therefore, when you present a simple singing call to an experienced group of dancers, you may find they have finished the figure before you have finished the call.

The singing call also limits the experienced caller in the number and size of the different trimmings and breaks that can be inserted between and during choruses. This limitation minimizes the possibility of adding an occasional unexpected call, a device which acts as a challenge to dancers and keeps them on their toes.

Despite these limitations, however, singing calls are the most popular. Whereas hoedown music merely provides rhythm for the patter calls and dancers are rarely aware of the melody, with singing calls, dancers are strongly aware of, and respond in lively fashion to, both the rhythm and the melody. Hoedown music can be boringly repetitive, but singing call music is generally upbeat and flamboyant, with its own particular flavor and character. It adds warmth and color to a dance program.

If you have difficulty presenting command and patter calls smoothly and rhythmically, the singing call should give you a helpful crutch. You won't have to concern yourself with the timing of the calls to suit the dance figures since the calls are already timed in the lyrics of the song. Your execution of the call is dependent only on your ability to learn and sing a tune so that the words can be clearly understood. Occasionally, too, in singing calls the dancers may be invited to join in the singing of a chorus or part of a chorus, as in "Marching Through Georgia." This type of audience participation always increases the dancers' enjoyment.

Here is a sample command call used to call four introductory figures: circle, swing, allemande left followed by a right and left grand, and promenade.

(1) CIRCLE LEFT ‾ ‾ ‾ ‾ ‾ ‾
      1   2   3 4 5 6 7 8

(2) SWING your PARTner ‾ ‾ ‾ ‾ ‾ ‾
      1   2   3 4 5 6 7 8

(3) ALLEmande left your CORners all ‾ ‾ ‾ ‾ ‾
      1   2   3   4 5 6 7 8

      GRAND RIGHT and LEFT ‾ ‾ ‾ ‾ ‾ ‾
      9   10   11   12 13 14 15 16

(4) MEET your PARTner and PROMenADE ‾ ‾ ‾ ‾ ‾
      1   2   3   4 5 6 7 8

      ‾ ‾ ‾ ‾ ‾ ‾ ‾ ‾
      9 10 11 12 13 14 15 16

The dashes following each call indicate the number of beats necessary to complete the figure. No provision is made for preparing the dancers for the next figure.

Here are the same figures as a patter-caller might call them. A new element of anticipation, or lead time, has been incorporated.

(1) CIRCLE LEFT around the hall,
      1   2   3   4

      Hurry 'round one and all.
      5   6   7   8

(2) SWING your PARTner, that pretty little thing,
      1   2   3   4

      Twirl her around and give her a fling.
      5   6   7   8

(3) ALLEmande LEFT on your ol' left hand
      1   2   3   4

      Right to your own and a RIGHT and left GRAND.
      5   6   7   8

      Now you're right and now you're wrong
      9   10   11   12

<u>MEET</u> your <u>PART</u>ner and <u>take</u> her <u>along</u>.
    13   14   15   16

(4) Tap your <u>heel</u> and <u>save</u> your <u>toe</u>,
      1   2   3   4

<u>Chicken</u> in the <u>bread</u> pan <u>scratchin'</u> <u>dough</u>,
   5   6   7   8

<u>Walk</u> her <u>home</u> and <u>don't</u> be <u>slow</u>
  9   10   11   12

<u> </u> <u> </u> <u> </u> <u> </u>.
13 14 15 16

An analysis of the patter in figures 3 and 4 above discloses an important technique. A skillful caller will space his calls so that the cue for the new figure will be given a few beats before the finish of the preceding figure. This effects a smooth transition from one figure to another, so that the dancers don't have to stop and wait for the next call. Although 8 beats are normally required for beginners to complete an allemande left, in figure 3 the cue "RIGHT and left GRAND" is given on beats 7 and 8, thus preparing for the next figure. Likewise, although it normally requires 8 beats from the beginning of the grand right and left until dancers meet their partners on opposite sides of the set, the cue "MEET your PARTner and take her along" is given on beats 13, 14, 15 and 16, in preparation for the promenading of partners back to their home positions.

Most beginner square dance groups feel comfortable and unhurried when dancing the figures mentioned above to the number of beats indicated. However, for experienced dancers who require less time to complete the figures, you should reduce the number of beats for certain figures. It is usually easiest to make this reduction in multiples of two beats. For example, in figure 4 above, you may find that by the time you have completed the second line, the dancers will be at their home positions, waiting for the next call. In this case, simply proceed to call the next figure on beats 9 through 16. If it is a visiting couple figure, the call might be:

Third <u>COUPLE</u> to the <u>RIGHT</u> with a <u>RIGHT</u> hand <u>STAR</u>
       9   10   11   12

It's <u>four</u> hands <u>'round</u>, don't <u>go</u> too <u>far</u>.
      13   14   15   16

Another procedure would be to substitute a simple figure like swinging during beats 9 through 16, as follows:

Now <u>SWING</u> her <u>high</u> and <u>swing</u> her <u>low,</u>
9   10   11   12

<u>Twirl around</u> on your <u>heel</u> and <u>toe.</u>
13   14   15   16

This slight addition to the call serves two purposes: first, the faster sets are kept active, while the slower sets are given the opportunity to reach their home positions. (It is true that slower sets may realize that they are not completing all of the called actions, but at least you give them the opportunity to proceed to their home positions and ready themselves for the next call.) Also, it retains the 16-beat sequence, which is desirable (although not essential for experienced callers) since a square dance melody usually has a 32-beat chorus—or 16 bars of 2 beats each —and feels a little more comfortable because it brings you to the end of the melodic phrase.

A slightly different method of effecting a smooth transition from one figure to another is shown in the following simple sequence:

(1) <u>SWING</u> your <u>PART</u>ner, <u>round</u> you <u>go</u>
1   2   3   4

<u> </u> <u> </u> and <u>now</u> your <u>COR</u>ner
5 6   7   8

(2) <u>DO-SA-DO</u> <u> </u> <u> </u>
9   10 11 12

<u> </u> <u> </u> now <u>take</u> your <u>PART</u>ner and
13 14   15   16

(3) <u>PROM</u>eno <u> </u> <u> </u> <u> </u>
1   2 3 4

<u> </u> <u> </u> <u> </u> <u> </u>
5 6 7 8

<u>Promenade</u> <u>eight</u> 'til <u>you</u> get <u>straight</u>
9   10   11   12

<u> </u> <u> </u> <u> </u> <u> </u>.
13 14 15 16

Here, the first figure, (1) "SWING your PARTner," requires 8 beats, and on beats 7 and 8, although the next call is not actually given, it directs the dancers to face a new person with whom the next figure will be danced, so that on beats 9 and 10 the next figure (2), "DO-SA-DO," can be danced without hesitation. Likewise, on beats 15 and 16, the last two beats of figure (2), attention is directed back to partners, although the actual call for promenade is not given until beat 1 of figure (3). This figure employs 16 beats although it could be reduced to 8 beats for experienced dancers. Note also in figure (3) that it is not necessary to use patter on every beat of the music throughout the figure. This can tire out both the dancers and the caller.

Practice blending one call into another as in figures (3) and (4), page 38, or figures (1), (2) and (3), page 40. You may also use a combination of both types of blending. Practice both command and patter calls to the music of a good hoedown record, and after a little experience, you will begin to know almost instinctively how many beats are required for the various figures. Here are some of the simpler figures which should be practiced to music before facing a group:

Honor your partners (or corners): 4 beats

Swing your partners (or corners): 4 to 8 beats

Allemande left: 8 beats

Grand right and left (halfway around the set—until partners meet): 8 beats

Promenade halfway around the set: 8 beats

Promenade completely around the set: 16 beats

Circle left or right (completely around the set): 16 beats

Here is a singing call, "Polly Wolly Doodle," which illustrates good lead time, or anticipation, technique. (The music is on page 108.)

(1) ALLEmande LEFT on your left hand
      1   2   3   4

(2) RIGHT HAND to your OWN and a RIGHT and left GRAND
      5   6   7   8

(3) Hand over hand around the hall
      9   10   11   12

(4)   You <u>MEET</u> your <u>PART</u>ner and <u>PROM</u>enade <u>all</u>.
   13   14   15   16

<u>Round</u> you <u>go</u>, <u>heel</u> and <u>toe</u>
 1   2 3   4

<u>PROM</u>enade <u>all</u> and <u>don't</u> be <u>slow</u>
 5   6 7   8

It's <u>hand</u> in <u>hand</u> <u>around</u> the <u>hall</u>
  9   10 11   12

Get <u>ready</u> <u>for</u> the <u>call</u> __ .
  13 14 15 16

The allemande left is done to 8 beats, and on line 2, beats 7 and 8, the dancers are readied to start a right and left grand, which actually starts on beat 9. Also, on line 4, beats 14 and 15, while the dancers are doing a right and left grand, they are told they will promenade before partners actually meet.

Rhythm

As the dancers' steps are guided by the musical beat, so it is essential for you to match your calls to the rhythm of the music. One of the quickest ways to alienate dancers is to present calls arrhythmically. If you find yourself straying from the beat you must quickly recover and return to the rhythmic pattern.

The essence of square dance music is the 4-beat phrase, and you must fit your calls into that phrase. To say "Allemande left to the lady standing on your left" takes 5 beats. You should say instead, "Allemande left to the lady on your left," which takes 4 beats. "A right hand star in the center" takes 3 beats. The proper call is "Into the center with a right hand star," which takes 4 beats. For the calls to remain rhythmically correct, you must fashion them so that the first beat of every 4-beat spoken phrase coincides with the first beat of every 4-beat musical phrase.

As you gain experience and facility with calls, you will find yourself putting more of a "lift" in your voice. And as your personality and enthusiasm begin to shine through the calls, the group response will become happier and livelier.

If you are able to work with the music, you'll make it as a square dance caller—it's the key factor.

Hash Calling

The patter square dances in this book follow specific choreographic patterns, and the caller need only memorize the calls and patter. A new type of calling has become popular recently where the caller presents figures and changes which dancers do not anticipate. This is known as hash. Hash calling has evolved into a kind of game that the caller plays with the dancers. The caller invents instant choreography. Dancers enjoy the challenge of responding immediately and smoothly to unexpected calls.

To become an effective hash caller, the caller must keep on top of every series of calls. It is a demanding skill that requires much practice to terminate the dance successfully, with all dancers having their original partners.

Hash calling is not dealt with in this book because it requires a detailed and involved analysis of changing formations and rotations which is much too lengthy to be included here. Anyway, I recommend that you familiarize yourself with the material in this book before attempting to learn hash calling techniques. At that time you may wish to consult the helpful booklet *The Mighty Module and Sight Calling Made Easy*, by Bill Peters, which can be purchased by writing to Bill Peters, 5046 Amondo Drive, San Jose CA 95129.

One-Night Stands

The factors that contribute to the success of a dance function are your responsibility alone. If the dance is not a success, the participants will point their fingers in one direction—at you!

When you are called upon to conduct a function, you should, wherever possible, visit the hall. If physical hazards exist—slippery floors or badly placed pillars—discuss them with the entertainment chairman and explain that certain types of dances cannot be performed. Arrange in advance for such details as adequate electrical extension wires and a sturdy, roomy table for equipment. The sheen on a highly waxed floor should be reduced so that it is smooth but not slippery. (A non-slip wax from any good hardware store can be applied over the existing wax.) Tables with sharp edges should be removed, or at least pushed into corners.

As far as the program for a one-night stand is concerned, you must assume that most guests have never participated in a square dance before. Thus you should make every effort to ensure that the group's first exposure to American square dancing is a pleasurable one.

You must be especially aware of, and sensitive to, those who appear to be hesitant and insecure about joining the group on the dance floor. Your friendly and outgoing personality will make it easier for the cautious to take the first step. Be forthright without being overbearing, and sympathetic without being saccharine. Express yourself clearly without being verbose. Your attitude should exude confidence so that beginners will put themselves completely in your hands.

By the same token, unseemly temperament and improper teaching devices are guaranteed to drive square dance hopefuls away from square dancing forever.

- Don't shout. Let your public address system do the work.
- Don't lose your patience. Nothing can erode a mood of good fellowship more than a harping, sarcastic caller.
- Don't be tactless. Remember, your dancers have fragile egos; they'll flower under a warm, encouraging leader. If you must single out those who make mistakes, do it in a tongue-in-cheek manner.
- Don't try to teach too much too fast. This creates frustration and leads to a general exodus from the squares to the sidelines.
- Don't use unfamiliar language. Assuming that your dancers already know basic square dance terminology can be disastrous.
- Don't allow dancers to stand on their feet too long by presenting interminable instructions before the dance begins. Select figures which can be taught quickly, and teach them to a soft hoedown musical background; in that way, the participants have the actual "feel" of dancing as they are being taught and as they walk through the figures.

One very important point: When planning the party, point out to the committee chairman that nothing can ruin a square dance function more quickly than the consumption of hard liquor. Stress that only nonalcoholic beverages should be served during the evening. Most party sponsors will be perfectly happy to go along with this ruling after you explain the problems that could ensue if an open bar is permitted.

Remember that as a caller you are also an entertainer. Your most useful attributes, other than your expertise, are patience, a sense of humor, and an ability to keep the group disciplined in an easygoing fashion. The element of fun should be emphasized. Never act annoyed when mistakes are made, but guide your group through the proper steps pleasantly and, where possible, with an element of comfortable banter.

Public Address System

A well-functioning public address system is indispensable. You'll need two good speakers, a microphone, an amplifier and a turntable. It is important to have a turntable that allows you to slow down a record for instructional purposes.

Proper use of the microphone and correct placement of the speakers are very important. Feedback (a screeching sound) occurs when the speakers are placed either too close to or behind the microphone. Position each speaker fifteen to twenty feet to the side and slightly in front of you, preferably above the heads of the group, so that the sound will carry to all parts of the hall. You should also slant them slightly in your direction so that you can hear the music without straining. Occasionally, when acoustical problems make it difficult for you to hear the music, a monitor amplifier must be used. This is a self-contained, small separate amplifier with a three- or four-inch speaker. It is plugged into the amplifier by means of a separate output jack and will amplify the music but not your voice. If it is placed on a small table at your elbow, you will be able to hear the music at all times. A monitor amplifier can be purchased at any electronics shop at nominal cost. Many new amplifiers today, however, have jacks that lead directly to a built-in monitor amplifier, thus doing away with the need for a separate monitor amplifier.

When calling, keep your mouth at least seven inches from the microphone. (Some microphones, however, are quite insensitive and must be used at closer quarters.) Use your natural speaking voice. If you desire more volume, adjust the amplifier volume control knob. Don't hold the microphone closer to your mouth to increase the volume. If you do that, your voice will become distorted and difficult to understand. The bass-treble control knob on the amplifier can be adjusted to suit the quality of your voice. Men usually need to use more treble control, whereas women should turn up the bass to add more resonance to their voice.

4

FOLK DANCING

How to Interpret a Folk Dance Description

Music is divided into *measures,* sequences of notes that add up to specific number of beats. A measure will usually have 2, 3 or 4 beats.

The number of beats per measure is indicated by the *meter,* which is written as a fraction, such as 2/4, 3/4 or 4/4, at the top of each dance description. The numerator refers to the number of beats to each measure in that piece of music. (The denominator refers to the type of note that receives the beat—not our concern here.)

A single movement—a step, a swing of the foot, a stamp—is usually done to one musical beat. Sometimes two dance movements are made during one beat or count. To time these two movements, the beat is divided into *half-beats,* and each of the movements is done to one of the half-beats. In the dance description, the word "and" is used to denote the second half-beat. For example, the dance may call for 4 walking steps to be done in 2 musical beats. This would be written as follows: first step (count 1); second step (count "and"); third step (count 2); fourth step (count "and").

An understanding of these three simple factors—measure, meter and half-beat—will give you a basis for properly timing the steps explained in a dance description. As a preliminary practice, play a record and count the beats out loud: "one, two," if the meter is 2/4, "one, two, three," if the meter is 3/4 or 3/8, "one, two, three, four," if the meter

46

is 4/4. Tap your foot to the beat. Next, practice calling out half-counts to these meters, tapping your foot on the accented beats. For example, for 4/4 meter music, you will call:

"One and two and three and four and."
(tap)   (tap)   (tap)   (tap)

Once you can do this, you are ready to move on to the dance descriptions that follow, and then to Chapter 7.

Some people have difficulty learning a dance from the printed page. This may happen because in their desire to learn quickly they tend to gloss over the instructions and try to learn the entire dance at one reading. This feat is quite impossible, even for experienced dancers. To learn a dance properly, first play the record four or five times and become familiar with the melody, tempo and general structure of the music. Check the meter to determine how many counts there are to each measure. The printed description will also indicate how many counts and/or measures are used for each step or step sequence.

Frequently Used Folk Dance Steps

The two-step, schottische, polka and waltz appear in many of the folk dances described in Chapter 7. After gaining some experience in teaching folk dances, in all likelihood the leader will invent teaching techniques which may prove more effective for a particular group. The novice leader, however, with no previous experience in this field, will find the following techniques helpful.

The Two-step

The two-step consists of three steps, progressing either forward, sideward or backward, starting with either foot, and is usually done to 2/4 meter. The first two steps are done to one half-beat each, and the third step is slower, being held for one full beat. In doing a two-step to the left, for example, the left foot steps to the left on the first half-beat (count 1), the right foot is placed alongside the left on the second half-beat (count "and"), then the left foot steps to the side again for one full beat (counts 2, "and"). The rhythm may be described as "quick-quick-slow."

Learning the Two-step

Form a single circle, hands joined, all facing the center. Using a good two-step record, such as "Oklahoma Mixer" (Folkraft 1035), take four sliding steps to the left, then four sliding steps to the right, doing each slide on one beat, as follows:

$$\frac{\text{Slide left together (R) left together (R) left together (R) left (hold)}}{1 \qquad \text{and} \qquad 2 \qquad \text{and} \qquad 1 \qquad \text{and} \qquad 2 \quad \text{and}}$$

$$\frac{\text{Slide right together (L) right together (L) right together (L) right (hold)}}{1 \qquad \text{and} \qquad 2 \qquad \text{and} \qquad 1 \qquad \text{and} \qquad 2 \quad \text{and}}$$

The letter (R) which appears after each "together" on the first line indicates that the right foot takes the body weight and touches the floor lightly on each unaccented half-beat. On the beat 4, the left foot remains on the floor for the full beat, and the right foot is not brought close to the left. The same procedure follows in the opposite direction, leading with the right and shifting the weight to the left foot lightly, on each unaccented half-beat. After the four sliding steps have been mastered in tempo, practice taking two sliding steps to the left, then two to the right, as follows:

$$\frac{\text{Slide left together (R) left (hold) slide right together (L) right (hold)}}{1 \qquad \text{and} \qquad 2 \text{and} \qquad 1 \qquad \text{and} \qquad 2 \quad \text{and}}$$

Next, take four sliding steps forward, to the center of the circle, then backward, away from the center, as follows:

$$\frac{\text{Forward left together (R) left together (R) left together (R) left (hold)}}{1 \qquad \text{and} \qquad 2 \qquad \text{and} \qquad 1 \qquad \text{and} \qquad 2 \quad \text{and}}$$

$$\frac{\text{Back right together (L) right together (L) right together (L) right (hold)}}{1 \qquad \text{and} \qquad 2 \qquad \text{and} \qquad 1 \qquad \text{and} \qquad 2 \quad \text{and}}$$

Follow this sequence by practicing two sliding steps forward, then two sliding steps back, as follows:

$$\frac{\text{Forward left together (R) left (hold) back right together (L) right (hold)}}{1 \qquad \text{and} \qquad 2 \quad \text{and} \qquad 1 \qquad \text{and} \qquad 2 \quad \text{and}}$$

All students now face right, so that the circle will move counterclockwise, and practice a forward two-step pattern around the circle, as follows:

$$\frac{\text{Left together (R) left (hold) right together (L) right (hold)}}{1 \qquad \text{and} \qquad 2 \quad \text{and} \quad 1 \qquad \text{and} \qquad 2 \quad \text{and}}$$

(The cue word "hold" may be dropped as soon as the class shows that it has the feel of the two-step rhythm.)

Now, alternating from side to side, take a sideward two-step to the left, then a two-step to the right, and continue to alternate to the left and then to the right until this side-to-side pattern has been mastered.

Next, take a two-step forward, then a two-step backward, and continue alternating forward and backward until this pattern has been mastered.

The Box Turn

From the single circle form a hollow square, all dancers facing the front of the hall (Fig. 11).

Fig. 11. Hollow square formed from single circle of couples

The box turn is made with alternating sideward two-steps. The first two-step will be taken to the left, leading with the left foot. As the second two-step starts, leading to the right with the right foot, make a quarter-turn to the right, and finish this two-step facing the right side wall. As the third two-step starts, leading to the left with the left foot, make a quarter-turn to the right, and finish this two-step facing the rear wall. Take two more two-steps, first leading with the right foot and making a quarter-turn to face the other side wall, then the last two-step, leading with the left foot and making the last quarter-turn to finish facing the front wall. This sequence may be cued as follows:

```
(face front wall)          (face right side wall)
Left together (R) left turn right together (L) right turn
 1      and        2  and  1        and         2   and

(face rear wall)           (face other side wall)
Left together (R) left turn right together (L) right turn
 1      and        2  and  1        and         2   and

(face front wall again)
Left together (R) left (hold)
 1      and        2   and
```

The Box Turn with Partners

Still in the hollow square formation, partners assume the closed or social dance position (see page 61), so that all men are facing the front wall and all women are facing the rear wall (Fig. 12). The step sequence is exactly the same as that described above, except that when the man leads out with his left foot, the woman leads out with her right. The cueing sequence for the box turn with partners might be:

```
Side together side turn side together side turn
 1    and     2    and  1    and     2    and
```

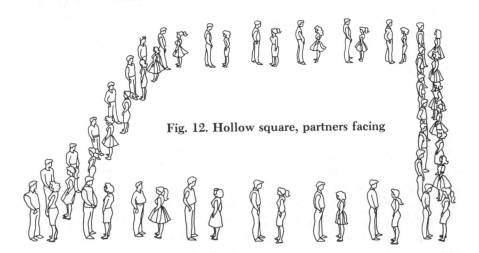

Fig. 12. Hollow square, partners facing

The Half-turn

The group starts in the same hollow square that begins the quarter-turn, all facing the front wall. The first two-step will be taken to the left, leading with the left foot. At the conclusion of this first two-step, toe the left foot in, making a half-turn to the right, pivoting on the left foot, to finish facing the rear wall. Now do another two-step, leading to the right with the right foot, and at the conclusion of this two-step, toe the right foot out, make a half-turn to the right, pivoting on the right foot, to finish facing the front wall. This sequence might be cued as follows:

Left	together (R)	left	pivot	right	together (L)	right	pivot
1	and	2	and	1	and	2	and

The Half-turn with Partners

The step sequence is exactly the same as that described above, except that as the man leads out with his left foot, the woman leads out with her right. The cueing sequence for the half-turn with partners might be:

Side	together	side	pivot	side	together	side	pivot
1	and	2	and	1	and	2	and

The Schottische

The schottische is danced to a 2/4 or 4/4 meter and has an even rhythmic pattern, with each of the four steps having equal time value. When the meter is marked 2/4, count the half-beats as separate beats. The schottische step is created simply by adding a hop on the last beat of a two-step. The step may be done forward, backward, or side to side. To do the schottische moving forward, step forward on the left foot (count 1); close the right foot to the left foot (count 2); step forward on the left foot (count 3); hop on the left foot (count 4).

Another more active method of doing the schottische step is to take three running forward steps and a hop, as follows: run forward on left foot (count 1); run forward on right foot (count 2); run forward on left foot (count 3); hop on left foot (count 4).

Learning the Schottische

Dancers stand at the rear of the dance area, in parallel lines, all facing the front wall (Fig. 13).

Fig. 13. All dancers facing in the same direction

Play a good schottische record such as "Road to the Isles" (Folkraft 1095), and tap your feet in time to the music to get the feel of the beat.

Standing in place and starting with the left foot, take three steps in place, and raise the right foot off the floor with bent knee on the fourth beat:

Left	right	left	raise right
1	2	3	4

Follow this sequence immediately with the same sequence starting on the right foot.

Right	left	right	raise left
1	2	3	4

Add forward movement by taking three steps forward, beginning with the left foot, and swing the right foot forward (off the floor) on the fourth beat. Continue this sequence by starting forward with the right foot:

Left	right	left	swing right
1	2	3	4

Right	left	right	swing left
1	2	3	4

(The group may have to move back to its original position several times during this practice, since the forward movement will advance the dancers in the direction of the front wall.)

Next, change the class formation to a single circle, all facing in the line of direction, and add the hop on the fourth beat as the free foot swings forward with slightly bent knee.

Left right left hop left
  1   2   3   4

Right left right hop right
   1   2   3   4

Do the same sequence going backward, except that on the hop step, do not swing the free foot. Merely raise it off the floor.

Now, moving forward, substitute three running steps for the three walking steps, still hopping on the fourth beat and swinging the free foot forward with slightly bent knee.

run run run hop
 1   2   3   4

Leading to the side with the left foot, do the schottische step, then repeat the pattern going to the right.

Left together (R) left hop left
 1   2   3   4

Right together (L) right hop right
  1   2   3   4

Finally, take partners, inside hands joined, all facing in the line of direction as in the circle of couples in Fig. 7, and practice all the variations described above. Repeat these sequences with partners in both skating and Varsouvienne positions (see the glossary).

And since two schottische steps are frequently followed by four step-hops, practice the following sequence in both skating and Varsouvienne positions:

Left right left hop left
  1   2   3   4

$$\frac{\text{Right}}{1} \quad \frac{\text{left}}{2} \quad \frac{\text{right}}{3} \quad \frac{\text{hop right}}{4}$$

$$\frac{\text{Left}}{1} \quad \frac{\text{hop left}}{2} \quad \frac{\text{right}}{3} \quad \frac{\text{hop right}}{4}$$

$$\frac{\text{Left}}{1} \quad \frac{\text{hop left}}{2} \quad \frac{\text{right}}{3} \quad \frac{\text{hop right}}{4}$$

The Polka

The polka step is done in 2/4 meter and consists of a quick hop followed by a two-step. Although both the schottische and the polka are characterized by a combination of three steps and a hop, the schottische rhythm is even, with each step receiving equal timing, whereas the polka's tempo is uneven. It is the position of the hop in the step sequence and the tempo of the hop that make the difference in the polka. The quick polka hop is done at the end of the measure, but it does not take a full half-beat. The number 2 beat of each measure is held just a fraction longer, into the "and" beat, and the hop is squeezed in just before the next number 1 beat, as follows:

$$\frac{\text{hop (R)}}{\text{and}} \quad \frac{\text{left}}{1} \quad \frac{\text{together (R)}}{\text{and}} \quad \frac{\text{left (hold)}}{2} \quad \frac{\text{hop (L)}}{\text{and}}$$

$$\frac{\text{right}}{1} \quad \frac{\text{together (L)}}{\text{and}} \quad \frac{\text{right(hold)}}{2} \quad \frac{\text{hop (R)}}{\text{and}}$$

Learning the Polka

Form a circle of couples, inside hands joined, facing in the line of direction as in Fig. 7. Review the two-step to polka music, starting on the outside foot. A good record to use for this is "A and E Rag" (Folkraft 1256).

Add the hop as described above, traveling forward in line of direction.

Next, form a single circle, partners facing, the man facing in the line of direction (Fig. 14).

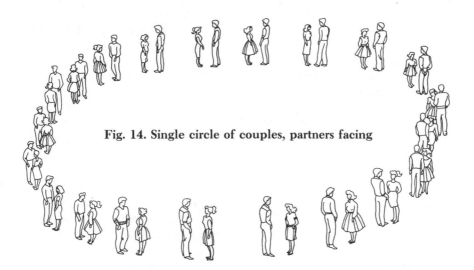

Fig. 14. Single circle of couples, partners facing

All dancers place their weight on the outside foot, with the inside foot pointing toward the center of circle. Take one polka step toward the center, starting with the hop on the outside foot, then do a polka step away from the center. Practice this side-to-side sequence.

Partners still facing, do a polka step toward the center; on the hop before the second polka step, make a quarter-turn to the right; continue doing polka steps from side to side, making a quarter-turn to the right on each hop, until the original position is reached. Partners should be facing each other, without contact, throughout this exercise. This sequence might be cued as follows:

		(turn right)				(turn right)			
Hop	side	together	side	hop	side	together	side	hop	etc.
and	1	and		2	and	1	and	2	and

Now do the same sequence with partners in the closed dance position (see page 61).

For the next exercise, start with a hollow square, all dancers facing the front wall (Fig. 11), to practice the half-turn. The first polka step is taken to the left, leading with the left foot. (Omitting the initial right foot hop will simplify this drill and enable the group to start in unison.) Toe the left foot in on the hop before the second polka step, at the same time turning to the right to face the rear wall on the step-together-step.

Toe the right foot out on the hop before the next polka step, and continue to turn to the right, to finish facing the front wall at the end of the step-together-step.

	(face rear wall)					(face front wall)		
Left	together (R)	left	hop (L)	(toe in)	right	together (L)	right	hop (R) (toe out)
1	and	2	and	1	and	2	and	

Now form a single circle, partners facing, in closed dance position (Fig. 14), and practice the half-turn. The step sequence is the same except that since partners are facing, the man leads toward the center of the circle with his left foot as the lady leads toward the center with her right foot.

The Waltz

The waltz step is done in 3/4 meter. It consists of three steps, each step being taken to one beat of the music. One can actually walk to waltz music, since there is neither hold nor hesitation nor hop nor any other break in the sequence of the walking steps to break the smooth "one-two-three" rhythm. It is the placement of the feet, together with the smooth flow of steps during the various turns, which gives the waltz its characteristic style and grace. The first of the three steps of each waltz step sequence corresponds to the first beat of the music in each measure, and it is accented. There is a complete transfer of weight on each of the three steps, with the first two steps being open and the third being a closing step. Moving in a forward direction, the waltz step may be described as follows: step forward on the left foot (count 1); step forward on the right foot (count 2); place the left foot alongside the right foot (count 3). Start the next sequence forward with the right foot.

Learning the Waltz

Form a single circle, all facing center. Play a slow waltz, such as "St. Bernard Waltz" (National 4528), and clap hands in time to the music, clapping most loudly on the first beat of each measure.

Substitute stepping in place for the clapping, and continue to accent the first beat of each measure by means of a light stamp:

$$\frac{\text{Stamp (L)}}{1} \quad \frac{\text{right}}{2} \quad \frac{\text{left}}{3} \quad \frac{\text{stamp (R)}}{1} \quad \frac{\text{left}}{2} \quad \frac{\text{right}}{3}$$

Next, take three steps forward toward the center of the circle, beginning with the left foot, making each succeeding step smaller. The first, or longest, step is the accented step. Repeat, going backward.

$$\frac{\text{Forward (L)}}{1} \quad \frac{\text{right}}{2} \quad \frac{\text{left}}{3} \quad \frac{\text{back (R)}}{1} \quad \frac{\text{left}}{2} \quad \frac{\text{right}}{3}$$

Repeat the sequence above, this time placing the left foot alongside the right foot on the third step forward, and placing the right foot alongside the left foot on the third step backward:

$$\frac{\text{Forward (L)}}{1} \quad \frac{\text{forward (R)}}{2} \quad \frac{\text{together (L)}}{3} \quad \frac{\text{back (R)}}{1} \quad \frac{\text{back (L)}}{2} \quad \frac{\text{together (R)}}{3}$$

Now all dancers face in the line of direction and do the basic "step-step-together" going forward:

$$\frac{\text{Forward (L)}}{1} \quad \frac{\text{forward (R)}}{2} \quad \frac{\text{together (L)}}{3}$$

$$\frac{\text{Forward (R)}}{1} \quad \frac{\text{forward (L)}}{2} \quad \frac{\text{together (R)}}{3}$$

Still facing in the line of direction, do the sequence going backward:

$$\frac{\text{Back (L)}}{1} \quad \frac{\text{back (R)}}{2} \quad \frac{\text{together (L)}}{3}$$

$$\frac{\text{Back (R)}}{1} \quad \frac{\text{back (L)}}{2} \quad \frac{\text{together (R)}}{3}$$

Form a hollow square, all facing the front wall (Fig. 11), and practice the waltz box step, as follows: step forward with left foot (count 1); step sideward to the right with right foot (count 2); bring the left foot along-side the right foot (count 3); step backward on the right foot (count 1); step sideward to the left on the left foot (count 2); bring the right foot alongside the left foot (count 3). The box step takes six beats, or two measures of music:

Forward (L) side (R) together (L)
    1   2   3

Back (R) side (L) together (R)
  1   2   3

The steps are smooth and should flow into one another, with the weight being kept on the balls of the feet. To prevent the box step from being stiff and awkward, on the second beat of the first measure, as the right foot is moving to the side, move the foot forward, close to the left foot, and then to the side, forming a slight arc. Likewise, on the second count of the second measure, first bring the left foot close to the right foot and then move it out to the side.

Still in hollow square formation, take partners in the closed dance position—men facing the front wall, ladies facing the rear wall (Fig. 12), and practice the waltz box step. Since partners are now facing, the lady's first step is back with her right foot.

Still in hollow square formation, all face the front wall again to practice the waltz step with a quarter-turn to the left: step forward diagonally on the left foot, and toe out (count 1); step sideward to the right with the right foot (count 2); bring left foot alongside right foot (count 3). All are now facing the left side wall. Step back on the right foot and toe in (count 1); step sideward to the left on the left foot (count 2); bring right foot alongside left foot (count 3). All are now facing the rear wall. Repeat the sequence to finish facing the front wall again:

(face left side wall)
Forward (L toe out) side (R) together (L)
       1   2   3

(face rear wall)
Back (R toe in) side (L) together (R)
    1   2   3

In the closed dance position again, practice the quarter waltz turn to the left with partners. On the first step, since partners are now facing, the lady takes her first step back with her right foot.

Now practice the quarter-turn going to the right. Use the hollow square formation, all facing the front wall: step forward diagonally on the right foot and toe out (count 1); step sideward to the left with the left foot (count 2); bring the right foot alongside left foot (count 3). All are now facing the right side wall. Step back on the left foot and toe in (count 1); step sideward to the right on the right foot (count 2); bring the left foot alongside right foot (count 3). All are now facing the rear wall. Repeat this sequence, making two more quarter-turns, to finish facing the front wall again:

(face right side wall)

Forward (R toe out) side (L) together (R)

1   2   3

(face rear wall)

Back (L toe in) (side (R) together (L)

1   2   3

In the closed dance position, practice the quarter waltz turn to the right with partners. The lady takes her first step back on her left foot.

The waltz exercises described above are designed to teach the basic waltz steps. However, in folk dances that are done in the closed dance position, the waltz turns are performed most effectively when each turn is a half-turn.

The two half waltz turns described below should be taught only after the exercises in the preceding instructions have been thoroughly mastered. The steps are described for the men. Two measures of music, or six counts, are used for two half-turns, or one full turn. Regardless of which foot the man leads with, the lady will always start with the opposite foot and move in the opposite direction. Thus, the footwork for the lady's half-turn will be the same as that described for the man's second half-turn, and the footwork for the lady's second half-turn will be the same as that described for the man's first half-turn.

Half Waltz Turn, Left

Practice this sequence in single circle, all facing in the line of direction. Then partners face each other (Fig. 14), assume the closed dance position, and do the step sequence progressing in the line of direction as the sequence continues.

Step forward diagonally on the left foot, toeing out, starting the half-turn to the left (count 1); step sideward on the right foot, continuing to turn to the left (count 2); bring the left foot alongside the right foot (count 3). The half-turn to the left has now been completed. Step back on the right foot, toeing in, starting another half-turn to the left (count 1); step sideward on the left foot, continuing the turn to the left (count 2); bring the right foot alongside the left foot (count 3). One full turn has now been completed, and couples are now facing the same direction as at the start.

$$\frac{\text{Forward (L toe out)}}{1} \frac{\text{side (R)}}{2} \frac{\text{together (L)}}{3}$$

(this completes half-turn)

$$\frac{\text{Back (R toe in)}}{1} \frac{\text{side (L)}}{2} \frac{\text{together (R)}}{3}$$

(this completes full turn)

Half Waltz Turn, Right

Practice this sequence in a single circle, all facing in the line of direction. Then partners face each other (Fig. 14), assume the closed dance position, and do the step sequence progressing in the line of direction as the sequence continues.

Step forward diagonally on the right foot, toeing out, starting the half-turn to the right (count 1); step sideward on the left foot, continuing to turn to the right (count 2); bring the right foot alongside the left foot (count 3). The half-turn to the right has now been completed. Step back on the left foot, toeing in, starting another half-turn to the right (count 1); step sideward on the right foot, continuing the turn to the right (count 2); bring the left foot alongside the right foot (count 3). A full turn to the right has been completed.

$$\frac{\text{Forward (R toe out)}}{1} \frac{\text{side (L)}}{2} \frac{\text{together (R)}}{3}$$

(this completes half-turn)

$$\frac{\text{Back (L toe in)}}{1} \frac{\text{side (R)}}{2} \frac{\text{together (L)}}{3}$$

(this completes full turn)

How to Add Grace and Style to Folk Dance Steps

Learning the steps of a dance is only part of learning the dance. Learning how to count out a beat or how to place one's feet to the different counts of a measure is a purely mechanical achievement and, although important, is but a means to the end. You must strive for the *feel* of the dance, and this can be achieved only through emphasis on style. Even the simplest of folk dances can be a joy to do when performed rhythmically, gracefully and with body control.

Position of Arms and Hands

The *closed,* or social or ballroom, *dance position* is used frequently in folk dancing and will be described here in some detail. Other folk dance positions are described in the glossary.

Partners face each other squarely, with the man holding the woman an inch or so to his right. The man holds his left hand, palm up, at about shoulder level, and the woman rests her right hand, palm down and fingers relaxed, in the man's left hand. The man holds the woman's hand lightly but firmly, with his left arm held out in an easy, graceful curve. The man's right hand is held just below the woman's shoulder blade; his elbow is out to the side a little below shoulder level. The woman's left arm rests easily on the man's upper arm, and her left hand is held rather firmly behind the man's right shoulder. At the same time, the man's right hand should maintain a constant pressure on the woman's back.

Movement of Legs and Feet

The most important clue to graceful foot movements is that the moving foot should pass close to the standing one as it passes it going either forward or backward. Short steps lead to greater ease of movement and grace, whereas long, reaching steps lead to awkward, lunging, jerky movements.

For the actual foot movements, there are two acceptable styles: either a light gliding step on the ball of the foot, with the heel lowered lightly to the floor at the conclusion of each step; or a walking step with the foot just an inch or so from the floor.

Awkward leg movements are frequently due either to stiff knees or to an exaggerated flexing at the knees. The one results in robotlike movements, the other in an up-and-down bobbing motion. Dancers should be encouraged to flex their knees naturally, in much the same manner as they do while walking.

The Torso

Normally the torso should be held easily erect, in its natural position. The military, ramrodlike, unbending torso leads to stiff, awkward movements. The hunched "question-mark" male torso looks even worse, as it forces the woman into an extremely uncomfortable back-bend position.

When turning, the torso should move smoothly to follow the direction of the feet, giving the impression of continuous, fluid movement. Dancers should be cautioned against overtwisting the torso during the turns. Excessive torso movements made for studied effect will often appear quite clumsy and ludicrous.

Style

It has been said that there are as many different styles of folk dancing as there are folk dancers. Although the basic elements of expression are the same for all dancers, the extent to which these elements affect the style of dancing varies widely among individuals.

What are the basic elements that determine style? The first and least easily defined is the enjoyment that dancers derive from dancing, and the extent to which this enjoyment is reflected not only in their facial expressions but in the relaxed feeling of abandon which is reflected in their body movements. Dancers who are really enjoying themselves will never appear dull and mechanical despite shortcomings in technique.

Good posture is another important factor in dancing with style. The elements of good posture stressed by health educators apply equally to dancers. "Stand tall," "Waist flat," "Chest high," "Head erect," "Weight on balls of the feet"—all these commonly used posture cues can prompt students to assume correct posture while dancing.

Correct body balance is closely allied to good posture. To assume a state of readiness for dancing, incline the body slightly forward but do not bend at the waist. Correct body balance is achieved when the weight is taken off the heels and passes to the balls of the feet. Keeping the weight on the balls of the feet aids immeasurably in the smoothness of body movements.

One might reasonably ask, "If all dancers have joyful expressions, good posture and correct body balance, won't their styles of dancing be quite similar?" Not necessarily. Although these factors unquestionably improve style, there are other considerations that enter the picture: the dancer blessed with a tall, slim body will tend to move about more gracefully than the short, wide-torsoed dancer; students who are members of a particular ethnic group, when called upon to perform dances indigenous to their national origin, often interpret these dances with a particularly authentic feeling; some students are naturally more agile and better coordinated than others, so that when they perform dances of a more active nature they almost invariably present a better picture; still others may have a natural feel for the flavor of a particular dance and thus interpret the movements with a greater air of authenticity.

Style, therefore, as it relates to basic foot and body movements, good posture and correct body balance, can and should be taught. Beyond this, the other factors that lead to variations in dance interpretations are inherent in the dancers themselves and make for the wide diversity in dance styling.

Additional Suggestions for Teaching Folk Dancing

By and large square dances are easier to learn than folk dances. It is advisable, therefore, to begin with square dances, to give the group an immediate feeling of success and achievement. After this has been accomplished, then proceed to teach folk dances. Start with the simple dances described at the beginning of Chapter 7 and then go on to the more difficult ones. As the group advances, select dances that have variety in structure, step pattern, formation and national origin, but avoid teaching two vigorous dances in succession during any one class session. Also, don't attempt to teach too many new dances without a sufficient review of those already learned. Groups frequently express preferences as to the types of dances they like to learn, and you should try to honor these preferences.

If you are seeing a group for a one-night stand, your objectives should be, of necessity, somewhat less demanding. The teaching principles are the same, but the stress should be on immediate achievement. Thus you should select square and folk dances that are just a bit challenging but quickly taught (see square dances "Red River Valley," "Buffalo Gals," and "Swing the Man from Arkansas," and folk dances "Patty Cake Polka," Put Your Little Foot," and "La Rinka").

Make sure the group has seen a folk dance danced completely at least once before you start to teach it. Not only should you be able to demonstrate the entire dance, but you should also be familiar with the introduction, tempo and phrasing of the music, so that you can cue the dancers right into the first step and through the dance as it progresses.

This may involve considerable pre-class preparation and is a must if the dance is to be taught effectively. If it is a couple dance, demonstrate it with a partner who is familiar with the dance. If this is not possible, be prepared to teach the footwork to both the men and the women.

Cueing

Proper cueing—calling out each succeeding step before the previous step has been completed—not only reminds the dancers of the sequence of steps but also helps smooth the transition from one step to the next. For example, let's analyze the first part of "Glowworm," which has four step sequences, to illustrate cueing directions.

Directions are for the man; the lady uses the opposite footwork. Dancers are in couple position, inside hands joined, facing counterclockwise around the circle (Fig. 7).

1. Walk forward three steps: left (count 1); right (count 2); left (count 3); touch right toe forward (count 4). Repeat this sequence beginning with the right foot.

2. Partners face each other, join both hands, and take a grapevine step to the left: step to left with left foot (count 1); cross right foot behind left foot (count 2); step to the left with left foot (count 3); swing right foot in front of left (count 4). Repeat this sequence going to the right, beginning with right foot and ending in original position.

3. Partners are still facing each other, right hands joined now. Beginning with the left foot, man and lady exchange places, taking three steps, turning and pointing, lady turning counterclockwise under man's raised right arm: left (count 1); right (count 2); left (count 3); touch right toe forward (count 4). Repeat this sequence, beginning on right foot, ending in original position.

4. In the closed dance position, take four two-steps: (a) step to left with left foot (count 1); place right foot alongside left foot (count and); step to left with left foot (count 2); hold (count and); (b) step to right with right foot (count 3); place left foot alongside right (count and); step to right with right foot (count 4); hold (count and). Repeat (a) and (b).

In the following cueing directions for this dance, examples of both incorrect and correct cues are given. To the inexperienced eye, the incorrect cueing directions will appear quite accurate, since all the cues are given on the proper beat. Notice, however, that the cues make no provision for *anticipating* subsequent steps.

Each step sequence—numbered (1), (2), (3), (4)—has eight beats, four beats to the line. The words in parentheses are unaccented words.

Incorrect cueing:

1.   Left right left (touch) right
          1   2   3   4

(1)

2.   Right left right (touch) left
          1   2   3   4

3.   Left right left (swing) right
              1   2   3   4

(2)

4.   Right left right (swing) left
              1   2   3   4

5.   Left right turn point
              1   2   3   4

(3)

6.   Right left turn point
              1   2   3   4

7.   Step together step hold Step together step hold
              1   and   2   and   3   and   4   and

(4)

8.   Step together step hold Step together step hold
              1   and   2   and   3   and   4   and

In contrast with the cueing directions above, an analysis of the following directions will show that preparatory cues are given at least one beat *before* the first beat of each new step sequence. The preparatory cues are in capital letters:

Correct cueing:

1.   Left right left (touch) right
              1   2   3   4

(1)

2.   Right left GRAPEVINE LEFT
              1   2   3   4

3.   Left right GRAPEVINE RIGHT
              1   2   3   4

(2)

4.   Right left FACE (YOUR) PARTNER
              1   2   3   4

5.   LADY (TURN) UNDER (and) POINT REPEAT
            1   2   3   4
   (3)

6.   LADY (TURN) UNDER (now) TWO-step 'round
            1   2   3   4

7.   Step together step REPEAT Step together step REPEAT
            1   and   2   and   3   and   4   and
   (4)

8.   Step together step REPEAT Step now ready (to) WALK
            1   and   2   and   3   and   4   and

   As the teacher, you should observe one important precaution in your
use of cueing directions. Cueing should not be continued for too long
a period of time, lest the dancers come to depend on it and stop think-
ing for themselves. For example, if you wish to have the class perform
a dance through all the choruses on a record, cue the dancers through
the steps for only half the record, then keep silent as the class attempts
to repeat the dance for the remaining choruses.

Suggested Group Formations for Teaching

For circle or line dances not involving partners, such as "Miserlou" or
"Mayim," or for dances in which partners do the same footwork, such
as "Put Your Little Foot," the group should be organized so that all
dancers are facing in the same direction (Fig. 13). This type of formation
is also best for teaching dances that are performed in single file or with
two or more people abreast, all dancers using the same footwork, such
as "Jessie Polka" or "Hot Pretzels." After the dance is taught with the
group in this line formation, then the group can be reorganized into a
single circle or any other type of circle arrangement that the dance may
call for, so that it may be performed in its original formation.
   Couple dances in which the ladies use opposite footwork to the gentlemen, such as "Lili Marlene" and "Patty Cake Polka," may be taught
in their original formation of a circle of couples (Figs. 7, 15).

Fig. 15. Double circle of couples, men's backs to the center

Sometimes, however, the group may find it confusing to learn a couple dance while in the circle because with the leader in the center demonstrating the steps, those students not facing in the same direction as the teacher may find it difficult to follow his footwork. In this case, divide the group into men and women and line them up on opposite sides of the hall, facing the center (Fig. 16).

Fig. 16. Group divided in half by sexes, teachers in the center

A dance like "Koroboushka," for example, may be taught from this formation.

Dances made up of several figures should be taught in stages, then put together. After each lengthy figure or series of simple figures is learned, the group should dance the figures to the music. If you find that the class has difficulty dancing to the music's original tempo, slow down the record until the steps are learned.

5

SQUARE DANCE
SINGING CALLS:
FOR THE STUDENT
AND TEACHER

As mentioned in Chapter 3, the two types of calls used today are singing calls and patter calls. Although traditionally singing calls were more popular in the eastern United States than they were in other parts of the country, in the last two decades there has been a decided increase in the popularity of this type of call throughout the entire country.

I have conducted several workshops for callers, and it has been my experience that beginners find singing calls easier to grasp than patter calls. Novice callers remember calls better when they fit a definite melodic line. Another advantage of singing calls is that the timing presents no problem to the novice, since the calls follow the same timing as the lyrics.

All singing calls are adapted from command or patter calls. I have included some of my own as well as those originated by other callers. I have simplified some singing calls to make them more suitable for beginners and revised others to make them more interesting to perform.

Dozens of record companies manufacture square dance records. As a result, there are frequently several different records available for the same square dance tune. I have attempted to select those that are recorded well, have a steady beat, and are pitched to suit the voices of most callers. The name of the record company and the number of the recommended record are listed next to the title of each square dance.

To assist the caller in fitting the calls to the music, the music for many singing calls is also included. The arrangements are quite simple, and if the prospective caller cannot read music, anyone with a rudimentary knowledge of music can play the tune for him; or if the caller already knows the tune, he can simply match the words of the calls with the musical notes above them.

The first time a figure is mentioned, it is described in detail. If you want to review the movements of a particular figure, consult the glossary, where they are described fully.

For the Teacher/Caller

The square dances are arranged in the order of increasing difficulty. If you reach the point where you feel your group is not ready to absorb the more advanced singing squares, skip to the chapter on patter calls and teach some of the simpler ones. At this stage, you may have developed a feeling for timing, so that after reviewing pages 31–42 in Chapter 3 on the techniques of calling, you may decide to proceed with the more advanced patter squares. You will now probably be able to handle both singing and patter calls with equal facility.

RED RIVER VALLEY   (Folkraft 1269)

This is a simple but popular version of one of the many square dances
done to "Red River Valley." Start the record again at call line 12. This
dance introduces the *swing* and the *promenade*.

The Calls

Introduction

1. Honor to your partners, now your corners,
2. Now you swing your little babies 'round and 'round.
3. Promenade your own gal 'round the hall,
   Hurry 'round to your places one and all.

Main Figure

4. First couple to the right and you circle
5. And you swing with the other feller's gal.
6. Then you step right back and you honor
7. And you swing your own Red River Gal.

8. Then it's on to the next and you circle
   And you swing with the other feller's baby.
   Now you step right back and you honor
   And you swing with your Red River Lady.

9. Then it's on to the last and you circle
   And you swing with the other feller's wife.
   Now you step right back and you honor
   And you swing with the joy of your life.

Break

10. (Repeat 1 through 3.)

11. Second couple to the right, etc. (Repeat 4 through 10.)
12. Third couple to the right, etc. (Repeat 4 through 10.)
13. Fourth couple to the right, etc. (Repeat 4 through 10.)

Red River Valley

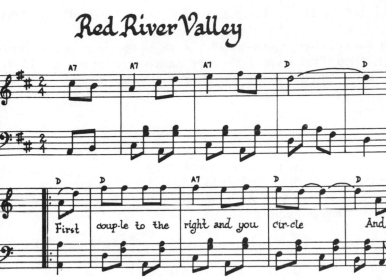

First couple to the right and you cir-cle And you

swing with the oth-er fell-er's gal. Then you step right

back and you hon-or and you swing your own

Red Riv-er Gal.

Explanation of Calls

1. All dancers honor their partners, then their corners.

2. All dancers swing their partners. In this movement, the gentleman holds the lady in closed dance position (see folk dance glossary). Both dancers place the balls of their right feet on the outside and to the right of the other's right foot, and move up alongside each other, so that the right hips are almost touching. The buzz step is now used to move around each other, clockwise. The ball of the right foot is used as the pivot. The right foot should be raised and lowered rhythmically, very close to the pivot point on the floor, as the left foot is used to propel the body around in a circle. The toes of the left foot push down and back with each step (Fig. 17).

Fig. 17. Buzz swing

3. Partners assume promenade position. They stand side-by-side, the lady to the right of the gentleman. The gentleman, with his palms up, holds the lady's left hand in his left hand and her right hand in his right hand. Thus their arms are crossed in front of them, with the gentleman's right arm positioned over the lady's left arm. Partners promenade once around the set, ending back at their home positions (Fig 18a). (In some parts of the country, the Varsouvienne promenade position is used) (Fig. 18b.)

4. Couple One leads out, joins hands with Couple Two to form a circle of four, and circles once around to the left.

5. The four dancers release hands. Gentleman One swings with Lady Two, and Gentleman Two swings with Lady One.

6. The four dancers stop swinging and drop hands. Each gentleman now faces the lady he was just swinging, takes one step away from her, then bows as she curtsies.

7. Couples One and Two now swing their own partners.

Fig. 18a. Promenade, skating position

Fig. 18b. Promenade, Varsouvienne position

8. Couple One leads on to Couple Three and performs the actions described in 4 through 7.

9. Couple One leads on to Couple Four and performs the actions described in 4 through 7.

10. Repeat actions described in 1 through 3.

11. Couple Two leads out and performs the actions described in 4 through 10, visiting each of the other couples in turn.

12. Couple Three leads out as in 11.

13. Couple Four leads out as in 11.

Buffalo Gals

BUFFALO GALS   (Folkraft 1145)

This dance gives dancers ample opportunity to "let off steam" as they "whoop it up" Indian-style. It introduces the *do-sa-do* and the *balance*.

The Calls

Introduction

(Music A)
1. All jump up and never come down,
    Circle wide around the town.
2. The other way back on the same old line,
3. Now promenade all you're doin' fine.

(Music A)
    Promenade around the hall,
    Hey, diddle diddle, the cow's in the stall.
    Grab the wheel of your Ford V eight
    Step on the gas and don't be late.

(Music B)
4. Honor to your partners all,
5. Now honor to your corners all,
6. And now that gal across the hall,
7. Your right-hand gal and that is all.

Main Figure One

(Music A)
8. First buffalo gal around the outside,
    Round the outside, 'round the outside,
    Buffalo Gal around the outside
    And do-sa-do your partners.

(Music A)
9. Do-sa-do your partners all,
    Swing your partners 'round the hall.
    Take your partners in your arms
    And promenade the hall.

(*Music B*)
10. Promenade around and 'round,
     The left foot up, the right foot down,
     Ace is high, the deuce is low,
     You promenade the row.

Main Figure Two

(*Music A*)
11. Balance to your corners all—step, swing, step, swing.
12. Balance to your partners all—step, swing, step, swing.

(*Music A*)
13. Indian style in single file,
     Whoop it up and stomp a while,
     Saddle your broncs and cinch 'em tight
     And home you go tonight.

(*Music B*)
14. Into the center you march all eight,
15. Back to the bar and don't be late.
16. Into the center with a great big yell,
17. Now back to the bar we're doin' swell.

18. Two buffalo gals 'round the outside, etc. (Repeat 8 through 17.)
19. Three buffalo gals 'round the outside, etc. (Repeat 8 through 17.)
20. Four buffalo gals 'round the outside, etc. (Repeat 8 through 17.)

Explanation of Calls

1. All dancers jump up in the air once, then join hands, form a circle of eight, and walk to the left.

2. All dancers reverse direction and walk to the right.

3. When dancers return to their home positions, partners promenade once around the set back to their home positions.

4. Gentlemen honor partners.

5. Gentlemen honor corners.

6. Gentlemen honor their opposite ladies.

7. Gentlemen honor their right-hand ladies.

8. Lady One takes one short step backward, faces right, and walks counterclockwise around the outside of the set.

9. When Lady One returns to her partner, all dancers do-sa-do partners. In this movement, partners pass each other's right shoulders. After

passing each other one step, both dancers sidestep to their right, passing back to back, then walk backward to their original positions. All dancers then swing partners.

10. All dancers promenade partners once around the set back to home positions.

11. All dancers face corners and hold corners' two hands. All dancers step on the left foot, then hop on the left foot as the right leg is kicked diagonally forward in front of the left foot. Now step on the right foot, then hop on the right foot as the left leg is kicked diagonally forward in front of the right foot.

12. All dancers face partners and perform the same movements described in 11.

13. All dancers take one big step into the center of the set and face right. Each dancer places his right hand on the right shoulder of the person standing in front of him, and all eight dancers promenade around the set, counterclockwise, in this single-file formation. As the dancers promenade, they whoop like Indians, tapping their left hands over their mouths and stamping their feet (Fig. 19).

Fig. 19. Single file, Indian style

14. All dancers take three steps forward, then

15. Three steps back to places.

16. All dancers take three steps forward, yelling loudly as they do so.

17. All dancers take three steps back to places.

18. Ladies One and Two take one short step backward, face right, and walk counterclockwise around the outside of the set, then all dancers repeat the actions described in 9 through 17.

19. Ladies One, Two and Three repeat movements in 18.

20. Ladies One, Two, Three and Four repeat movements in 18.

COMIN' ROUND   (Windsor 4115)
THE MOUNTAIN

The figures in this version are danced to a number of different tunes but most frequently to "Comin' 'Round the Mountain." The calls are longer than the record; start the record again at call line 14.

The Calls

Introduction

1. Let's form a ring and circle round the hall,
   Now go back the other way to your own stall,
   Then you ask her if she loves you true
2. And promenade her, yes you do,
   You promenade your partners one and all.

Main Figure

3. Oh! the first old gent you lead out to the right
   And you swing that little mountain girl around.
4. Then you take her back home,
   Circle three hands with your own
   And you leave her with your own sweet mountain girl.

5. Now you lead on to the next across the way,
   Swing that girl and here is what I say,
6. Take her right back to your home,
   Circle four hands with your own
   And you leave her with your own sweet mountain girl.

7. Now go over to the girlie on your left.
   You swing her boy and try to guess her heft,
8. Then you take her back home,
   Circle five hands with your own,
   Yes, you circle with those four sweet mountain girls.

9. It's the first gent to the center of the ring
   And the ladies circle four hands 'round and 'round,
10. Now the gent hop out and swing his own,
    The other three run right on home
    And swing your handsome mountain boy alone.

11. Promenade them one and all you do,
    Yes you keep on going 'til you're almost through,
12. And when you get back home
    Everybody swing your own,
    Swing the sweetest little girl you've ever known.

13. Oh! the second old gent, etc. (Repeat 3 through 12.)
14. Oh! the third old gent, etc. (Repeat 3 through 12.)
15. Oh! the fourth old gent, etc. (Repeat 3 through 12.)

Explanation of Calls

1. All dancers join hands, form a circle of eight, and walk to the left. Dancers then reverse direction and walk to the right.

2. When all dancers return to their home positions, they break the circle, and partners promenade completely around the set.

3. Gentleman One leads out and swings Lady Two.

4. Gentleman One takes Lady Two, puts her on his right, takes her back to his home position, forms a circle of three and circles three hands round with Lady Two and his partner.

5. Gentleman One leaves the circle of three, walks across the set and swings Lady Three. Lady Two remains standing alongside Lady One, at her left, in Couple One's home position.

6. Gentleman One takes Lady Three, puts her on his right, takes her back to his home position, forms a circle of four and circles four hands around with the three ladies.

7. Gentleman One leaves the circle of four, walks to his left and swings Lady Four. Lady Three remains standing to the left of the line of three ladies, in Couple One's home position.

8. Gentleman One takes Lady Four, puts her on his right, takes her back to his home position, forms a circle of five and circles five hands around with the four ladies.

9. Gentleman One goes to the center of the set, and the four ladies join hands and circle to their left around him.

10. The four ladies break the circle, go back to their home positions, and all four couples swing.

11. All couples promenade once around the set.

12. When they arrive at their home positions, all dancers swing their partners.

13. Repeat all movements described in 3 through 12, with Gentleman Two leading out to the right.

14. Repeat all movements described in 3 through 12, with Gentleman Three leading out to the right.

15. Repeat all movements described in 3 through 12, with Gentleman Four leading out to the right.

Comin' Round The Mountain

Oh! the first old gent you lead out to the right. And you swing that lit-tle moun-tain girl a-round. Then you take her back home, Cir-cle three hands with your own And you leave her with your own sweet moun-tain girl.

EL RANCHO GRANDE   (Grenn 12148)
Version 1

Here are a few simple square dance figures arranged to a hit tune of 1927, to suit the needs of beginners. This dance introduces the *star* and the *sashay*.

The Calls

(Music B)
1. Head couples circle left round the rancho,
2. Now circle right with your Sancho.
3. Side couples circle left round the rancho,
4. Now circle right with your Sancho.

(Music A)
5. You honor to your corner, then swing your Señorita,
6. Now promenade el rancho up to your own casita,
7. Then honor your chiquita.

(Music B)
8. You circle left round the rancho
9. Now circle right with your Pancho.
10. You do-sa-do your corner lady,
11. Now do-sa-do your own sweet lady.

(Music A)
12. (Repeat 5 through 7.)

(Music B)
13. Head couples star round the rancho,
    You star around with your Pancho.
14. Side couples star round the rancho,
    You star around with your Sancho.

(Music A)
15. (Repeat 5 through 7.)

(*Music B*)
16. Head couples sashay 'cross the prairie,
    Now sashay back, don't be wary.
17. Side couples sashay 'cross so dandy,
    Then right back to Rancho Grande.
18. (Repeat 5 through 17.)

(*Music A*)
19. You honor to your corner, then swing your Señorita,
20. Now promenade el rancho to your own casita,
21. Now swing your corner lady,
22. And then you hug your own sweet lady. (Call 22 is an 8-bar tag at
    the end of Music A, to finish the record.)

Explanation of Calls

1. Couples One and Three walk to the center of the set, join hands and circle left.

2. Couples One and Three circle right, then step back to home positions.

3. Couples Two and Four walk to the center of the set, join hands and circle left.

4. Couples Two and Four circle right, then step back to home positions.

5. All dancers honor their corners, then swing their partners.

6. All dancers promenade partners once around the set, back to home positions.

7. All dancers honor partners when they return to home positions.

8. All dancers join hands, form a circle of eight, and circle to the left.

9. All dancers circle right until home positions are reached.

10. All dancers do-sa-do their corners.

11. All dancers do-sa-do their partners.

12. Repeat movements described in 5 through 7.

13. Couples One and Three advance to the center of the set, form a right hand star and walk once around, clockwise. In this movement, the inside hands are joined in a "palm star" position, with the hands touching at about eye level, the palm of one dancer's hand resting on the back of the hand of the dancer standing in front of him (Fig. 20).

El Rancho Grande

round the ran-cho, Now cir-cle right with your Pan-cho. You do-sa- do cor- ner la-dy, Now do-sa- do own sweet la-dy.

Fig. 20. Couples star

They then release right hands and step back to their home positions.

14. Couples Two and Four perform the same movement described in 13, then return to their home positions.

15. Repeat movements described in 5 through 7.

16. Lady One faces Gentleman One, and they join both hands. They extend arms sideward, shoulder height, parallel to the floor. At the same time, Couple Three does the same thing. Couples One and Three now exchange places with each other by sliding across the set, the gentlemen passing back to back as they do so (Fig. 21).

Fig. 21. Head couples sashay across

These same two couples now return to their home positions by sliding across the set in the opposite direction, this time the ladies passing back to back. When these two couples return to their home positions, they drop their hands and face into the center of the set.

17. Couples Two and Four exchange places, then return to their home positions as described in 16.

18. Repeat all movements described in 5 through 17.

19. All dancers honor their corners, then swing partners.

20. All dancers promenade partners once around the set, back to home positions.

21. All dancers swing their corners.

22. All dancers face and hug partners.

Turkey In The Straw

TURKEY IN THE STRAW (Worldtone 10023)

This simple visiting couple dance includes the right hand and left hand *star*. Start the record a second time at call line 13.

The Calls

Introduction

1. Oh! you all join hands and circle south,
   Put a little moonshine in your mouth,
2. Now you turn right back, you're goin' all wrong,
   You go back home where you belong.
3. Now promenade 'em two by two,
   You strut around as you always do,
   Two by two around the hall,
   You're right back home, so ready for the call.

Main Figure

4. First couple out with a right hand star,
   It's a right hand round and there you are.
5. Now a left hand back and don't be slack
   Around you go on the same ol' track.
6. Now give your corner lady a twirl,
   You swing around that cute little girl.
7. Treat your partner with a swing,
   You twirl around your pretty little thing.

8. On to the next with a right hand star, etc.
   (Repeat 4 through 7.)
9. On to the last with a right hand star, etc.
   (Repeat 4 through 7.)

Break

10. (Repeat 1 through 3.)

11. Second couple out, etc. (Repeat 4 through 10.)
12. Third couple out, etc. (Repeat 4 through 10.)
13. Fourth couple out, etc. (Repeat 4 through 10.)

Explanation of Calls

1. All dancers join hands, form a circle of eight, and walk to the left.

2. All dancers reverse direction and walk back to their home positions.

3. All dancers promenade their partners once around the set.

4. Couple One leads out and forms a right hand star with Couple Two, and both couples turn the star around clockwise.

5. Couples One and Two drop their right hands, form a left hand star, and turn the star around counterclockwise.

6. The four dancers now swing their opposites. Thus, Gentleman One swings Lady Two, and Gentleman Two swings Lady One.

7. The four dancers now swing their partners.

8. Couple One leads on to Couple Three and performs all of the movements described in 4 through 7.

9. Couple One leads on to Couple Four and performs all of the movements described in 4 through 7.

10. Repeat all movements described in 1 through 3.

11. Couple Two leads out, visits each of the other couples in turn, and performs the movements described in 4 through 10.

12. Couple Three leads out, as in 11.

13. Couple Four leads out, as in 11.

MARCHING THROUGH GEORGIA

(Folkraft 1145)

Dancers invariably sing the chorus of this lively old tune as they promenade single file around the set. This dance introduces the *allemande left*
and the *right and left grand.*

The Calls

Introduction

(*Music A*)
1. All join hands and circle left, all around the hall.
2. Circle back on the same old track and hurry one and all.
3. Left hand round your corner lady, all the way around,
   Now a grand right and left 'round the town.

(*Music B*)
4. You meet your belle and swing her high and low
5. Now promenade, boys, hurry don't be slow,
   And when you get home
6. Everybody swing your own,
   That's the way they do it down in Georgia.

Main Figure

(*Music A*)
7. First old lady promenade the inside of the ring,
8. You hurry home and give your man a great big healthy swing
   Now everybody swing your partners, swing 'em 'round and 'round,
9. Single file promenade the town.

(*Music B*)
Hooray, hooray, around and away.
10. Go back, go back, go back the other way,
    And when you get back home
11. Everybody swing your own.
    That's the way they do it down in Georgia!

12. Second old lady promenade, etc. (Repeat 7 through 11.)
13. Third old lady promenade, etc. (Repeat 7 through 11.)
14. Fourth old lady promenade, etc. (Repeat 7 through 11.)

Terminating Call

15. (Repeat 1 through 6.)

Marching Thru Georgia

First old la-dy prom-en-ade the in-side of the ring. You
hur-ry home and give your man a great big heal-thy swing. Now
ev-'ry- bod- y swing your part-ners, swing 'em round and round,
Sin-gle file prom-en ade the town. Hoo-

Explanation of Calls

1. All dancers join hands, form a circle of eight, and circle to the left.
2. All dancers circle to the right and return to their home positions.
3. All dancers allemande left with their corners: each dancer gives his left hand to his corner; they walk completely around each other in counterclockwise direction, and return to their original position (Fig. 22).

Fig. 22. Allemande left

Then, for the right and left grand, partners face each other, join right hands and walk forward, passing right shoulders. Each gives the left hand to the next dancer and walks past that dancer, passing left shoulders. This weaving movement continues until the dancers meet their partners (Fig. 23).

4. When dancers meet their partners (on the opposite side of the set), all swing partners.
5. Partners promenade around the set, back to home positions.

Fig. 23. Right and left grand

6. When dancers arrive at their home positions, all swing their partners.

7. Lady One promenades around the inside of the set, counterclockwise, flirting with each gentleman as she passes.

8. When Lady One returns to her partner, all dancers swing their partners.

9. All dancers stop swinging, square the set, and take one step into the center. All dancers face right, so that everyone is facing counterclockwise. All place their right hand on the right shoulder of the person standing in front of them and promenade around the set, single file.

10. Dancers drop hands and about-face, so that all are now facing clockwise. As before, they place their right hand on the right shoulder of the person standing in front, and promenade, single file, back to their home positions.

11. All dancers swing their partners.

12. Lady Two leads out and performs all movements described in 7 through 11.

13. Lady Three leads out and performs all movements described in 7 through 11.

14. Lady Four leads out and performs all movements described in 7 through 11.

15. All dancers repeat the movements described in 1 through 6.

DARLING NELLIE GRAY

(Square Dance Music SJB-6A)*

This dance, done to an old folk tune, is simple and easy to learn.

The Calls

Introduction

(Music A)
1. Oh, you all join hands and you circle to the left,
   Now, you circle back, the other way around.
2. Then when you get back home, you will swing your very own,
   Yes, you swing with your Darling Nellie Gray.

(Music B)
3. Then it's allemande left all around with your left hand
   And a grand right and left around the land,
   And when you meet your partner, then you promenade her home,
   Promenade with your Darling Nellie Gray.

Main Figure

(Music B)
4. First couple to the right and you circle to the left,
   Then you circle right, the other way around.
5. It's a right hand over and a left hand back,
6. And you both swing your Darling Nellie Gray.

(Music B)
7. Then it's on to the next and you circle to the left,
   Then you circle right, the other way around.
   It's a right hand over and a left hand back,
   And you both swing your Darling Nellie Gray.

8. Then it's on to the last and you circle four hands round, etc.
   (Repeat 7.)

---

*This record can be obtained only from:
    Twelgrenn Enterprises, Inc.   or   Shirley J. Boyd
    2775 Yellow Creek Rd.   1020 N.W. Boulevard B
    Akron, OH 44313   Columbus, OH 43212

Break

9.   (Repeat 3.)

10. Second couple to the right, etc. (Repeat 4 through 9.)
11. Third couple to the right, etc. (Repeat 4 through 9.)
12. Fourth couple to the right, etc. (Repeat 4 through 9.)

Explanation of Calls

1. All dancers join hands, form a circle and walk to the left, then reverse direction and walk back to their home positions.

2. All dancers swing their partners.

3. All dancers do an allemande left with their corners; then a grand right and left until they meet their partners; then promenade to their home positions.

4. Couple One joins hands with Couple Two, forms a circle of four, and circles to the left, then to the right.

5. The four dancers break the circle, then Gentleman One joins right hands with Lady Two, and Lady One joins right hands with Gentleman Two. The persons holding right hands change places with each other, passing right shoulders. The persons who just changed places with each other release right hands, and hold left hands. They walk past each other again, passing left shoulders, and change places.

6. Couples One and Two swing their partners.

7. Couple One leads out to Couple Three and repeats all movements described in 4 through 6.

8. Couple One leads out to Couple Four and repeats all movements described in 4 through 6.

9. All dancers repeat the movements described in 3.

10. Couple Two leads out to the right and repeats movements 4 through 9.

11. Couple Three leads out to the right and repeats movements 4 through 9.

12. Couple Four leads out to the right and repeats movements 4 through 9.

Darling Nellie Gray

First coup-le to the right and you cir-cle to the left, Then you cir-cle right the o-ther way a-round. It's a right hand o-ver and a left hand back, And you both swing your Dar-ling Nel-lie

Honolulu Baby

HONOLULU BABY   (Folkraft 1280)

There are a number of variations to this dance, the simplest of which
is presented in this version. The calls are longer than the record; start
the record again at call line 10.

The Calls

Introduction

1. Allemande left the lady on the left,
    Now grand right and left half around.
    When you meet your own
    You promenade her home,
    Promenade your Spanish Cavaliero.

Main Figure

2. First lady go right and swing that gent around,
    You swing him around and around, dear.
    After you have swung
3. Go back where you begun,
    Swing with your Spanish Cavaliero.

4   Now lead cross the hall
    And swing that man so tall,
    You swing him around and around, dear.
    Listen to my call,
5. Go back across the hall,
    Swing with your Spanish Cavaliero.

6. Now lead to the left
    And swing the one that's left,
    You swing him around and around, dear.
    After you have swung,
7. Go back where you begun,
    Swing with your Spanish Cavaliero.

Break

8. (Repeat 1.)

9. Second lady go right, etc. (Repeat 2 through 8.)
10. Third lady go right, etc. (Repeat 2 through 8.)
11. Fourth lady go right, etc. (Repeat 2 through 8.)

Explanation of Calls

1. All dancers do an allemande left; then a grand right and left until they meet their partners; then promenade to their home positions.

2. Lady One goes to her right and swings with Gentleman Two.

3. The same lady goes home and swings with her partner.

4. The same lady walks across the set to Gentleman Three and swings with him.

5. She returns to her home position and swings with her partner.

6. She goes to her left, to Gentleman Four, and swings with him.

7. She returns home and swings with her partner.

8. All dancers repeat the movements described in 1.

9. Lady Two leads out and repeats the same figures with each of the other gentlemen in turn. Then all dancers repeat the movements described in 1.

10. Lady Three leads out as in 9. Then all dancers repeat the movements described in 1.

11. Lady Four leads out as in 9. Then all dancers repeat the movements described in 1.

PISTOL PACKIN' MAMA   (Old Timer 1103)
Version 1

I have written the calls of this well-known square dance to fit a tune that was quite popular in the early 1940s.

The Calls

Introduction

1. Allemande left on your left wing
    All around that sweet li'l thing.
    Right hand out, grand chain all,
    Hurry round the hall.
2. Meet your own and swing her so,
    High and low on heel and toe.
3. Then promenade, one and all,
    Now ready for the call.

Main Figure

4. First old lady lead to the right
    To the gent with a right hand round.
5. Back to your own with left hand round,
    Left hand all around.

6. Across the set to the opposite gent
    With a right hand all around.
7. Now go back to your partner
    With a left hand all around.

8. Move along to the left-hand gent
    With a right hand all around.
9. Back to your own with the same ol' left,
    left hand all around.

10. Birdie in the cage, it's seven hands round,
    Circle seven around the town.
11. Birdie hop out, crow hop in,
    Seven hands round and you're off again.

12. Crow hop out and all eight swing,
13. Now promenade around the ring.
    Strut around, strut all eight,
    Promenade 'til you get straight.

14. Second old lady lead to the right, etc. (Repeat 4 through 13.)
15. Third old lady lead to the right, etc. (Repeat 4 through 13.)
16. Fourth old lady lead to the right, etc. (Repeat 4 through 13.)

Terminating Call

17. (Repeat 1 and 2, then end with:)
    Then promenade one and all
    And that's the end of this old call.

Explanation of Calls

1. All dancers allemande left with their corners, then do a grand right and left.

2. All dancers swing their partners when they meet them at the opposite side of the set.

3. All dancers promenade their partners back to their home positions.

4. Lady One leads out and does an allemande right with Gentleman Two.

5. She returns to her partner and does an allemande left with him.

6. She walks across the set to Gentleman Three and does an allemande right with him.

7. She returns to her partner and does an allemande left with him.

8. She walks to her left to Gentleman Four and does an allemande right with him.

9. She returns to her partner and does an allemande left with him.

10. Lady One walks to the center of the set, and the other seven dancers join hands and circle to their left, around Lady One.

11. Lady One takes her partner's place in the circle of seven as he leaves the circle and walks to the center. The seven dancers now circle to their left around Gentleman One.

12. Gentleman One joins his partner in the circle, and all eight dancers swing their partners.

13. All dancers promenade once around the set, back to their home positions.

14. Lady Two leads out to Gentleman Three and performs the movements described in 4 through 13.

15. Lady Three leads out as in 14.

16. Lady Four leads out as in 14.

17. All dancers repeat the movements described in 1 through 3.

Pistol Packin' Mama

Polly Wolly Doodle

first coup-le out and it's

four hands round, Yes it's four hands a-cross as you go round. Now the la-dies bow and the

gents know how And you basket swing a- round. Now it's high, now it's

low And you swing 'em a-round don't be slow. Now you break that bas-ket and

cir-cle four, You cir-cle four once more.

POLLY WOLLY DOODLE   (E-Z 5002)
Version 1

Here is another square dance figure which has been arranged to fit a lively old tune. Warning: to avoid an accident, dancers shouldn't swing too rapidly while doing the *basket swing!* Start the record a second time at call line 11; then start it a third time at call line 12, main figure 9.

The Calls

Introduction

1. Allemande left on your left hand,
   Right hand to your own and a right and left grand.
   Hand over hand around the hall
2. You meet your partner and promenade all.
   Round you go, heel and toe,
   Promenade all and don't be slow.
   It's hand in hand all around the hall,
   Get ready for the call.

Main Figure

3. First couple out and it's four hands round,
4. Yes it's four hands across as you go round.
5. Now the ladies bow, and the gents know how
6. And you basket swing around,
   Now it's high, now it's low
   And you swing' em around don't be slow.
7. Now you break that basket and circle four,
   You circle four once more.

8. On to the next, it's four hands round, etc.
   (Repeat 3 through 7.)
9. On to the last, it's four hands round, etc.
   (Repeat 3 through 7.)

Break

10. (Repeat 1 and 2.)

11. Second couple out, etc. (Repeat 3 through 10.)
12. Third couple out, etc. (Repeat 3 through 10.)
13. Fourth couple out, etc. (Repeat 3 through 10.)

Explanation of Calls

1. All dancers allemande left with their corners, then do a grand right and left.

2. When the dancers meet their partners on the opposite side of the set, they promenade back to their home positions.

3. Couple One leads out and circles four hands around to the left with Couple Two.

4. The two couples release hands. Lady One joins both hands with Lady Two, and Gentleman One joins both hands with Gentleman Two, above the ladies' joined hands (Fig. 24).

Fig. 24. Four hands across

5. The two gentlemen raise their joined hands and lower them behind the ladies' backs. The two ladies then raise their joined hands and lower them behind the gentlemen's backs. An interlocking "California breadbasket" has now been formed.

Fig. 25. Basket swing

6. The four dancers place their right feet slightly ahead of their left feet, and pushing with their left feet, as in the regular buzz swing, circle to the left. They start slowly, but gain momentum as they continue to circle (Fig. 25).

7. They stop the basket swing, release hands, then join hands to form a regular circle of four, and circle to the left.

8. Couple One goes to Couple Three and performs the same figures described in 3 through 7.

9. Couple One advances to Couple Four and repeats the figures described in 3 through 7.

10. Repeat the movements described in 1 and 2.

11. Couple Two leads out to the right and performs the movements described in 3 through 10.

12. Couple Three leads out as in 11.

13. Couple Four leads out as in 11.

POLLY WOLLY DOODLE   (E-Z 5002)
Version 2

This is an add-a-couple version of the preceding square dance, with the California breadbasket being formed first with two couples, then three couples, then four couples. Start the record a second time at call line 11; then again at call line 12, main figure 9.

The Calls

(Repeat calls 1 through 7, page 110; then substitute the calls as follows:)
8. On to the next, it's six hands round, etc. (Repeat 3 through 7, substituting "six" for "four" throughout.)
9. On to the last, it's eight hands round, etc. (Repeat 3 through 7, substituting "eight" for "four" throughout.)

Explanation of Calls

8. Gentleman One frees his left hand, and Couples One and Two lead on to Couple Three and include them in the circle to form a circle of six. The circle of six circles clockwise. The six dancers release hands and the three ladies join hands to form a circle of three, as the three gentlemen join hands to form a circle of three around the three ladies. The three ladies raise their joined hands and bring them down around the backs of the gentlemen standing alongside of them to form a California breadbasket of six dancers. The six dancers place their right feet slightly ahead of their left feet, as in the regular buzz swing, and circle to the left, picking up momentum as they circle around clockwise. They stop the basket swing, release hands, then join hands to form a regular circle of six, and circle clockwise.

9. Gentlemen One frees his left hand, and Couples One, Two and Three lead on to Couple Four and include them in the circle to form a circle of eight. The eight dancers then perform all of the movements described in 8 and form a California breadbasket. At this point, if the caller is working with advanced dancers, he may permit them to do the "fly-away," in which the breadbasket gains such momentum that the ladies' feet leave the floor (Fig. 26).

Fig. 26. Fly away

(Before the caller permits this, however, he must make certain that all of the gentlemen have a very firm hold of one another's hands behind the ladies' backs! The sets must also be far enough apart to allow for the extra room necessary for the "fly-away.")

Mañana

MAÑANA   (Mac Gregor 1017)

I have arranged this simple dance figure to fit a tune which was quite popular in the early 1940s. Dancers should join in singing the refrain at the end of each chorus.

The Calls

Introduction

(*Music A*)
1. Allemande left your corner, you go all around I theenk,
2. Allemande right your partner, go around her with a wink.
3. Now allemande left your corner, and give your own a swing
4. And promenade to Mexico and everybody sing,

(*Music B*)
   Mañana, Mañana, Mañana is good enough for me.

(*Music A*)
5. Honor to your partners, then you honor corners all,
6. Now all join hands and circle left, it's once around the hall,
7. And when you get back home you give your corner girl a whirl,
8. The same to señorita, she's your pretty little girl.

Main Figure

(*Music A*)
9. Head couples to the right and then you take a little peek.
10. Now go back to the center and you swing your honey sweet.
11. You go around again and you take a peek once more.
12. You go back to the center and you circle 'round all four.

(*Music B*)
   Mañana, Mañana, Mañana is good enough for me.

13. Head couples to the left, etc. (Repeat 9 through 12.)

Break

(*Music A*)
14. (Repeat 5 through 8.)

15. Side couples to the right, etc. (Repeat 9 through 12.)
16. Side couples to the left, etc. (Repeat 9 through 12.)

Terminating Call

17. Now promenade your chiquitas all back home.
(*Note:* This call is done to a 16-beat fading musical tag.)

Explanation of Calls

1. All dancers do an allemande left with their corners.
2. All dancers do an allemande right with their partners.
3. All dancers do an allemande left with their corners again, then all swing their partners.
4. All dancers promenade once around the set, back to their home positions.
5. All dancers honor their partners, then their corners.
6. All dancers join hands and circle left.
7. All dancers swing their corners.
8. All dancers swing their partners.
9. Couples One and Three lead out to their right so that Couple One faces Couple Two, and Couple Three faces Couple Four. Lady One bends forward slightly and peeks at her partner behind Gentleman Two, while Gentleman One bends forward slightly and peeks at his partner behind Lady Two (Fig. 27).

Fig. 27. Take a peek

While Couple One is taking a peek behind Couple Two, Couple Three is performing the same action with Couple Four.

10. Couples One and Three return to the center of the ring and swing partners.

11. Couple One peeks again behind Couple Two, and Couple Three peeks again behind Couple Four.

12. Couple One returns to the center of the set and circles around with Couple Two (singing the refrain as they do so). At the same time, Couple Three performs the same action with Couple Four. All couples quickly return to their home positions at the end of the refrain.

13. Couple One leads out to Couple Four and performs the actions described in 9 through 12. At the same time, Couple Three performs these actions with Couple Two.

14. All dancers repeat the actions described in 5 through 8.

15. Couple Two leads out to Couple Three, and Couple Four leads out to Couple One, repeating the actions described in 9 through 12.

16. Couple Two leads out to Couple One, and Couple Four leads out to Couple Three, repeating the actions described in 9 through 12.

17. All dancers promenade partners once around the set.

Pop Goes The Weasel

The first ol' lady out to the right And don't you dare to blun-der, You cir-cle three hands round and round And pop the la-dy un-der. The la-dy moves on, the gent goes right, You cir-cle round like thun-der, Doub-le three hands round and round, Pop them both on un-der.

POP GOES THE WEASEL   (Folkraft 1329)

"Pop Goes the Weasel" is another popular tune to which a number of square dances are called. This is one of the more frequently called versions. Start the record a second time at call line 12.

The Calls

Introduction

1. Allemande left your corners all, (wait 4 beats)
   Grand right and left around the hall, (wait 4 beats)
   Meet your partner and promenade,
   Give her a glass of lemonade,
   Promenade eight 'til you get straight,
   Pop Goes the Weasel.

Main Figure

2. The first ol' lady out to the right
   And don't you dare to blunder,
   You circle three hands round and round,
3. And pop the lady under.
4. The lady moves on, the gent goes right,
   You circle round like thunder,
   Double three hands round and round,
5. Pop them both on under.

6. Then she goes on, the gent goes on,
   Now is it any wonder
   That after double three hands round
7. You pop them both on under.
8. The lady comes back, the gent goes on,
   It's more than easy, it's easier,
   Circle four hands round and round,
9. Pop them both on under.

Break

10. (Repeat 1.)

11. The second ol' lady out to the right, etc. (Repeat 2 through 10.)
12. The third ol' lady out to the right, etc. (Repeat 2 through 10.)
13. The fourth ol' lady out to the right, etc. (Repeat 2 through 10.)

Explanation of Calls

1. All dancers allemande left with their corners, then do a grand right and left. When they meet their partners, they promenade back to their home positions.

2. Lady One leads out to the right, joins hands with Couple Two, and circles clockwise three hands round with them, one and a half times, so that she ends standing on the outside of the set, facing into the center.

3. Couple Two now raises its inside hands to form an arch, and Lady One ducks through the arch, releases hands with Couple Two, and leads on to Couple Three.

4. Lady One joins hands with Couple Three to form a circle of three. At the same time, Gentleman One leads out and forms a circle of three with Couple Two. Both circles of three circle around one and a half times until Gentleman One is standing on the outside of his circle and Lady One is standing on the outside of her circle, both facing into the center of the set.

5. Lady One ducks under the arch made by the inside hands of Couple Three, as Gentleman One ducks under the arch made by the inside hands of Couple Two (Fig. 28).

Fig. 28. Pop them both on under

6. Lady One advances to Couple Four. At the same time Gentleman One advances to Couple Three. Lady One circles one and a half times with Couple Four, as Gentleman One circles one and a half times with Couple Three.

7. Lady One ducks under the arch formed by the inside hands of Couple Four, as Gentleman One ducks under the arch formed by the inside hands of Couple Three.

8. As Gentleman One advances to Couple Four, Lady One turns around and goes back to stand alongside her partner, on his right. Couple One now joins hands with Couple Four to form a circle of four and circles around one and a half times clockwise.

9. Couple One ducks under the arch formed by the inside hands of Couple Four and goes back to its home position.

10. All dancers repeat the movements described in 1.

11. With Lady Two leading out, all dancers repeat the movements described in 2 through 10.

12. With Lady Three leading out, all dancers repeat the movements described in 2 through 10.

13. With Lady Four leading out, all dancers repeat the movements described in 2 through 10.

Hot Time In The Old Town Tonight

HOT TIME IN THE   (Windsor 4115)
OLD TOWN TONIGHT

Both the main figure and the break are well known and quite popular.
This dance introduces the *rip 'n' snort*. Start the record a second time
at call line 12.

The Calls

Introduction

1. First two rip 'n' snort
    Through the center of the ring,
    And now you turn right and left
    Round the outside of the ring.
2. And now the next two rip 'n' snort,
    Don't you dare to change a thing,
    There'll be a Hot Time in the Old Town Tonight.

3. Third two rip 'n' snort, etc. (Repeat 1.)
4. And now the fourth two rip 'n' snort, etc. (Repeat 2.)

Main Figure

5. All four gals to the center of the ring,
6. And now the gents promenade round the outside of the ring,
7. Be sure you pass your own,
    Swing the next as you come down,
    There'll be a Hot Time in the Old Town Tonight.
8. (Repeat 5 through 7.)
9. (Repeat 5 through 7.)
10. (Repeat 5 through 7.)

Break

11. (Repeat 1 through 4.)

12. All four gents to the center of the ring,
13. And now the ladies promenade round the outside of the ring.

14. (Repeat 7.)
15. (Repeat 12 through 14.)
16. (Repeat 12 through 14.)
17. (Repeat 12 through 14.)

Terminating Call

18. (Repeat 1 through 4.)

Explanation of Calls

1. All dancers join hands and form a circle of eight. With everybody still holding hands, Couple One walks across the set and stands directly in front of Couple Three. Couple Three raises its inside hands and forms an arch, and Couple One walks through the arch, leading the other dancers through (everyone is still holding hands). Couple One now separates. Lady One goes to her right (pulling the dancers through the arch) and walks around the outside of the set back to her home position; at the same time Gentleman One goes to his left (pulling the dancers through the arch) and walks around the outside of the set back to his home position (Fig. 29),

Fig. 29. Rip 'n' snort

where he joins hands with Lady One to re-form the circle. In the meantime, as the last dancers pass through the arch, Couple Three turns under its own inside arms to "wring the dishrag" (Fig. 30) and faces into the center of the circle again. (To make it easier to understand this movement, Figs. 29 and 30 show the set turned around, so that Couple Three is standing with their backs to the caller.)

Fig. 30. Wring the dishrag

2. Couple Two rip 'n' snort by walking across the set and leading the dancers under the arch formed by Couple Four. Follow the same directions outlined in 1.

3. Couple Three rip 'n' snort by walking across the set and leading the dancers under the arch formed by Couple One. Follow the same directions outlined in 1.

4. Couple Four rip 'n' snort by walking across the set and leading the dancers under the arch formed by Couple Two. Follow the same directions outlined in 1.

5. The four ladies advance to the center of the set, do an about-face, stand back to back, and face their home positions.

6. The gentlemen face right and promenade single file, counterclockwise, around the outside of the set.

7. The four gentlemen pass by their partners and swing the first lady standing on their partner's left.

8. Repeat the movements in 5 and 6. This time the gentlemen pass their partners and swing the second lady to the left of their partners.

9. Repeat the movements in 5 and 6. This time the gentlemen pass their partners and swing the third lady to the left of their partners.

10. Repeat the movements in 5 and 6. The gentlemen walk completely around the ladies in the center, then swing their partners.

11. Repeat the movements outlined in 1 through 4.

12. The four gentlemen advance to the center of the set, do an about-face, stand back to back, and face their home positions.

13. The ladies face right and promenade single file, counterclockwise, around the outside of the set.

14. The four ladies pass by their partners and swing the first gentleman standing on their partner's left.

15. Repeat the movements in 12 and 13. This time the ladies pass their partners and swing the second gentleman standing to the left of their partners.

16. Repeat the movements in 12 and 13. This time the ladies pass their partners and swing the third gentleman standing to left of their partners.

17. Repeat the movements in 12 and 13. The ladies walk completely around the gentlemen standing in the center, then swing their partners.

18. Repeat the actions described in 1 through 4.

SOLOMON LEVI (Lloyd Shaw 502)

Here is a dance that almost invariably ends with the dancers laughing uproariously. Start the record a second time at call line 12.

The Calls

Introduction

1. Say "Hi Ya" to your partners and "Hi Ya" corners all.
2. Now join hands and circle left, go halfway round the hall.
3. The other way back you're going wrong
4. And everybody swing.
   Swing your partner round and round
5. And promenade the ring.

(There are no calls for the last eight bars of the chorus, as the dancers promenade.)

Main Figure

6. The first couple separate, go round the outside track.
7. Say "Hi Ya" to your partner when you pass her coming back.
8. Now pass right by your partner,
   Do-sa-do your corners all.
9. You face about and swing your own
10. And promenade the hall.

(As in 5, there are no calls for the last eight bars of the chorus, as the dancers promenade.)

11. The second couple separate, go round the outside track, etc. (Repeat 6 through 10.)
12. The third couple separate, go round the outside track, etc. (Repeat 6 through 10.)
13. The fourth couple separate, go round the outside track, etc. (Repeat 6 through 10.)
14. The head couples separate, go round the outside track, etc. (Repeat 6 through 10.)
15. The side couples separate, go round the outside track, etc. (Repeat 6 through 10.)
16. Now all couples separate, go round the outside track, etc. (Repeat 6 through 10.)

Terminating Call

17. Left hand to your corners and the right hand to your own,
    Right and left around that track until you meet your own.
    When you meet your partner you will promenade on high.
    Now that's the end we always use for Solomon Levi.
(As in 5 and 10, there are no calls for the last eight bars of music, as the dancers promenade.)

Explanation of Calls

1. All dancers face their partners, wave right hands or salute, and say "Hi ya." Dancers then do an about-face, face corners, and greet corners in the same manner.

2. All dancers join hands, form a circle of eight, and walk to the left.

3. Dancers reverse direction and walk to the right.

4. All dancers swing their partners.

5. All dancers promenade their partners once around the set until they return to their home positions.

6. Couple One separates and walks around the outside of the set, the lady walking to the right, the gentleman walking to the left.

7. When Couple One meets on the opposite side of the set, behind Couple Three, Lady One and Gentleman One wave to each other and say, "Hi ya," pass right shoulders and continue to their home position.

8. When they arrive at their home position, they pass right shoulders, then all dancers do-sa-do their corners.

9. All dancers swing their partners.

10. All dancers promenade their partners once around the set.

11. Couple Two repeats the movements described in 6 through 10.

12. Couple Three repeats the movements described in 6 through 10.

13. Couple Four repeats the movements described in 6 through 10.

14. Couples One and Three simultaneously repeat the movements described in 6 through 10, saying, "Hi ya" each time they pass another person. As dancers pass each other, they should pass right shoulders at all times.

15. Couples Two and Four repeat the movements described in 6 through 10, as in 14.

16. All couples perform the movements described in 6 through 10, simultaneously. When this figure starts, the ladies are walking counter-clockwise in a circle on the inside of the set, as the gentlemen walk clockwise in a circle on the outside of the set. All dancers say, "Hi ya" to each person they meet.

17. All dancers do an allemande left, then a grand right and left until they meet their partners, and then promenade to their home positions.

Solomon Levi

The first coup-le sep-a-rate, go round the out-side track. Say "Hi Ya" to your part-ner when you pass her com-ing back. Now pass right by your part-ner, do-sa-do your cor-ners all. You face a-bout and swing your own And prom-en-ade the hall. [Eight bars of music for the promenade..... No calls]

PISTOL PACKIN' MAMA   (Old Timer 1103)
Version 2

The pleasing pattern of this dance invariably intrigues those doing it for the first time. Once they have learned it, dancers enjoy performing the figures with precise timing. Start the record a second time at call line 16. (The music is on page 107.)

The Calls

Introduction

1. Allemande left your corners all,
    You hurry, hurry, round.
2. A grand old right and left you do,
    All around the town.

3. Meet your own and promenade all
    Walk your gal around the hall,
    Promenade eight 'til you get straight,
    Now ready for the call.

Main Figure

4. First couple out and circle four,
    Four hands round and round.
5. Leave her there, go on to the next,
    Circle three hands round.

6. Take that lady on with you,
    Circle four hands round.
7. Leave her there, go home alone,
    Back to your stamping ground.

8. Forward six and fall back six,
9. The lone gents do-sa-do.
10. Pass the left-hand lady under,
    On to the next you go.

11. (Repeat 8 through 10.)
12. (Repeat 8 through 10.)
13. (Repeat 8 through 10.)
14. (Repeat 1 through 3.)

15. Second couple out, etc. (Repeat 4 through 14.)
16. Third couple out, etc. (Repeat 4 through 14.)
17. Fourth couple out, etc. (Repeat 4 through 13.)

Terminating Call

18. Allemande left on your left hand,
    Grand chain eight around the land.
    Hand over hand around the ring
    And then you meet your pretty little thing.

19. When you meet your partners, boys,
    Whoop it up and make some noise
    Take her away to an easy chair,
    Take her away and give her some air.

Explanation of Calls

1, 2. All dancers allemande left with their corners, then do a grand right and left.

3. When partners meet at the opposite side of the set, they promenade back to their home positions.

4. Couple One leads out, joins hands with Couple Two, and circles four hands round with them.

5. Gentleman One leaves his partner with Couple Two, leads on to Couple Three, and circles three hands round with Couple Three.

6. Gentleman One transfers Lady Three to his right, takes her with him to Couple Four, and circles four hands round with them.

7. Gentleman One leaves Lady Three with Couple Four and returns to his home position. Gentlemen One and Three are now standing alone in their home positions, and Gentlemen Two and Four each have their partner standing on their right and another lady on their left, to form two lines of three.

8. The two lines of three take four steps forward and bow, then four steps back.

9. Gentlemen One and Three walk to the center of the set, do-sa-do, then return to their home positions.

10. With the lines of three holding hands, the two ladies on either side of Gentlemen Two and Four take a short step forward and face each other. Gentlemen Two and Four raise their right hands to form an arch, and the ladies on their left duck under the arch and advance in the direction of the head gentlemen nearest them. At the same time, the right-hand ladies cross in front of Gentlemen Two and Four and advance in the direction of the head gentlemen nearest them (Fig. 31).

Fig. 31. Pass the left-hand lady under

Gentlemen One and Three now hold hands with the ladies who have just arrived at these head gentlemen's home positions, and form new lines of three.

11. Repeat all the movements described in 8 through 10. The head gentlemen will pass their left-hand ladies under, and new lines of three will be formed at the side gentlemen's home positions.

12. Repeat all the movements described in 8 through 10. At the conclusion of these movements, lines of three will again be formed at the head gentlemen's home positions.

13. Repeat all the movements described in 8 through 10. Lines of three will again be formed at the side gentlemen's home positions.

14. Repeat the action described in 1 through 3.

15. Repeat all movements described in 4 through 14, with Couple Two leading out.

16. Repeat all the movements described in 4 through 14, with Couple Three leading out.

17. Repeat all the movements described in 4 through 13, with Couple Four leading out.

18. All dancers do an allemande left with their corners, then a grand right and left until they meet their partners.

19. When used as the last dance in a tip, this call directs all dancers to disband the set and walk off the dance floor.

RIG A JIG (Folkraft 1415)

The continuous "dip and dive" figure appeals as much to spectators as it does to dancers. I have arranged this figure to fit a lively square dance tune, "Rig a Jig." Start the record a second time at call line 14.

The Calls

Introduction

1. Swing your corners, don't you fret,
   She's the best that you've swung yet.
2. Right to your own and a grand chain all,
   You hurry round the hall.
3. You meet your own half round the ring
   Then promenade that pretty thing.
   You promenade all while you hold her tight
   As home you go tonight.

Main Figure

4. First couple out and you circle four,
   The inside couple arch, you do.
5. It's dip and dive and away we go,
6. The inside high, the outside low.
7. Now hurry, hurry, hurry, let's go,
8. You duck on over and below.
9. You duck right on through and go on to the next
   And circle four hands round.

10. You duck on through, visit with the next,
    The inside couple arch, you do.
11. It's dip and dive and away we go,
    The inside high, the outside low.
    Now hurry, hurry, hurry, let's go,
    You duck on over and below.
    You duck right on through and go back home alone,
    Right to your places all.

Break

12. (Repeat 1 through 3.)

13. Second couple out, etc. (Repeat 4 through 12.)
14. Third couple out, etc. (Repeat 4 through 12.)
15. Fourth couple out, etc. (Repeat 4 through 12.)

Rig A Jig

First coup- le out and you cir-cle four, The in- side coup- le arch you do. It's dip and dive and a- way we go, The in- side high, the out-side low. Now hur- ry, hur- ry, hur-ry let's go, You duck on o - ver and be - low, You duck right on thru and go on to the next And cir-cle four hands round.

Explanation of Calls

1. All dancers swing their corners.
2. All dancers face their partners and do a grand right and left.
3. Partners meet at the opposite side of the set, and promenade back to their home positions.
4. Couple One leads out to the right, joins hands with Couple Two to form a circle of four, and they circle to the left, halfway around, so that Couple One is standing on the outside of the set, facing into the center. Couple Two raise their inside hands to form an arch. (At this point a continuous "dip-and-dive" figure begins, with Couples One, Two and Four being active, until Couple One returns to its home position. See 5 through 11, below.)
5. Couple One ducks under the arch formed by the raised hands of Couple Two and proceeds to the center of the set (Fig. 32).

Fig. 32. The inside couples arch

Couple One raises its hands to form an arch, and Couple Four ducks through and goes to the center of the set. As this is happening, Couple Two turns to face the center of the set, with the lady staying on her partner's right as she turns around with him (Fig. 33).

Fig. 33. It's dip and dive

6. Couple Four now forms an arch, and Couple Two ducks through and goes to the center of the set. As this is happening, Couple One turns to face the center.

7. Couple Two forms an arch, and Couple One ducks through to the center of the set. As this is happening, Couple Four turns to face the center.

8. Couple One forms an arch and Couple Four ducks through to the center of the set. As this is happening, Couple Two turns to face the center. Couple Four forms an arch and Couple Two ducks through to the center, while Couple One turns to face the center.

9. Couple Two forms an arch and Couple One ducks through, then leads on to Couple Three; they circle four hands around, halfway, so that Couple One is standing on the outside, facing the center of the set. As this is happening, Couples Two and Four turn to face the center of the set.

10. Couple Three raises its hands to form an arch and Couple One ducks through, leads on to Couple Four, and circles halfway around with Couple Four to finish standing on the outside of the set, facing into the center. Couple Four raises its inside hands to form an arch.

11. Couple One now repeats all of the movements described in 4 through 10 and finishes in its home position.

12. Repeat the actions described in 1 through 3.

13. Couple Two leads out and performs the dip-and-dive figure with couples Three and One, employing the same series of movements described in 4 through 12.

14. Couple Three leads out and performs the dip-and-dive figure with Couples Four and Two, as in 4 through 12.

15. Couple Four leads out and performs the dip-and-dive figure with Couples One and Three, as in 4 through 12.

Oh Susannah

la-dy right, the gent go left And cir-cle three hands round. Go
right and left through home you go And ev-ery-bo-dy swing. You

to the next and bal-ance there, You bal-ance up and down. Cir-cle half,
swing your part-ner round and round And prom-en-ade the ring. Tap your heel

la-dies chain, Hur-ry don't be slack, And chain a-gain go
save your toe, chick-en scratch-in' dough, Now pla-ces all and

right straight back to the out-side of the track,
hear my call And once more here we go.

OH SUSANNAH (Folkraft 1186)

The "Ladies Chain," which is introduced here, is one of the most charming of all square dance figures. This figure includes the *courtesy turn*. This dance also introduces the *right and left thru*, which is done in combination with the *ladies chain*.

The Calls

Introduction

1. All jump up and don't come down,
2. You circle left around.
3. The other way back on the same ol' track,
   It's all the way around.
4. Swing your partners high and low
   Round and round you go
   Swing 'em round one and all
   Now ready for the call.

Main Figure

5. First lady right, the gent go left
   And circle three hands round.
6. Go to the next and balance there,
   You balance up and down.
7. Circle half, ladies chain,
   Hurry, don't be slack,
   And chain again, go right straight back
   To the outside of the track.

8. A right and left thru home you go
9. And everybody swing
   You swing your partner round and round
10. And promenade the ring.
    Tap your heel, save your toe,
    Chicken scratchin' dough.
    Now places all and hear my call
    And once more here we go.

Break

11. Allemande left your corners all,
    Your corners left allemande.
    Your partner right and grand chain all,
    All around the land.
    Meet your own, swing' em round,
    Everybody swing,
    Now promenade your pretty maid
    All around the ring.

12. Second lady right, etc. (Repeat 5 through 11.)
13. Third lady right, etc. (Repeat 5 through 11.)
14. Fourth lady right, etc. (Repeat 5 through 11.)

Explanation of Calls

1. All dancers join hands, form a circle of eight, and jump up in the air.
2. All dancers circle to the left.
3. All dancers reverse direction and walk back to their home positions.
4. All dancers swing their partners.
5. Lady One goes to Couple Two, joins hands with them and forms a circle of three. At the same time, Gentleman One goes to Couple Four and forms a circle of three with them. Both circles of three circle once around, clockwise.
6. Lady One leaves her circle of three, and Gentleman One leaves his circle of three. Couple One advances to Couple Three and joins hands with that couple to make a circle of four, and all four dancers do a step-swing balance in four counts.
7. Couples One and Three circle halfway around, so that Couple One is on the outside of the circle. Ladies One and Three chain to their opposite gentlemen. In this movement, the two ladies pass each other's right shoulder, joining right hands briefly as they do so (Fig. 34).

Then the two gentlemen each take their opposite lady's left hand in their left hand, place their right arm around her waist, and turn her around, in place, counterclockwise (Fig. 35). This is called the "courtesy turn." Ladies now chain back to their partners. Couple One is on the outside of the circle again.

8. Couple One does a right and left through with Couple Three and goes back to its home position. In this movement, facing dancers step

Fig. 34. Ladies chain

Fig. 35. Courtesy turn

Fig. 36. Right and left thru

forward, join right hands with dancers directly ahead, and pull by. Thus, Gentleman One pulls by Lady Three and Gentleman Three pulls by Lady One (Fig. 36). Each couple does a courtesy turn to face the center of the set.

9. All dancers swing partners.

10. All couples promenade once around the set back to their home positions.

11. All dancers do an allemande left with their corners, then a grand right and left, meet their partners, swing them, then promenade back to their home positions.

12. Lady Two leads out to Couple Three, and Gentleman Two leads out to Couple One. They repeat the actions described in 5 through 11.

13. Lady Three leads out to Couple Four, and Gentleman Three leads out to Couple Two. They repeat the actions described in 5 through 11.

14. Lady Four leads out to Couple One, and Gentleman Four leads out to Couple Three. They repeat the actions described in 5 through 11.

MY PRETTY GIRL (Windsor 4112)

This dance presents a very pretty picture, with a continuous flow of ladies chaining in various directions. Two figures are introduced in this dance: *all around the left-hand lady* and *seesaw your partner.*

The Calls

Introduction

1. Honor your partner, honor your corner,
2. Then you circle left, round and round.
3. Allemande left with the left hand
   And a grand right and left all around.
4. You do-sa-do your honey when you meet her
5. And then you promenade her home.
6. And when you're home you swing your lady
   For she's the gal that you adore.

Main Figure

7. Head couples promenade around the outside,
   Around the outside of the ring.
8. Head ladies chain right down the center,
   And then you chain right back again.
9. Head ladies chain right, your right-hand lady
   And then you chain right back again.
10. Head ladies chain left your left-hand lady
    And then you chain right back again.

Break

11. And now it's all around your left-hand lady,
12. See-saw your pretty little taw.
13. Allemande left with the left hand,
    And a grand right and left all around.
14. You swing your partner when you meet her
15. Then you promenade her home.
16. And when you're home you swing your baby,
    For she's the gal that you adore.

17, 18, 19, 20. Side couples promenade, etc. (Repeat 7 through 10, substituting the words "side ladies" for "head ladies," and "side couples" for "head couples.")

21. (Repeat 11 through 16.)

22. All couples promenade around the outside,
    Around the outside of the ring.

23. (Repeat 8 through 16.)

Explanation of Calls

1. All dancers honor their partners, then honor their corners.
2. All join hands, form a circle, and walk to the left.
3. All dancers do an allemande left with their corners, then a grand right and left.
4. When partners meet on the opposite side of the set, all dancers do-sa-do their partners.
5. All dancers promenade their partners back to their home positions.
6. All dancers swing their partners in their home positions.
7. Couples One and Three promenade around the outside of the set, counterclockwise, back to their home positions.
8. Ladies One and Three chain across the set, then chain back to their partners.
9. Lady One chains with Lady Two; at the same time, Lady Three chains with Lady Four. All ladies chain back to their partners.
10. Lady One chains with Lady Four; at the same time Lady Three chains with Lady Two. All ladies chain back to their partners.
11. All dancers face their corners and walk forward, around each other keeping right shoulders adjacent. When dancers return to their original positions they face their partners (Figs. 37–40).

Fig. 37. All   Fig. 38. around

Fig. 39. your left-hand   Fig. 40. lady.

12. Partners walk forward around each other keeping left shoulders adjacent, return to their starting positions and face their corners (Figs. 41–44).

Fig. 41. See-saw   Fig. 42. your

Fig. 43. pretty little   Fig. 44. taw.

13. All dancers do an allemande left with their corners, then a grand right and left.

14. When partners meet at the opposite side of the set, all dancers swing their partners.

15. Partners promenade to their home positions.

16. All dancers swing their partners.

17. Couples Two and Four promenade around the outside of the set, counterclockwise, back to their home positions.

18. Ladies Two and Four chain across the set, then chain back to their partners.

19. Ladies Two and Four chain with their respective right-hand ladies, then back to their partners.

20. Ladies Two and Four chain with their respective left-hand ladies, then back to their partners.

21. Repeat all the movements described in 11 through 16.

22. All four couples promenade once around the set.

23. Repeat all the movements described in 8 through 16.

IRISH WASHERWOMAN   (Folkraft 1155)

This dance, done to a peppy old tune, adds a change-partner feature to the ladies chain figure.

The Calls

1. Oh! the head ladies chain to the opposite side,
   Then you turn all around with the gent by your side.
   Now you chain back across to the man you adore,
2. Then you all join your hands and you circle the floor.
   First you go to your left on your heel and your toe,
   Yes you hurry around, folks, and don't be so slow.
3. Now the other way back to your home you advance
   And when you got back home you are ready to dance.

4. Oh! It's all 'the four gents to the right of the ring, boys,
   And when you get there you just take her and swing, boys,
   And when you are done, just remember the call,
5. It's an allemande left and a promenade all.
   (Promenade for the second half of the chorus. There
   are no calls during these eight measures.)

6. Oh! The head ladies chain etc. (Repeat 1 through 5)
7. Oh! The head ladies chain etc. (Repeat 1 through 5.)
8. Oh! The head ladies chain etc. (Repeat 1 through 5.)

Explanation of Calls

1. Ladies One and Three chain across the set, then back to their partners.

2. All dancers join hands and circle to the left.

3. All dancers circle to the right and walk back to their home positions.

4. The four gentlemen step behind their partners, walk over to their right-hand ladies, and swing their right-hand ladies. Thus, Gentleman One swings with Lady Two; Gentleman Two swings with Lady Three; Gentleman Three swings with Lady Four; and Gentleman Four swings with Lady One.

5. Each gentleman now does an allemande left with his original partner, comes back to the lady he was just swinging, then promenades that lady back to the gentleman's home position. For example, Gentleman One (who is now standing in Couple Two's position, because he has just been swinging Lady Two) does an allemande left with his partner, Lady One. He then returns to Lady Two and promenades her around the set, back to home position of Couple One. Each lady has now moved one position to the left in the set.

6. The head ladies, who are now Ladies Two and Four, chain across the set, then chain back to their partners. Then all dancers repeat the movements described in 2 through 5.

7. Gentleman One now has Lady Three as his partner and Gentleman Three has Lady One as his partner. Ladies One and Three chain across the set, then chain back to their partners. Then all dancers repeat the movements described in 2 through 5.

8. Gentleman One now has Lady Four as his partner, and Gentleman Three has Lady Two as his partner. Ladies Two and Four chain across the set, then chain back to their partners. Then all dancers repeat the movements described in 2 through 5. All dancers now have their original partners.

Irish Washerwoman

Oh! the head la-dies chain to the op-po-site side, Then you turn all a-round with the gent by your side. Now you chain back a-cross to the man you a-dore Then you all join your hands, and you cir-cle the floor. First you go to your left on your heel and your toe,Yes you hur-ry a-round folks and don't be so slow. Now the o-ther way back to your home you ad-vance And when you get back home you are read-y to dance.

Life On The Ocean Wave

The head two gents cross o-ver and by the la-dies stand. The side two gents cross o-ver and you all join hands. Now bow to the cor-ner la-dy and then to your part-ners all. Swing the cor-ner la-dy and prom-en-ade the hall. If I had a gal who would n't dance, I tell you what I'd do. I'd buy her a boat and set her a-float And pad-dle my own ca-noe

LIFE ON THE OCEAN WAVE   (Folkraft 1251)
Version 1

The dancers need very little prodding when invited to join in singing the promenade chorus of this simple change-partner dance!

The Calls

Introduction

1. All join your hands and circle, you make the circle eight,
2. The other way back you circle 'til you all get straight.
3. You swing your partners round, it's round and round you go.
4. Allemande left on the corners, and grand chain round the row.
   All the way round the circle, you make the circle eight,
   You meet your sweet Sue and promenade until you all get straight.

Main Figure

5. The head two gents cross over and by the ladies stand.
6. The side two gents cross over and you all join hands.
7. Now bow to the corner lady and then to your partners all.
8. Swing the corner lady and promenade the hall.
   If I had a gal who wouldn't dance, I tell you what I'd do.
   I'd buy her a boat and set her afloat, and paddle my own canoe.

9. The head two gents cross over etc. (Repeat 5 through 8.)
10. The head two gents cross over, etc. (Repeat 5 through 8.)
11. The head two gents cross over, etc. (Repeat 5 through 8.)

Terminating Call

12. (Repeat 1 through 4.)

Explanation of Calls

1. All dancers join hands and circle to the left.
2. All dancers circle to the right and return to their home positions.
3. All dancers swing their partners.
4. All dancers allemande left with their corners, then do a grand right and left. When partners meet at the opposite side of the set, they promenade back to their home positions.

5. Gentlemen One and Three walk across the set, passing right shoulders, exchange places, and stand next to their opposite ladies.

6. Gentlemen Two and Four walk across the set, passing right shoulders, exchange places, and stand next to their opposite ladies.

7. All dancers join hands and form a circle of eight. While holding hands, all dancers bow to their corners, then to their partners.

8. Each gentleman now swings the lady on his left, then takes her as his new partner and promenades her to his new position (the one to which he had crossed on the opposite side of the set). During the promenade, the dancers may sing the promenade chorus.

9. Gentleman One and Three walk across the set back to their original positions, then Gentlemen Two and Four do the same. Repeat all movements described in 7 and 8.

10. Repeat all movements described in 5 through 8.

11. Repeat all movements described in 9. At this point, all gentlemen have their original partners and are back in their home positions.

12. Repeat movements described in 1 through 4.

GOLDEN SLIPPERS
(Old Timer 8002)

(Uptown and Downtown)

Although this is a fairly simple change-partner dance, it is fast moving and provides considerable action. It introduces *split the ring* and *elbow swing*. Start the record a second time at call line 14.

The Calls

Introduction

(Music A)
1. All join hands and circle left,
    You circle left around the hall.
2. Circle right on the same old track,
    Make your feet go whickety whack.
3. Now promenade your partners round
    It's two by two around the town.
    Promenade eight around the line,
    Keep on going, you're doin' fine.

(Music B)
4. Left hand round your corners,
    All the way around,
    A grand right and left you do,
    All around the town.
5. You meet your partners
    And you promenade a while,
    About half a mile,
    Then ready for the call.

Main Figure

(Music A)
6. First couple up center to the couple uptown
    And you bring that other couple down.
    Pick them up and bring them back
    And here you go around the track.
7. Now the lady go right and gent go wrong,
8. Right elbow swing as you come 'long,
    Elbow swing where you belong,
    Now swing your corner lady.

Golden Slippers

First couple up center to the
Now the la-dy go right and the

coup-le up town And you bring that o-ther coup-le down. Pick them up and
gent go wrong, Right el-bow swing as you come 'long. El- bow swing where

bring them back and here you go a- round the track.   la- dy.
you be-long, Now swing your cor-ner

Round and round you go And twirl on heel and toe, Now all prom-en
Take her for a stroll And pledge your all your soul, Now give her a

ade cor-ners all a-round the row.   hug and here we go a- gain.

(Music B)

9. Round and round you go
   And twirl on heel and toe,
10. Now all promenade corners all around the row.
    Take her for a stroll
    And pledge your all, your soul,
    Now give her a hug and here we go again.
11. (Repeat 6 through 10.)
12, 13. Second couple up center, etc. (Repeat 6 through 10 twice.)
14, 15. Third couple up center, etc. (Repeat 6 through 10 twice.)
16, 17. Fourth couple up center, etc. (Repeat 6 through 10 twice.)

Terminating Call

18. (Repeat 1 through 5.)

Explanation of Calls

1. All dancers join hands, form a circle of eight, and circle to the left.
2. All dancers circle to the right and return to their home positions.
3. Partners promenade once around the set, back to their home positions.
4. All dancers do an allemande left with their corners, then a grand right and left.
5. When partners meet at the opposite side of the set, they promenade back to their home positions.
6. Couple One, holding inside hands, walks across the set and joins hands with Couple Three to form a circle of four. Both couples walk back to Couple One's position, then walk across the set again to return to Couple Three's home position. The two couples release hands. Couple Three separates and Couple One splits the ring by walking through them (Figs. 45, 46).

Fig. 45. Split

Fig. 46. the ring.

7. Lady One turns to her right and walks around the outside of the set, as Gentleman One turns to his left and walks around the outside of the set.

8. When Couple One meets at its home position, Lady One and Gentleman One do a right elbow swing (Fig. 47).

Fig. 47. Right elbow swing

9. All gentlemen swing their corner ladies.

10. The gentlemen take the ladies they were just swinging as their new partners and promenade them once around the set, back to the gentlemen's home positions. All ladies have now moved one position to their right in the set. Thus, Lady Four is Gentleman One's partner; Lady Three is Gentleman Four's partner; Lady Two is Gentleman Three's partner; and Lady One is Gentleman Two's partner.

11. With his new partner, Gentleman One repeats the movements described in 6 through 10. The gentlemen now have their original opposite ladies as their new partners.

12, 13. Gentleman Two repeats the movements described in 6 through 10 twice. All gentlemen have their original partners again.

14, 15. Gentleman Three repeats the movements described in 6 through 10 twice. As in 11, the gentlemen have their original opposite ladies as their partners again.

16, 17. Gentleman Four repeats the movements described in 6 through 10 twice. All gentlemen have their original partners again.

18. Repeat the actions described in 1 through 5.

LIFE ON THE OCEAN WAVE   (Folkraft 1251)
Version 2

The following more complicated movements are added to the standard version of this dance (page 153) to make it suitable for more advanced dancers. This introduces the *ocean wave* formation. Start the record a second time at the beginning of call line 16.

The Calls

1–8. (Calls 1 through 8, page 153.)
9. Head two gents give right hands 'cross, you're doin' mighty fine.
10. On with your left, don't let go, and balance four in line.
11. Now break in the center, pass halfway round and balance your line again,
12. Then break that line and swing your doe, round and round you go.
13. The head two ladies chain across, hurry, don't be slow,
    Now chain right back across the hall, back to your partners you go.

14. Side two gents give right hands 'cross, etc.
    (Repeat 9 through 13.)
15. (Repeat 5 through 8, page 153; then 9 through 14.)
16. (Repeat 5 through 8, page 153; then 9 through 14.)
17. (Repeat 5 through 8, page 153; then 9 through 14.)

Terminating Call

18. (Repeat 1 through 4.)

Explanation of Calls

   1–8. See "Explanation of Calls," page 153.
   9. Gentlemen One and Three walk across the set and exchange places with each other, touching right hands as they pass.
   10. Gentlemen One and Three walk toward each other again and join left hands. Still holding left hands, they walk past each other and join right hands with their partners. The four dancers holding hands are now standing in a line of four, straight across the set, facing in alternate directions. This is an ocean wave formation. Since the end dancers and the dancers adjacent to them have right hands joined, it is a right-hand wave. At the call "balance four in line," all take one step forward and

Fig. 48. Balance four in line

Fig. 49. Break in the center, pass halfway round

pause while bringing the other foot forward, touching it to the floor without transferring weight. Each steps back on the free foot and pauses while touching the other foot beside it (Fig. 48).

11. Gentlemen One and Three release each other's left hand but continue to hold on to their partner's right hand. The gentlemen do a right allemande with their partners, just halfway around, so that the ladies finish this movement in the center of the set (Fig. 49).

The ladies join left hands, and once again the dancers are standing in a line of four, straight across the set, facing in alternate directions, forming another wave. At the call "balance your line again," all four take one step forward, then one step backward.

12. The two ladies release left hands and both couples swing partners back to their original positions.

13. The same two ladies chain across the set, then chain back to their partners.

14. Gentlemen Two and Four and their partners repeat the actions described in 9 through 13. On call 13, the side two ladies chain across the set, then back to their partners.

15, 16, 17. Repeat the movements described in 5 through 8 (page 154), then 9 through 14, three times.

18. Repeat the movements described in 1 through 4.

EL RANCHO GRANDE (Grenn 12148)
Version 2

This is a change-partner version of "El Rancho Grande" which employs an interesting combination of figures. (The music is on page 86.)

The Calls

Introduction

(*Music B*)
1. Allemande left your corner lady
   Grand right and left around the rancho.
2. And when you meet your handsome Pancho,
   You promenade around the Rancho.

(*Music A*)
3. Left hand to your corner, then swing your Señorita.
4. Promenade el rancho to your own casita,
5. Honor your Chiquita.

Main Figure

(*Music B*)
6. The ladies star, the gents promenade,
7. You turn your partner when she's handy.
8. The same old star and when you meet her,
   You swing your own at Rancho Grande.

(*Music A*)
9. Then do-sa-do your corner, swing corner Señorita,
10. Now promenade Rosita, that lovely Señorita
    To your own casita.

11. (Repeat 6 through 10.)
12. (Repeat 6 through 10.)
13. (Repeat 6 through 10.)

Terminating Call

(*Music B*)
14. Allemande left your corner lady
    Grand right and left around the rancho.
15. And when you meet your handsome Pancho,
    You promenade around the rancho.

Explanation of Calls

1. All dancers allemande left with their corners, then do a grand right and left.

2. When partners meet at the opposite side of the set, they promenade back to home positions.

3. All dancers allemande left with their corners, then swing partners.

4. Partners promenade once around the set.

5. All dancers honor their partners.

6. The four ladies walk to the center of the set, form a right hand star, and turn the star clockwise (Fig. 50).

Fig. 50. The ladies star, the gents promenade,

At the same time, the gentlemen promenade counterclockwise around the outside of the set. Partners pass each other on the opposite side of the set. The ladies continue to star and the gentlemen continue to promenade.

7. The second time partners meet (at the opposite side of the set), the ladies break the right hand star, and each lady does an allemande left with her partner (Figs. 51, 52).

Fig. 51. You turn your partner   Fig. 52. when she's handy.

8. The ladies form a right hand star again, turning the star clockwise, as the gentlemen promenade counterclockwise around the outside of the set (Fig. 53).

Fig. 53. The same old star and when you meet her,

Partners swing when they meet at their home positions (Fig. 54).

Fig. 54. You swing your own at Rancho Grande.

9. All dancers do-sa-do their corners, then swing their corners.

10. The gentlemen now promenade the ladies they were just swinging back to the gentlemen's home positions. Each lady has now advanced one position to her right in the set. Thus, Lady Four is Gentleman One's partner; Lady Two is Gentleman Three's partner; and Lady One is Gentleman Two's partner.

11. Repeat the movements described in 6 through 10. Each lady has now advanced one more position to her right in the set. The ladies are now partners with their opposite gentlemen.

12. Repeat 6 through 10 again. The ladies are now partners with their left-hand gentlemen.

13. Repeat 6 through 10 again. The ladies are now dancing with their original partners.

14. All dancers allemande left with their corners, then do a grand right and left.

15. When partners meet at the opposite side of the set, they promenade back to their home positions.

Some Contemporary Square Dance Calls

At this point you have seen a number of singing calls that include many traditional and some modern movements. Many professional callers have written and choreographed their own singing calls to modern country, jazz and rock melodies as well as to traditional tunes. Their singing styles and delivery vary, but they still rely on basic calling techniques.

The five singing calls in this next section introduce some additional Callerlab basic and mainstream movements, and they are presented very effectively on records. One side of the record has the calls, and the flip side contains just the music. Teacher/callers can study the calls, then practice their delivery using the instrumental side of the record as the musical background. At first, you will find yourself emulating the style and intonation of the originator of the calls, but with practice and application, your individual style will emerge.

The figures presented in the five records are somewhat more difficult than those described in the preceding pages. For this reason, diagrams of the sets are shown in order to clarify the more complicated movements. They indicate the positions of all dancers in the set at the conclusion of each figure (① for Lady One, ③ for Gentleman Three, etc.). For the first two records, however, "Houston" and "Easy on My Mind," since the figures are not overly complicated diagrams are not used.

These records are representative of the hundreds that have been pressed over the past several years. The figures, all of which are shown in the Callerlab handbook, are merely a sampling of the entire list of mainstream movements (see page 4).

HOUSTON

(Wagon Wheel 302)

CALLER: Beryl Main

This dance introduces the *Four ladies chain, do-paso,* and *weave the ring.*

The Calls

(*Sequence:* Introduction, Figure twice, Break, Figure twice)

Introduction and Break

1. Circle left and around you go, left allemande, come home and do-sa-do,
2. The men star right, go walking around that land
3. Left allemande and you weave that old ring.
4. I've got holes in both of my shoes, do-sa-do and then you swing her too—
5. You swing her round and do an allemande
6. Come back and promenade that old land.
   Promenade to Houston, Houston, Houston.

Figure

7. Four ladies chain, across you know, star right back and do a do-paso
8. Your corner right and turn your partner left,
9. The men star right, go walking round that old set.
10. Left allemande and do a right and left grand
    Go in and out and around that land,
11. Do-sa-do and then your corner swing
12. And then you promenade that old ring.
    Going back to Houston, Houston, Houston.

Explanation of Calls

1. All dancers circle left. When halfway around the set, allemande left corners, then do-sa-do partners.

2. Gentlemen form a right hand star, and turn it clockwise.

3. When gentlemen meet their corners they allemande left, then wave the ring. This figure is the same as a grand right and left, but dancers do not hold hands.

4. When dancers meet partners in home positions, they do-sa-do, then swing.

5. All dancers allemande left their corners.

6. All dancers return to their partners and promenade once around the set.

7. The four ladies do a grand chain by forming a right hand star. When the ladies reach their opposite gentlemen, they give them their left hands and all dancers do a courtesy turn (Figs. 55–58).

Fig. 55. Four ladies

Fig. 56. chain

Fig. 57. across

Fig. 58. you know

The ladies form a right hand star again (Fig. 59), turn it, and do a 180-degree left forearm turn with their partners, starting a do-paso (Fig. 60).

Fig. 59. Star right back   Fig. 60. and do-paso. Left to your partner,

8. All dancers complete the do-paso by doing a 180-degree right forearm turn with their corners (Figs. 61, 62), then a 180-degree left forearm turn with their partners (Figs. 63, 64).

Fig. 61. your corner   Fig. 62. right and

Fig. 63. turn your partner   Fig. 64. left,

(Instead of this left forearm turn, when a do paso finishes so that partners are standing in a basic square set formation, the gentlemen do a courtesy turn with their partners.)

9. The gentlemen form a right hand star (Fig. 65), and walk completely around the set.

Fig. 65. the men star right . . .

10. When they reach their corners, they allemande left and grand right and left.

11. All dancers do-sa-do their partners when they meet them, then swing their corners.

12. Gentlemen take their corners as their new partners, and promenade once around the set, back to the gentlemen's home positions.

13. Repeat the movements in 7 through 12. Gentlemen now have original opposite ladies as their new partners.

14. Repeat 1 through 6.

15. Repeat 7 through 12. Gentlemen now have original right-hand ladies as their new partners.

16. Repeat 7 through 12. All dancers now have their original partners.

EASY ON MY MIND   (Wagon Wheel 133)

CALLER: Don Franklin

This dance introduces *star thru* and *California twirl*.

The Calls

(*Sequence:* Introduction, Figure twice for heads, Break, Figure twice for sides, Ending)

Introduction/Break/Ending

1. Circle left around the floor, you're the one I'm living for,
   And the best I'll ever get you've given me,
2. Walk around that corner girl, see-saw your own,
3. Men star by the right one time around,
4. Left allemande, you do-sa-do,
5. Left allemande her and promenade,
   Whenever I need you all I have to do is close my eyes.

Figure

6. Heads (Sides) you promenade halfway around,
7. Sides (Heads) go right and left thru,
8. Star thru, California twirl, swing corner girl,
9. Left allemande and weave the ring,
10. Easy on my mind, do-sa-do her and promenade,
    Whenever I need you all I have to do is close my eyes.

Explanation of Calls

1. All dancers join hands and circle left, once around the set.

2. All dancers face their corners and walk forward around each other, keeping right shoulders adjacent. When dancers return to their original positions, they face their partners and walk forward around each other, keeping left shoulders adjacent, all dancers finish this figure by facing their corners.

3. Gentlemen form a right hand star and turn it around.

4. Gentlemen allemande left their corners when they meet them, then do-sa-do their partners.

5. Gentlemen allemande left their corners again, then all promenade their partners once around the set.

6. Head couples promenade halfway around the set and stand in each other's original positions.

7. Side couples change places by doing a right and left thru.

8. All dancers star thru. In this figure, partners face each other, and the gentleman's right hand is placed against the lady's left, palms touching, fingers pointed up, to form an arch. Partners move forward and the lady does a 90-degree left turn under the arch, as the gentleman does a 90-degree right turn moving behind the lady. They finish side by side, with the lady on the gentleman's right. All dancers now have their backs to the center of the set (Figs. 66–68).

Fig. 66. Star thru   Fig. 67. gentleman turns right,   Fig. 68. lady turns left.

All dancers California twirl. In this figure, the gentleman's right hand holds his partner's left hand as the hands are raised to form an arch. The lady walks forward under their joined hands, making a 180-degree left turn, as the man walks around the lady in a clockwise direction, turning 180 degrees to his right. Dancers have exchanged places and all are now facing the center of the set (Figs. 69–73). All dancers swing their corners.

Fig. 69. California twirl   Fig. 70. gentleman turns

Fig. 71. right,   Fig. 72. lady turns   Fig. 73. left.

9. Gentlemen allemande left with the lady to the left of their corners (opposite lady), then come back, pass right shoulders by their corners and weave the ring (grand right and left without hand contact).

10. When the gentlemen meet the ladies they were swinging in movement 8 (their original corners), all dancers do-sa-do, then the gentlemen take these ladies as their new partners, and promenade them back to the positions the gentlemen occupied after completing movements 6 and 7.

11. Repeat movements 6 through 10. All gentlemen now have original opposite ladies as new partners, and all gentlemen are standing in their original positions in the set.

12. Repeat movements 1 through 5.

13. Repeat movements 6 through 10, with side couples promenading halfway around the set and head couples doing a right and left thru. Gentlemen now have their right-hand ladies as their new partners.

14. Repeat movements 6 through 10, with side couples promenading halfway around the set and head couples doing a right and left thru. All gentlemen now have their original partners in their original home positions.

15. Repeat movements 1 through 5.

I DON'T LIVE THERE ANYMORE

(Blue Star 2194)

CALLER: Johnnie Wykoff

This dance introduces the *rollaway, square-thru four hands* and *turn thru.*

The Calls

(*Sequence:* Introduction, Figure with heads active, Figure with sides active, Break, Figure with heads active, Figure with sides active, Ending)

Introduction/Break/Ending

1. Four ladies chain go straight across that ring,
2. You rollaway, circle left around and then
3. Four ladies rollaway, you circle round that land,
4. Left allemande that corner gonna weave the ring,
   Weave in and out around and when you meet that maid
   Swing that pretty little girl. Everybody promenade.
   You didn't want the lovin' that now you're beggin' for,
   But that's all in the past, I don't live there anymore.

Figure

5. Head (Side) couples square thru four hands around you go.
6. You make a right hand star once around you know.
7. Heads (Sides) star left one time around will do
8. To the same two get a right and left thru, turn the lady to.
9, 10. Everybody rollaway and turn thru and go left allemande,
11. Come back and swing, promenade the land,
   But I'm giving up our dream house and roses by the door
   But that's all in the past, I don't live there anymore.

Explanation of Calls

Introduction

1. The four ladies chain to the opposite side of the set.

2. Ladies all rollaway. Each lady rolls across a full left turn (360 degrees) in front of the dancer on her left, as he sidesteps to his right to exchange places. All dancers circle left.

3. Ladies do another rollaway in front of the gentlemen on their left. All dancers circle left.

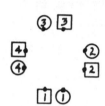

4. All dancers allemande left with their corners, weave the ring, swing their partners when they meet them, then promenade to home positions.

Figure (Heads active)

5. Head couples square thru four hands around. This means that Couples One and Three do the square thru figure four times. (All dancers are in home positions at the start of this figure.)

The first time, the facing dancers (Gentleman One and Lady Three, and Gentleman Three and Lady One) join right hands and pull by, exchanging places. Each dancer turns in one quarter (90 degrees) (Figs. 74–78).

Fig. 74. Square thru

Fig. 75. Right hand

Fig. 76. pull

Fig. 77. by,

Fig. 78. face in.

The second time (two hands square thru or square thru one half), facing dancers (Gentleman One and Lady One, and Gentleman Three and Lady Three) join left hands and pull by (Figs. 79–81) and turn in one quarter (90 degrees).

Fig. 79. Left hand

Fig. 80. pull by,

Fig. 81. face in.

The third time (three hands square thru or square thru three quarters), facing dancers (Gentleman One and Lady Three, and Gentleman Three and Lady One) join right hands and pull by, and turn in one quarter (90 degrees).

The fourth time (full square thru or square thru four hands), facing dancers (Gentleman One and Lady One, and Gentleman Three and Lady Three) join left hands and pull by, but do not turn in. Note that Couple One is standing back to back, and Couple Three is standing back to back.

(The square thru movement requires the dancers to give their right hands to their opposites, pull by, turn a quarter, and continue until the figure is completed.

6. Facing couples (Gentleman One facing Lady Four, Gentleman Four facing Lady Three; and Gentleman Two facing Lady One, Gentleman Three facing Lady Two) form a right hand star and turn it once around.

7. Couples One and Three form a left hand star and turn it once around, then drop hands and return to original positions (as in 6).

8. Facing couples do a right and left thru.

9. Ladies rollaway one position to their left.

10. All dancers face partners and turn thru. In this movement, facing dancers step forward and join right forearms. They turn right one half (180 degrees), release armholds and step forward, passing each other's right shoulder. They are now facing in the opposite direction from which they started the turn (Figs. 82–85).

11. All dancers allemande left with the dancers they are facing, go back and swing their new partners, then all promenade once around the set, back to the gentlemen's home positions.

Fig. 82. Turn thru

Fig. 83. Right forearm

Fig. 84. 180-degree turn,

Fig. 85. step forward.

Figure (Sides active)

Repeat the movements in 5 through 7, with side couples doing the square thru four times, facing dancers doing a right hand star and side couples doing a left hand star.

8. Facing couples do a right and left thru.

9. Ladies rollaway.

10. All turn thru.

11. Left allemande, swing new partners and promenade.

Break

1. Four ladies chain.

2. Ladies rollaway, all dancers circle left.

3. Ladies rollaway again, all dancers circle left.

4. All dancers allemande left, weave the ring, swing their partners and promenade.

Figure (Heads active)

Repeat the movements in 5 through 7, with head couples doing the square thru four times, facing dancers doing a right hand star and head couples doing a left hand star.

8. Facing couples do a right and left thru.

9. Ladies rollaway.

10. All turn thru.

11. All allemande left, swing new partners and promenade.

Figure (Sides active)

Repeat movements in 5 through 7, with Couples
Two and Four doing the square thru four times, facing couples doing a right hand star and side couples
doing a left hand star.

8. Facing couples do a right and left thru.

9. Ladies rollaway.

10. All turn thru.

11. All allemande left, swing original partners and
promenade.

Ending

Repeat all movements in 1 through 4.

IF THEY COULD SEE ME NOW   (Wagon Wheel 600)

CALLER: Ken Bower

This dance introduces *box the gnat* and *square thru three hands*.

The Calls

(*Sequence:* Introduction, Figure twice for heads, Break, Figure twice for sides, Ending)

Introduction/Break/Ending

1. Why don't you circle left, go walking 'round that old ring.
2. You allemande your corner, then your partner swing,
3. Four ladies promenade, go one time and then,
4. Hey box the gnat, with a right and left grand.
   All I can say is Wowie, look at where I am.
5. Do-sa-do your partner, promenade that old land,
   Hey, what a set-up, Holy Cow! they'd never believe it,
   If my friends could see me now.

Figure

6. Why don't those heads (sides) square thru, four hands around that old town,
7. Do-sa-do, one time around,
8. Star thru, forward eight and back to the land,
9. Square thru and count three hands,
10. Do a left allemande.
11. Well do-sa-do,
12. And to that corner go,
    Swing that girl around and promenade her back home.
    You promenade her 'round, just struttin',
    High with that gal, oh, if my friends could see me now.

Explanation of Calls

Introduction

1. All dancers join hands and circle left.
2. All allemande left their corners, then swing their partners.
3. Gentlemen stand still as the four ladies promenade around the inside of the set.
4. As the ladies return to their partners, they extend right hands to their partners and box the gnat. In this figure, partners join right hands and walk forward, exchanging positions, the ladies making a left turn under their joined right hands (Figs. 86–88). All dancers right and left grand.
5. When partners meet, all do-sa-do, then promenade to their home positions.

Fig. 86. Box

Fig. 87. the

Fig. 88. gnat.

Figure (Heads active first time)

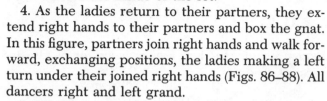

6. Head-couples square thru four times (see pages 176–177, or see glossary). Note that Couple One is standing back-to-back, and Couple Three is standing back-to-back.

7. All dancers do-sa-do those they are facing and finish in the same formation as 6, above.

8. All facing dancers star thru. The two lines of four take three steps forward, then three steps back to places.

9. The four dancers on the left half of the lines (Gentleman Four facing Lady Four and Gentleman One facing Lady Three), and the four dancers on the right half of the lines (Gentleman Three facing Lady One and Gentleman Two facing Lady Two) square thru three times (see page 176 or glossary).

10. All gentlemen allemande left with the lady on their right. Thus, Gentleman Four does an allemande left with Lady Three, Gentleman Three with Lady Two, Gentleman One with Lady Four, and Gentleman Two with Lady One.

11. The center four dancers do-sa-do those they are facing (original partners), and the end dancers do-sa-do those in the opposite line (original partners). As the gentlemen complete the do-sa-do, they move toward their original corners.

12. All gentlemen swing their original corners, then promenade those ladies back to the gentlemen's home positions.

Figure (Heads active second time)

6. Head couples square thru four times.

7. All dancers do-sa-do those they are facing and finish in the same formation as 6, above.

8. All facing dancers star thru. The two lines of four take three steps forward, then three steps back to places.

9. The four dancers on the left half of the lines and the four dancers on the right half of the lines square thru three times.

10. All gentlemen allemande left with the lady on their right.

11. The center four dancers do-sa-do those they are facing (original corners), and the end dancers do-sa-do those in the opposite line (original corners). As gentlemen complete the do-sa-do, they move toward their original opposite lady.

12. All gentlemen swing their corners (original opposite ladies), then promenade them as new partners back to the gentlemen's home positions.

Break

Repeat movements in 1 through 5, all couples starting from and ending in positions indicated in 12.

Figure (Sides active first time)

6. Side couples square thru four times.

7. All dancers do-sa-do those they are facing and finish in the same formation as 6, above.

8. All facing dancers star thru. The two lines of four take three steps forward, then three steps back to places.

9. The four dancers on the top half of the lines and the four dancers on the bottom half of the lines square thru three times.

10. All gentlemen allemande left with the lady on their right.

11. Center four dancers do-sa-do those they are facing (original opposites) and end dancers do-sa-do those in the opposite line (original opposites). As gentlemen complete the do-sa-do, they are moving toward their original right hand lady.

12. All gentlemen swing their corners (original right-hand ladies), then promenade them as new partners back to the gentlemen's home positions.

Figure: (Sides active second time)

6. Side couples square thru four times.

7. All dancers do-sa-do those they are facing and finish in the same formation as 6, above.
8. All facing dancers star thru. The two lines of four take three steps forward, then three steps back to places.

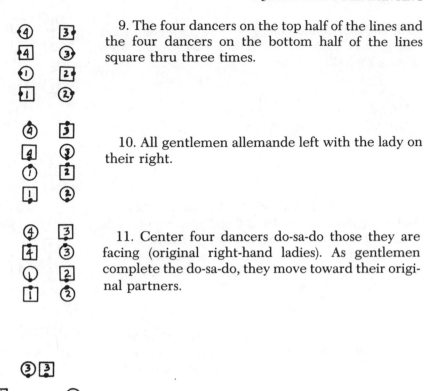

9. The four dancers on the top half of the lines and the four dancers on the bottom half of the lines square thru three times.

10. All gentlemen allemande left with the lady on their right.

11. Center four dancers do-sa-do those they are facing (original right-hand ladies). As gentlemen complete the do-sa-do, they move toward their original partners.

12. All gentlemen swing their corners (original partners), then promenade their corners back to the gentlemen's home positions.

Ending

Repeat movements in 1 through 5, all couples starting from original home positions and ending in original home positions.

AFTER THE LOVIN' (Continental 20001)

CALLER: Jack Drake

This dance introduces *circle (break) to a line, pass thru, boys run, slide thru* and *chase right.*

The Calls

(*Sequence:* Introduction, Figure twice for heads, Break, Figure twice for sides, Ending)

Introduction/Break/Ending

1. (*Circle left*)
   So, I'll sing you to sleep after the lovin'
   With a song I just wrote yesterday.
2. Walk around your corner, seesaw your own.
3. Left allemande, weave the ring.
4. You're all I wanted, you're all I hoped for,
   Do-sa-do and promenade.
   After the lovin' I'm still in love with you.

Figure

5. Heads (sides) promenade halfway around there,
6. Lead to the right, circle up four,
7. Break to a line and then
8. Pass thru, chase right,
9. Boys run right around that girl
10. Right and left thru,
11. Slide thru,
12. Square thru three quarters,
13. Swing the corner, promenade.
    After the lovin' I'm still in love with you.

Explanation of Calls

Introduction

1. All join hands and circle left once around the set.

2. All dancers walk forward around their corners, keeping right shoulders adjacent, then face their partners and walk forward around their partners, keeping left shoulders adjacent. (See glossary: All Around the Left Hand Lady, See Saw Your Partner.)

3. All dancers allemande left their corners, then weave the ring.

4. When partners meet they do-sa-do, then promenade to home positions.

Figure (Heads active first time)

5. Head couples promenade halfway around the set.

6. Head couples lead out to the side couples and circle four hands with the side couples, turning the circle 180 degrees (Figs. 89–91).

Fig. 89. Circle

Fig. 90. up

Fig. 91. four,

7. Each of the two circles break to a line. In this maneuver, the men who started on the inside of their respective circles (Gentleman One and Gentleman Three) release their left hand but retain the hand of the dancer on their right, so that the gentlemen become the left end dancers of their respective lines. The ladies at the right end of these lines turn under the raised hands of their partners while advancing to the right end of their lines (Figs. 92–94).

Fig. 92. break

Fig. 93. to a

Fig. 94. line.

8. The two lines pass thru. In this movement, facing dancers in each of the two lines move forward, opposites passing right shoulders. Each line ends in the other's starting position. The dancers do not change facing position, so that the two lines now have their backs toward each other (Figs. 95–97).

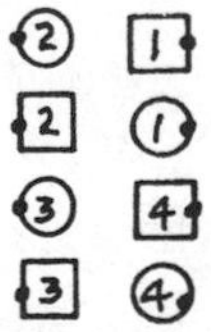

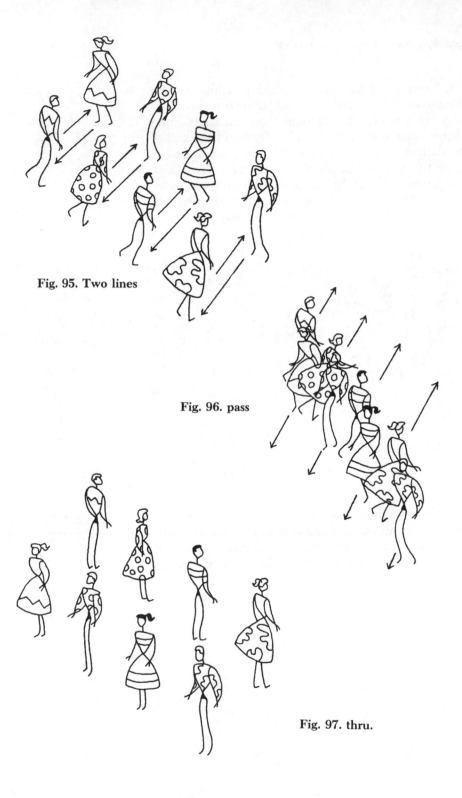

Fig. 95. Two lines

Fig. 96. pass

Fig. 97. thru.

To chase right, each lady walks to her right in a full circle (360 degrees) to finish in the position of the lady who was diagonally behind her and facing in the same direction as when she started the action. Her partner follows her and turns 180 degrees to his right to stand next to her to finish facing out. Partners are now facing in opposite directions.

9. At the call "Boys run right," gentlemen move forward in a semicircle to their right, around their partners, to end in their partners' starting positions. At the same time, their partners sidestep (without changing facing direction) into the positions vacated by the gentlemen (Figs. 98–100).

Fig. 98. Boys

Fig. 99. run

Fig. 100. right.

10. Both lines of four do a right and left thru.

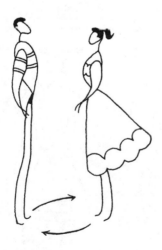

11. Facing dancers in opposite lines slide thru. To do this, both lines pass thru and occupy the other lines' positions. All gentlemen turn right one quarter (90 degrees), as all ladies turn left one quarter (90 degrees). At this point, all dancers are facing their original partners within the lines of four (Figs. 101–104).

Fig. 101. Slide   Fig. 102. thru.

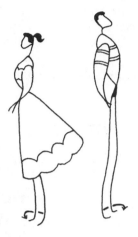

Fig. 103. Boy turns   Fig. 104. right, girl turns left.

12. Square thru three quarters (or three times).

Square thru first time.

Square thru second time.

Square thru third time.

13. Gentlemen swing their corner ladies. Thus Gentleman One swings Lady Four, Gentleman Two swings Lady One, Gentleman Three swings Lady Two and Gentleman Four swings Lady Three. Gentlemen promenade these ladies back to their home positions. Gentlemen now have their original corners as their partners.

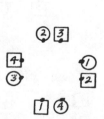

Figure (Heads active second time)

5. Head couples promenade halfway around the set.

6. Head couples lead to the right and circle four.

7. Each of the two circles break to a line.

8. The two lines pass thru, chase right.

9. Boys run right.

10. Both lines of four do a right and left thru.

11. Facing dancers in opposite lines slide thru.

12. Square thru three quarters.

13. All swing their corners and promenade back to the gentlemen's home positions. Gentlemen now have their original opposite ladies as new partners.

Break

Repeat the movements in 1 through 4. Dancers finish
in the same positions as 13.

Figure (Sides active first time)

5. Side couples promenade halfway around the set.

6. Side couples lead to the right and circle four.

7. Each of the two circles break to a line.

8. The two lines pass thru,
chase right.

9. Boys run right

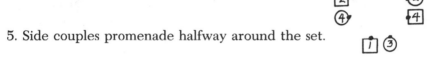

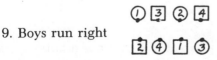

④ ② ③ ①   10. Both lines of four do a right and left thru.

③ ① ④ ②

③ ① ④ ②   11. Facing dancers in opposite lines slide thru.

④ ② ③ ①

④ ② ③ ①   12. Square thru three quarters.

③ ① ④ ②

④ ③

④   ③   13. All swing their corners and promenade back to

①   ②   the gentlemen's home positions. Gentlemen now
                     have their original right hand ladies as new partners.

① ②

④ ③   *Figure (Sides active second time)*

② ①

③ ④   5. Side couples promenade halfway around the set.

① ②

① ④

③ ④

② ①   6. Side couples lead to the right and circle four.

② ③

④ ③ ① ④
                     7. Each of the two circles break to a line.
② ③ ① ②

8. The two lines pass thru, chase right.

9. Boys run right.

10. Both lines of four do a right and left thru.

11. Facing dancers in opposite lines slide thru.

12. Square thru three quarters.

13. All swing their corners and promenade around the set back to the gentlemen's home positions. Gentlemen now have their original partners.

Ending

Repeat movements in 1 through 4. Dancers finish in original positions with original partners.

6

SQUARE DANCE PATTER CALLS: FOR THE STUDENT AND TEACHER

As was explained on page 17, the introductions, breaks and terminating movements of patter calls may be interchanged at the caller's discretion and used in any square dance. For this reason, only the calls for the main figures of the square dances are included in this chapter. A variety of introductory calls, breaks and terminating calls may be found on pages 32–36; the caller should choose among the less complicated figures for the simple square dances and use the more involved ones in the advanced square dances.

The square dances in this chapter include some maneuvers not employed in the chapter on singing calls. All new terms are explained fully where they appear for the first time; they are also explained in the glossary.

Many of the selections in this chapter are traditional, frequently performed dances, and regardless of the section of the country in which they are called, the execution of the figures is pretty much the same. This applies particularly to the simple square dances such as "Split the Ring," "Duck for the Oyster," and "Birdie in the Cage."

On the other hand, the more advanced dances (and even some of the simple ones) have tended to vary somewhat from place to place as local callers added their personal touches and interpretations to the many square dance figures. With the advent of Callerlab, however, this tendency toward differentiation is fast disappearing. This chapter presents a sampling of Callerlab formations. For the complete listing, consult the Callerlab handbook (see page 4).

Recommended Hoedown Records for Patter Calls

Bake Them Hoecakes Brown	Folkraft 3301
Chinese Breakdown	Sets in Order 2123
Little Brown Jug	Worldtone 10023
Mississippi Sawyer	Folkraft 1334
Old Joe Clark	Folkraft 1071
Rakes of Mallow	Folkraft 1425
Soldier's Joy	Folkraft 1152
Flop Ear Mule	Folkraft 1319
Miss McLeod's Reel	Folkraft 1043
White Cockade	Folkraft 1005
Hootenany Hoedown	Wagon Wheel 105
Billy John	Wagon Wheel 121
Devil's Dream	Wagon Wheel 124
Jim Jam	Sets in Order 2147
Rubber Dolly	Blue Star 1767
Sherbrooke	Grenn 12052
Whiffletree	Top 25068
Wild Cat	Windsor 4186
Dance All Night	Kalox 1277
River Boat Run	Kalox 1275
Airmail Special	Kalox 1279

SWING THE MAN FROM ARKANSAS

In this dance, the active lady gets to swing every person in the set!

The Calls

1. First lady out to the right of the ring
   And swing your Maw and then your Paw.
2. Now swing the man from Arkansas.
3. On to the next and swing your Maw
   And then your Paw.
   Now swing the man from Arkansas.
4. On to the last and swing your Maw
   And then your Paw.
   Now swing the man from Arkansas.
5. Now swing your partners one and all
   Swing 'em be they short or tall.
6. Second lady lead out, etc. (Repeat 1 through 5.)
7. Third lady lead out, etc. (Repeat 1 through 5.)
8. Fourth lady lead out, etc. (Repeat 1 through 5.)

Explanation of Calls

1. Lady One leads out and swings Lady Two, then swings Gentleman Two. Meanwhile Gentleman One walks to the center of the set.

2. Lady One now swings her partner in the center of the set.

3. Lady One leads on to Couple Three and performs the movements described in 1 and 2.

4. Lady One leads on to Couple Four and performs the movements described in 1 and 2.

5. Couple One returns to their home positions and all dancers swing their partners.

6. Lady Two leads out and performs the movements described in 1 through 5.

7. Lady Three leads out and performs the movements described in 1 through 5.

8. Lady Four leads out and performs the movements described in 1 through 5.

TWO LITTLE LADIES FORM A RING

In this square, the active lady "picks up" a lady from each couple she visits, until all four ladies are dancing together.

The Calls

1. First couple balance and swing,
   Twirl around that pretty little thing.
2. First lady out to the right and
   Two little ladies form a ring.
   Circle two then home you swing.

3. Three little ladies form a ring and
   Circle three, then home you swing.

4. Four little ladies form a ring and
   Circle four, then home you swing.

5. Second couple balance and swing, etc. (Repeat 1 through 4.)
6. Third couple balance and swing, etc. (Repeat 1 through 4.)
7. Fourth couple balance and swing, etc. (Repeat 1 through 4.)

Explanation of Calls

1. Couple One does a step-swing balance, then swings.
2. Lady One leads out to her right and stands in front of Couple Two. She joins hands with Lady Two and both ladies circle once around, clockwise. The ladies release hands, return to their home positions and swing their partners.
3. Ladies One, Two and Three walk to the center of the set, join hands to form a circle of three and circle once around, clockwise. The three ladies release hands, return to their home positions and swing their partners.
4. All four ladies walk to the center of the set, form a circle of four and circle once around, clockwise. The ladies release hands, return to their home positions and swing their partners.
5. Repeat all of the movements described in 1 through 4, with Lady Two leading out.
6. With Lady Three leading out, repeat as in 5.
7. With Lady Four leading out, repeat as in 5.

GENTLEMEN JIG

In this simple visiting dance, the gentlemen have an opportunity to show off as the others chuckle at their antics.

The Calls

1. First gent lead out to the right of the ring
   And bow real low to that pretty little thing.
2. Now jig around on heel and toe
   Then swing around that pretty little doe.

3. Move along to the next boy and girl
   And bow to the lady with the cute spit curl.
   Now jig around on heel and toe
   Then swing her high and swing her low.

4. Now visit with the lady on the left
   And bow real low, so nice and deft.
   Strut your stuff, boy, jig and whirl
   Then twirl around that last little girl.

5. Second gent lead out, etc. (Repeat 1 through 4.)
6. Third gent lead out, etc. (Repeat 1 through 4.)
7. Fourth gent lead out, etc. (Repeat 1 through 4.)

Explanation of Calls

1. Gentleman One leads out, stands in front of Lady Two and executes a low, exaggerated bow.

2. He then "shows off" in front of the lady by improvising a short jig step. Gentleman One then swings Lady Two.

3. Gentleman One leads on to Lady Three and performs the movements described in 1 and 2.

4. Gentleman One leads on to Lady Four and performs the movements described in 1 and 2.

5. Gentleman Two leads out and performs the movements described in 1 through 4.

6. Gentleman Three leads out and performs the movements described in 1 through 4.

7. Gentleman Four leads out and performs the movements described in 1 through 4.

SPLIT THE RING

This is the simplest of all "split the ring" dances.

The Calls

1. First couple bow, first couple swing,
2. Go down the center and split the ring,
   Cut off six.
   Lady go gee and gent go haw,
3. Go on back home and swing your maw.

4. Now down the center and cut off four,
   Lady go right, gent go wrong,
5. Swing back home where you belong.

6. Down center again and cut off two.
   Lady go east, gent go west
7. Now swing the gal that you like best.

8. Second couple bow, etc. (Repeat 1 through 7.)
9. Third couple bow, etc. (Repeat 1 through 7.)
10. Fourth couple bow, etc. (Repeat 1 through 7.)

Explanation of Calls

1. Couple One honors, then swings.
2. Couple One walks across the set and passes through Couple Three (who separate to let them through). This movement splits the six stationary dancers into two groups of three—hence the name of the call, "cut off six." Lady One walks to her right around the outside of the set, and Gentleman One walks to his left around the outside of the set.
3. When Lady One and Gentleman One meet at their home position, they swing.
4. Lady One leads out again and passes between Couples Two and Three, as Gentleman One leads out and passes between couples Three and Four.
5. Both walk back, around the outside of the set, to their home position and swing.
6. Lady One now walks through Couple Two and returns to her home position as Gentleman One walks through Couple Four and returns to his home position.
7. Couple One swings.
8. Couple Two leads out and performs the movements described in 1 through 7.
9. Couple Three leads out as in 8.
10. Couple Four leads out as in 8.

DUCK FOR THE OYSTER

Although quite simple, this is one of the most popular of all square dances.

The Calls

1. First couple out and circle four,
   It's four hands halfway round the floor.
2. Duck for the oyster, duck!
3. Dig for the clam, dig!
4. Kick a hole in the ol' tin can,
5. It's four hands half around the land.
   Duck for the oyster, duck!
   Dig for the clam, dig!
   Duck for the oyster and on you go,
6. Four hands half around and don't be slow.
   Duck for the oyster, duck!
   Dig for the clam, dig!
   Duck on through and home you go.

7. Second couple out, etc. (Repeat 1 through 6.)
8. Third couple out, etc. (Repeat 1 through 6.)
9. Fourth couple out, etc. (Repeat 1 through 6.)

Fig. 105. Duck for the oyster

Explanation of Calls

1. Couple One leads out, forms a circle of four with Couple Two, and circles halfway round, clockwise, to finish facing the center of the set.

2. With all four dancers still holding hands, Couple Two raises its inside hands to form an arch and Couple One walks two steps under the arch, then two steps back to place (Fig. 105).

3. Couple One now raises its inside hands to form an arch and Couple Two takes two steps under the arch, then two steps back to place.

4. Couple Two raises its hands to form an arch again. Couple One releases the hands joined with Couple Two, walks completely through the arch and leads on to Couple Three.

5. Couple One repeats all the movements with Couple Three as described in 1 through 4.

6. Couple One repeats all the movements with Couple Four as described in 1 through 4.

7. Couple Two leads out and repeats the movements described in 1 through 6.

8. Couple Three leads out as in 7.

9. Couple Four leads out as in 7.

BIRDIE IN THE CAGE

This is one of the simplest of all visiting couple square dances.

The Calls

1. First couple out and circle four,
   It's four hands all around the floor.
2. Birdie in the cage, it's three hands round,
   Cage her in, go round and round.
3. Birdie hops out, the crow hops in,
   It's three hands round and you're gone again.
4. Crow hops out, both couples swing,
   Twirl around your pretty little thing.

5. On to the next and circle four, etc. (Repeat 1 through 4.)
6. On to the last and circle four, etc. (Repeat 1 through 4.)

7. Second couple out, etc. (Repeat 1 through 6.)
8. Third couple out, etc. (Repeat 1 through 6.)
9. Fourth couple out, etc. (Repeat 1 through 6.)

Explanation of Calls

1. Couple One leads out to the right and circles four hands round with Couple Two, clockwise.

2. Lady One releases her hands and steps into the center of the circle of four. The other three dancers join hands and circle clockwise around the lady, as she turns to her left inside the circle.

3. Lady One now leaves the center and joins the circle as her partner goes into the center. The three dancers circle clockwise around the gentleman as he turns to his left inside the circle.

4. Gentleman One now leaves the center of the circle of three and joins his partner. Couples One and Two swing partners.

5. Couple One leads on to Couple Three and performs all the movements described in 1 through 4.

6. Couple One leads on to Couple Four and performs all the movements described in 1 through 4.

7. Couple Two leads out and repeats 1 through 6.

8. Couple Three leads out as in 7.

9. Couple Four leads out as in 7.

LADY GO SEE

The lady of the active couple is left alone for a moment and she surveys the situation to see how her partner is faring with another couple.

The Calls

1. First couple out to the couple on the right,
    Circle three and the lady go see.
2. Meet your partner comin' round
    And swing that gal right off the ground.
3. Two in the center and circle up six,
    Watch 'em show their bag of tricks!

4. Lead right on to the couple on the right, etc.
    (Repeat 1 through 3.)
5. Lead right on, etc. (Repeat 1 through 3.)

6. Second couple out, etc. (Repeat 1 through 5.)
7. Third couple out, etc. (Repeat 1 through 5.)
8. Fourth couple out, etc. (Repeat 1 through 5.)

Explanation of Calls

1. Couple One leads out to Couple Two and Gentleman One joins hands with Couple Two and circles three hands round with them, clockwise. Meanwhile, Lady One walks around the outside of the circle of three, in the opposite direction.

2. Lady One passes her partner once, as the circle of three moves around. The second time she meets her partner, he detaches himself from the circle of three and swings his partner in the center of the set.

3. The remaining three couples join hands and circle clockwise, six hands around the swinging couple. When Couples Two, Three and Four return to their home positions, they release their hands and break the circle.

4. Couple One leads on to Couple Three and repeats all the movements described in 1 through 3.

5. Couple One leads on to Couple Four and repeats all the movements described in 1 through 3. Couple One returns to its home position.

6. Couple Two leads out and performs all the movements described in 1 through 5.

7. Couple Three leads out as in 6.

8. Couple Four leads out as in 6.

GRAPEVINE TWIST

This is an add-a-couple dance, with the figure eight increasing in size as the lead couple picks up additional couples.

The Calls

1. First gent take your lady by the wrist,
   Go around that lady with a grapevine twist.
2. Now around the gent, you're not through yet,
   Right straight back to the center of the set.
3. Circle four in the center of the floor.

4. Break at the head and on once more.
   Go through the next and around that doe,
   Now around the gent, to the center you go.
   Circle up six and don't be slow.

5. Now break at the head and on through the last,
   Around the lady with a hey-diddle-diddle,
   Now around that gent and back to the middle
   And circle up eight in the center of the floor.

6. Second gent take your lady, etc. (Repeat 1 through 5.)
7. Third gent take your lady, etc. (Repeat 1 through 5.)
8. Fourth gent take your lady, etc. (Repeat 1 through 5.)

Explanation of Calls

1. Gentleman One takes his partner by the wrist and leads her through Couple Two. He turns to his left, walks around Lady Two and leads his partner back to the center of the set (Figs. 106, 107).

Fig. 106. First gent take
your lady by the wrist,

Fig. 107. Go around that lady

Fig. 108. with a grapevine twist.

Fig. 109. Now around the gent,

Fig. 110. you're not through yet,

Fig. 111. Right straight back
to the center of the set.

2. Still holding his partner's wrist, he leads her through Couple Two again. He turns to his right, walks around Gentleman Two and leads his partner back to the center of the set (Figs. 108–111).

3. Couples One and Two now join hands, form a circle of four and circle once around, clockwise (Figs. 112, 113).

Fig. 112. Circle four   Fig. 113. in the center of the floor.

4. Gentleman One frees his left hand and leads the other three danc-ers through Couple Three. Couples One and Two now repeat all the movements described in 1 through 3. Couples One, Two and Three have now formed a circle of six.

5. Gentleman One frees his left hand and leads the other five dancers through Couple Four. Couples One, Two and Three now repeat the movements described in 1 through 3. All four couples have now formed a circle of eight.

6. Gentleman Two leads out and performs all the movements de-scribed in 1 through 5.

7. Gentleman Three leads out as in 6.

8. Gentleman Four leads out as in 6.

FOUR IN LINE

This square dance employs a simple but effective pattern in which opposites swing on either side of a standing line of four.

The Calls

1. First couple balance and swing,
2. Now promenade half round the ring,
    Line up four on the opposite track.
3. Forward four and four come back,
4. Forward four and there stand pat.
5. Two end couples lead on down
    And swing the opposite round and round.
6. Move along to the end of the line,
    Swing your own, you're doing fine.
7. Go down that line on the other side
    And swing your opposite high and wide.
8. Then home you go and all eight swing.

9. Second couple balance, etc. (Repeat 1 through 8.)
10. Third couple balance, etc. (Repeat 1 through 8.)
11. Fourth couple balance, etc. (Repeat 1 through 8.)

Explanation of Calls

1. Couple One balances, then swings.

2. Couple One walks halfway around the set, passes behind Couple Three, then turns left to face the center of the set and stands alongside Couple Three, to their right, to form a line of four.

3. Couples One and Three, still standing in a line of four, join hands and take four steps forward, then four steps back to their places.

4. The line of four takes four steps forward again to the center of the set and stands still (Figs. 114, 115).

Fig. 114. Forward four and there stand pat.

Fig. 115. Two end couples

5. Couples Two and Four separate and walk along the line toward the center of the set. The ladies walk along the right side of the line as they face it from their home positions, and the gentlemen walk along the left side. Halfway along the line, the side couples swing their opposites when they meet (Figs. 116, 117).

Fig. 116. lead on down

Fig. 117. and swing the opposite round and round.

6. The opposites stop swinging, separate, and continue to move along the line in the same direction as before. Partners meet and swing when they reach the end of the line (Figs. 118, 119).

Fig. 118. Move along to the end of the line,

Fig. 119. Swing your own, you're doing fine.

7. Partners separate again and move along the other side of the line, in the opposite direction. They meet their opposites again in the center of the line and swing.

8. Opposites separate, return to their home positions and swing their partners. At the same time, the line of four releases hands and Couples One and Three swing back to their home positions.

9. Couple Two leads out and performs all the movements described in 1 through 8. During these movements, the line of four is formed by Couples Two and Four.

10. Couple Three leads out and performs all of the movements described in 1 through 8. During these movements, the line of four is again formed by Couples One and Three.

11. Couple Four leads out and performs all the movements described in 1 through 8. During these movements, the line of four is again formed by Couples Two and Four.

FORWARD SIX, FALL BACK SIX

This is one of the simplest of all line formations. It introduces *U turn back*. For a more complicated line dance using the same formation, see the singing square "Pistol Packin Mama," Version Two, page 130.

The Calls

1. First couple out to the couple on the right
   And circle four 'til the middle of the night.
2. Leave her there with he and she,
   Go on to the next and circle three.
3. Steal the gal that you just found
   And on to the next with four hands round.
4. Leave that gal who ain't done wrong,
   Go on back home where you belong.

5. Forward up six and fall back six,
6. Forward up two and fall back two.
7. Six pass thru and U turn back,
8. The two lone gents cross over too.

9. (Repeat 5 through 8.)

10. All eight swing,
    Now promenade around the ring.

11. Second couple out, etc. (Repeat 1 through 10.)
12. Third couple out, etc. (Repeat 1 through 10.)
13. Fourth couple out, etc. (Repeat 1 through 10.)

Explanation of Calls

1. Couple One leads out, joins hands with Couple Two, and circles four hands round with them.

2. Gentleman One leaves his partner with Couple Two, leads on to Couple Three and circles three hands with them.

3. Gentleman One transfers Lady Three to his right, takes her with him to Couple Four and circles four hands round with Couple Four.

4. Gentleman One leaves Lady Three with Couple Four and returns to his home position. Gentlemen One and Three are now standing alone in their home positions, and Gentlemen Two and Four each have their partner standing on their right and another lady on their left, to form two lines of three.

5. The two lines of three, holding hands, take three steps forward, bow, then walk backward to their places.

6. Gentlemen One and Three take three steps forward, bow to each other, then walk backward to their places.

7. The two lines of three release hands and walk toward each other. Each person in the lines of three passes right shoulders with the opposite person (Fig. 120).

Fig. 120. Forward six and pass right thru

Each line of three continues across the set until it occupies the position of the other line, and then each person turns around in place to face the center of the set.

8. Gentlemen One and Three exchange places, passing right shoulders as they do so, then turn around to face the center of the set.

9. All dancers now repeat all the movements described in 5 through 8, to finish with the lines of three and Gentlemen One and Three back in their original positions.

10. All dancers swing their partners, then promenade once around the set.

11. Couple Two leads out and performs all the movements described in 1 through 10. At the conclusion of these movements, Gentlemen Two and Four are standing alone in their home positions and two other lines of three are formed, with Gentlemen One and Three each standing with their partner on their right and another lady on their left.

12. Couple Three leads out and performs all the movements described in 1 through 10. During these movements, lines are formed as described in 4.

13. Couple Four leads out and performs all the movements described in 1 through 10. During these movements, lines are formed as described in 11.

FORWARD UP AND BACK

This is a good square dance for practicing the right and left through and the ladies chain.

The Calls

1. First old couple go round the ring,
    Right back home and there you swing.
2. Head two couples forward and back,
3. Forward again and right and left through,
    Right and left back on the same old track.
4. The two ladies chain across,
    Now chain right back and don't get lost.
5. All eight swing on heel and toe,
    Then promenade around the row.

6. Second old couple, etc. (Repeat 1 through 5, with the side couples active.)
7. Third old couple, etc. (Repeat 1 through 5, with the head couples active.)
8. Fourth old couple, etc. (Repeat 1 through 5, with the side couples active.)

Explanation of Calls

1. Couple One promenades once around the set and back to its home position, then swings.

2. Couples One and Three take four steps forward, then four steps back to places.

3. Couples One and Three do a right and left thru, then a right and left back.

4. Ladies One and Three chain across the set, then chain back to their places.

5. All dancers swing partners, then promenade once around the set and back to their home positions.

6. Couple Two leads out and the side couples perform all the movements described in 1 through 5.

7. Couple Three leads out and the head couples perform all the movements described in 1 through 5.

8. Couple Four leads out and the side couples perform all the movements described in 1 through 5.

SWING AND TAKE HER ALONG

This is a change-partner square dance in which the active gentleman visits each couple in turn, leaves his old partner and picks up a new one.

The Calls

1. First couple out to the right of the ring,
   Change your partners and there you swing.
2. Take her along to the next ol' two,
   Gents swing new gals as you always do.
3. Take her along and change and swing
4. Then home you go with that pretty little thing.
5. Now you're home and everybody swing.

6. Second couple out, etc. (Repeat 1 through 5.)
7. Third couple out, etc. (Repeat 1 through 5.)
8. Fourth couple out, etc. (Repeat 1 through 5.)

Explanation of Calls

1. Couple One leads out to Couple Two. Gentleman One swings Lady Two, and Gentleman Two swings Lady One.

2. Gentleman One leaves his partner with Gentleman Two and takes his new partner, Lady Two, along to Couple Three. Gentleman One and Gentleman Three now exchange partners and swing new partners.

3. Gentleman One takes his new partner, Lady Three, along to Couple Four. Gentleman One and Gentleman Four now exchange partners and swing new partners.

4. Gentleman One takes his new partner, Lady Four, along to his home position.

5. The four gentlemen swing their new partners at their home positions.

6. Couple Two leads out and performs the movements described in 1 through 5.

7. Couple Three leads out as in 6.

8. Couple Four leads out as in 6.

FOUR GENTS STAR

This is a simple change-partner square dance in which the gentlemen do a right hand star twice before taking a new partner.

The Calls

1. Four gents in with a right hand star
    A right hand round and there you are.
2. Meet your partner with a left hand round,
    It's all the way round.
3. Then star by the right around once more,
    a four hand star around the floor.
4. Come back to your own with a left-hand twirl
5. Then all run away with the corner girl.

6. Four gents in, etc. (Repeat 1 through 5.)
7. Four gents in, etc. (Repeat 1 through 5.)
8. Four gents in, etc. (Repeat 1 through 5.)

Explanation of Calls

1. The four gentlemen step to the center of the set, form a right hand star and turn the star clockwise.

2. When the gentlemen arrive at their home positions, they break the star by releasing right hands and do an allemande left with their partners.

3. The gentlemen return to the center of the set again, form a right hand star and turn the star clockwise.

4. They allemande left with their partners again when they arrive at their home positions.

5. The gentlemen now take their corner ladies as their new partners and promenade their new partners back to the gentlemen's home positions.

6. Repeat all the movements described in 1 through 5. At the conclusion, each gentleman will have his original opposite lady as his new partner.

7. Repeat all the movements described in 1 through 5. At the conclusion, each gentleman will have his original right-hand lady as his new partner.

8. Repeat all movements described in 1 through 5. Gentlemen now have their original partners.

FORWARD UP FOUR, SIX, EIGHT

Dancers are intrigued by the almost military precision with which the figures can be performed in this square dance.

The Calls

1. First couple bow and now you swing,
   Separate, go around the ring
   And join the opposite in a line of four.
2. Forward up four, fall back four,
3. Sashay four to the right.
4. Forward up six, fall back eight,
5. Forward up eight, fall back six,
6. Sashay four to the right.
7. Forward up four, fall back four,
8. Sashay four to the right.
9. Forward up six, fall back eight,
10. Forward up eight, fall back six,
11. Sashay four to the right.
12. Forward up four and circle four,
13. Swing your partners one and all,
14. Then promenade around the hall.

15. Second couple bow, etc. (Repeat 1 through 14.)
16. Third couple bow, etc. (Repeat 1 through 14.)
17. Fourth couple bow, etc. (Repeat 1 thrugh 14.)

Explanation of Calls

1. Couple one honors, then swings. Lady One faces right and Gentleman One faces left, and they walk in opposite directions around the outside of the set. Gentleman One stops walking when he reaches Couple Three. He stands to the right of Lady Three and faces the center of the set. When Lady One reaches Gentleman Three, she stands to his left and faces the center of the set. Couples One and Three are now standing in a line of four, in Couple Three's home position, holding hands and facing the center of the set.

2. The line of four takes four steps forward, then four steps back to place.

3. The line takes four sliding steps to the right and stands behind Couple Four. Gentleman One and Lady One, each standing at opposite ends of the line of four, reach forward and grasp the free hands of Couple Four, to form a sort of elongated circle.

4. The elongated circle of six dancers takes four steps forward and finishes standing opposite Couple Two. The six dancers take four steps

Fig. 121. Forward up six, fall back eight.

back to place and Couple Two follows them by taking four steps forward.

5. All eight dancers now take four steps in the direction of Couple Two's position, the six dancers walking forward and Couple Two walking backward. Couple Two remains in its home position and the six dancers take four steps back to place.

6. The original line of four leaves its position behind Couple Four by taking four sliding steps to the right, to stand in Couple One's home position.

7. The line of four takes four steps forward, then four steps back to place.

8. They take four sliding steps to the right to stand behind Couple Two.

9. They form an elongated circle with Couple Two, take four steps forward to Couple Four (Fig. 121), then four steps back to place, with Couple Four following.

10. The eight dancers take four steps toward Couple Four's home position. Couple Four remains there as the six dancers take four steps back to place.

11. The original line of four takes four sliding steps to the right, to stand in Couple Three's home position.

12. They take four steps forward, join hands to form a circle of four and circle once around, clockwise.

13. Couples One and Three return to their home positions and all four couples swing their partners.

14. Partners promenade once around the set and return to their home positions.

15. Couple Two leads out and performs all the movements described in 1 through 14.

16. Couple Three leads out as in 15.

17. Couple Four leads out as in 15.

LADY GO HALFWAY ROUND AGAIN

In this square dance, the active gentleman takes the spotlight as he quickly maneuvers with each lady in the set.

The Calls

1. First couple balance, first couple swing
2. Then promenade around the ring.
3. The lady leaves her gent right there
4. And walks around to the opposite pair.
5. Forward three and fall back three,
    Forward three and three stand pat.
6. The lonesome gent with a do-sa-do
    Around those three to the center go.
7. Turn the left-hand lady with a right hand round,
8. Now the right-hand lady with a left hand round.
9. The opposite lady with both hands round.
10. Now swing your partner, home you go,
11. All eight swing on heel and toe.

12. Second couple balance, etc. (Repeat 1 through 11.)
13. Third couple balance, etc. (Repeat 1 through 11.)
14. Fourth couple balance, etc. (Repeat 1 through 11.)

Explanation of Calls

1. Couple One balances, then swings.

2. Couple One promenades around the set, back to its home position.

3. Gentleman One remains in his home position as Lady One walks counterclockwise around the outside of the set.

4. Lady One stands alongside Couple Three, to the left of Gentleman Three, to form a line of three.

5. The three dancers hold hands and take four steps forward, then four steps back to place. The line of three takes four steps forward again and remains standing in a line in the center of the set.

6. Gentleman One does a do-sa-do around the line of three. He passes right shoulders by Lady Three, stands back to back with her, then moves to his right. When he gets to the other end of the line of three, he walks backward to the center of the set, passing left shoulders by Lady One.

7. Gentleman One leads on to Lady Four, does an allemande right with that lady, then returns to the center of the set.

8. He leads on to Lady Two, does an allemande left with that lady, then returns to the center of the set.

9. He then advances to Lady Three, joins both hands with that lady and walks around her, clockwise, to return to the center of the set.

10. He swings his partner back to his home position.

11. All dancers swing their partners.

12. Couple Two leads out as in 1 through 5, then Gentleman Two repeats the movements described in 6 through 11.

13. Couple Three leads out as in 1 through 5, then Gentleman Three repeats the movements described in 6 through 11.

14. Couple Four leads out as in 1 through 5, then Gentleman Four repeats the movements described in 6 through 11.

CIRCLE ROUND THE CIRCLE

When little circles rotate around each other in sets all over the floor, they give the impression of fast-moving pinwheels.

The Calls

1. First lady out to the second boy and girl
    And circle three hands round the world.
2. The lady move on and the gent begin,
    Two circles of three and we're gone again.
    Round and round the circles go,
    One around the other you circle so.
3. The lady move on and the gent also,
    Two circles of three and around you go,
    Round and round the circles go,
    One around the other you circle so.
4. The lady stand pat and the gent move on,
    And now you form two rings of four.
    Round and round the circles go,
    One around the other you circle so.
5. Run along home and everybody swing.

6. Second lady out, etc. (Repeat 1 through 5.)
7. Third lady out, etc. (Repeat 1 through 5.)
8. Fourth lady out, etc. (Repeat 1 through 5.)

Explanation of Calls

1. Lady One leads out to Couple Two, joins hands with them to form a circle of three, and they circle once around clockwise.

2. Lady One detaches herself from Couple Two, leads on to Couple Three and forms a circle of three with them. At the same time, Gentleman One leads on to Couple Two and forms a circle of three with them. The two circles of three turn clockwise. While they are turning clockwise, they revolve around each other, counterclockwise, until they arrive at their starting points (Fig. 122), then all dancers release hands.

Fig. 122. Circle around the circle

3. Lady One leads on to Couple Four and joins hands with them, as Gentleman One leads on to Couple Three and joins hands with them. Both circles of three revolve around each other, as explained in 2.

4. Lady One remains with Couple Four and Gentleman One leaves Couple Three to join his partner; they form a circle of four with Couple Four. Meanwhile, Couples Two and Three move toward each other, join hands and form a circle of four. Both circles of four revolve around each other as explained in 2. Both circles of four release hands when they near their home positions.

5. All dancers swing their partners at their home positions.

6. Lady Two leads out and she and her partner perform all the movements described in 1 through 5.

7. Lady Three leads out and she and her partner perform all the movements described in 1 through 5.

8. Lady Four leads out and she and her partner perform all the movements described in 1 through 5.

TEXAS STAR

Everyone is kept active throughout this highly popular, interesting change-partner square dance which introduces the *Texas star.*

The Calls

1. Ladies to the center and back to the bar.
2. Gents to the center and form a star,
   It's right hand round and there you are.
3. Back with your left, don't go too far,
   Just meet your partner, pass her by,
   Hook the next gal on the fly.
4. The gents swing out, the ladies swing in,
   Form that Texas Star again.
5. Break the star, the new girl swing,
6. Now promenade around the ring.

7. Ladies to the center, etc. (Repeat 1 through 6.)
8. Ladies to the center, etc. (Repeat 1 through 6.)
9. Ladies to the center, etc. (Repeat 1 through 6.)

Explanation of Calls

1. The four ladies take three steps in to the center of the set, bow, then walk backward to their places.

2. The four gentlemen walk to the center of the set, from a right hand star and turn the star clockwise.

3. The four gentlemen release right hands, form a left hand star and turn the star counterclockwise. While turning the star in this direction, they walk past their partners and place their right arms around the waist of the next lady they meet, to form a Texas star, and continue to walk counterclockwise (Fig. 123).

4. With their right arms still around the ladies' waists, the gentlemen break the star by releasing left hands. The gentlemen now back up to the outside of the set as the ladies walk forward to the inside, reversing the Texas star by forming a right hand star. The Texas star now turns clockwise.

5. The ladies break the Texas star by releasing right hands and the gentlemen swing their new partners.

6. Partners promenade once around the set, back to the gentlemen's home positions. Each gentleman now has his original right-hand lady as his new partner.

7. Repeat all the movements described in 1 through 6. At the conclusion, each gentleman has his original opposite lady as his new partner.

8. Repeat all the movements described in 1 through 6. At the conclusion, each gentleman has his original left-hand lady as his new partner.

9. Repeat all the movements described in 1 through 6, with all gentlemen finishing the dance with their original partners.

Fig. 123. Texas star

LADIES GRAND CHAIN

This change-partner square dance, employing the *ladies grand chain* (or *four ladies chain*), enables the ladies to quickly maneuver to their opposite gentlemen.

The Calls

1. Ladies forward and back to the bar,
2. In you go with a right hand star.
   Ladies grand chain just halfway round
   To the opposite gent then come on down,
   Back to the center with right hands crossed,
   Go home to your partners, don't get lost.
3. Turn the right-hand lady with the right hand round,
4. Your own with the left just halfway round,
5. Swing your corner as she comes down
   And promenade around the town.

6. (Repeat 1 through 5.)
7. (Repeat 1 through 5.)
8. (Repeat 1 through 5.)

Explanation of Calls

1. The four ladies take four steps forward, then four steps back to places.

2. The four ladies go forward again, form a right hand star and turn the star clockwise until they reach the opposite side of the set, where they stand in front of their opposite gentlemen. The ladies release right hands. Each gentleman does a courtesy turn by taking his opposite lady's left hand in his left hand and placing his right arm around the lady's waist, turning her counterclockwise, once around, so that each couple is facing the center of the set. The ladies form the right hand star again and continue to turn the star clockwise until they reach their partners. Each gentleman does a courtesy turn with his partner, just as he did with his opposite lady.

3. Each gentleman advances to his right-hand lady and does an allemande right with her.

4. Each gentleman gives his partner his left hand and turns halfway around with her, exchanging places.

5. Each gentleman swings his corner lady, takes her as his new partner, and promenades her once around the set back to his home position. Thus, Gentleman One has Lady Four as his new partner; Gentleman Two has Lady One as his new partner; Gentleman Three has Lady Two as his new partner; and Gentleman Four has Lady Three as his new partner.

6. Repeat all the movements described in 1 through 5. At the conclusion, all gentlemen have their original opposite ladies as their new partners.

7. Repeat all the movements described in 1 through 5. At the conclusion, all gentlemen have their original right-hand ladies as their new partners.

8. Repeat all the movements described in 1 through 5. At the conclusion, all dancers are in their home positions with their original partners.

WAGON WHEEL
Version 1

Although the starting formation of this square dance is the same as in "Pistol Packin' Mama," page 130, the action is somewhat different and dancers have to "keep on their toes" if they wish to finish the dance with their original partners!

The Calls

1. First couple out and circle four,
    Just once around, no more.
2. Leave her there, go on to the next,
    Circle three hands round.
3. Take that lady on with you
    And circle four hands round.
4. Leave her there, go home alone.

5. Forward up six, fall back six,
6. Forward up two, fall back two.
7. Forward up six and wheel around,
8. Two lone gents go across the town.
9. Four ladies cross over on an even keel,
    New lines of three and you're ready to wheel.

10. Forward up six, etc. (Repeat 5 through 9.)
11. Forward up six, etc. (Repeat 5 through 9.)
12. Forward up six, etc. (Repeat 5 through 9.)
13. Swing your partners and promenade.

14. Second couple out, etc. (Repeat 1 through 13.)
15. Third couple out, etc. (Repeat 1 through 13.)
16. Fourth couple out, etc. (Repeat 1 through 13.)

Explanation of Calls

1. Couple One leads out, joins hands with Couple Two and circles four hands once around, clockwise.

2. Gentleman One leaves his partner with Couple Two, leads on to Couple Three and circles three hands once around, clockwise, with that couple.

3. He takes Lady Three, transfers her to his right hand, leads on to Couple Four with that lady, and they circle four hands once around, clockwise.

4. Gentleman One leaves Lady Three with Couple Four and returns to his home position, alone.

5. Gentlemen Two and Four hook elbows with the ladies on either side of them, to form two lines of three. The lines of three take four steps forward, then four steps back to places.

6. Gentlemen One and Three take four steps forward, then four steps back to places.

7. The lines of three take four steps forward again and the two gentlemen join hands; they pivot their parallel lines halfway around, clockwise, until the lines have changed places (Figs. 124, 125). The gentlemen drop hands and each line of three backs up into the position originally occupied by the other line.

Fig. 124. Six wheel

Fig. 125. around.

8. Gentlemen One and Three cross the set and change places.

9. Gentlemen Two and Four pass the lady on their right in front of them and to the lone gentlemen on their left, and then they pass the lady on their left in front of them and to the lone gentlemen on their right. Two new lines of three are now formed, with Gentlemen One and Three in the center of the lines and Gentlemen Two and Four standing alone.

10. Repeat all the movements described in 5 through 9. At the conclusion of these movements, Gentlemen Two and Four are standing in the center of the two lines of three.

11. Repeat all the movements described in 5 through 9. At the conclusion, Gentlemen One and Three are standing in the center of the two lines of three.

12. Repeat all the movements described in 5 through 9. At the conclusion, Gentlemen Two and Four are standing in the center of the two lines of three, as in the original formation in 5.

13. All dancers swing their partners, then promenade once around the set.

14. Couple Two leads out and performs all the movements described in 1 through 13.

15. Couple Three leads out as in 14.

16. Couple Four leads out as in 14.

CHARLESTON ARCH

Originated by William Carr of Charleston, West Virginia, this square dance employs the old figure-eight movement in a unique formation.

The Calls

1. Head two couples forward and back,
2. Forward again and the ladies hook.
3. Clockwise now around you march
   'Til the gents get home then form an arch.
5. Side men under with your date,
   Turn to the left go figure eight.
6. Through the other arch and don't get sore,
   Make a figure eight then circle up four.
7. Head girls reel with the right elbow,
8. When the sides get home all do paso.
9. Side two couples forward and back, etc.
   (Repeat 1 through 8.)

Explanation of Calls

1. Couples One and Three take four steps forward, then four steps back to places.

2. Couples One and Three hook partners' inside elbows (gentlemen's right and ladies' left elbows), walk forward again and stand in a line of four, the ladies standing right shoulder to right shoulder. Ladies One and Three hook right elbows (Fig. 126).

Fig. 126. Head two couples forward and the ladies hook.

3. The line of four now wheels around clockwise, three quarters of a turn, until Gentlemen One and Three are standing closest to their home positions (Figs. 127-129).

Fig. 127. Clockwise now

Fig. 128. and around you march

Fig. 129. 'Til the gents get home

4. Gentlemen One and Three release their partners' elbows and join hands instead, then raise their hands to form an arch. Ladies One and Three still have their right elbows hooked (Fig. 130).

Fig. 130. then form an arch.

5. Each side gentleman takes his partner's hand and leads her through the arch formed by the couple with its back to him. Thus, Couple Two ducks under Couple One's arch and Couple Four ducks under Couple Three's arch (Fig. 131).

Fig. 131. Side men under with your date,

Each side gentleman turns to the left around the man to come under the same arch again (Figs. 132, 133).

Fig. 132. Turn to the left

Fig. 133. go figure

6. Each side gentleman, still followed by his partner, continues the figure-eight movement under the other arch. Thus, Couple Two ducks under Couple Three and Couple Four ducks under Couple One (Figs. 134, 135).

Fig. 134. eight.

Fig. 135. Through the other arch

Each side gentleman turns to the left around the man to come under the same arch again (Figs. 136, 137).

Fig. 136. and don't get sore,

Fig. 137. Make a figure

Couples Two and Four join hands to form a circle of four around couples One and Three, who are still standing in a line of four, and circle clockwise (Fig. 138, 139).

Fig. 138. eight

Fig. 139. then circle up four.

7. As the side couples start to circle around the center line, Ladies One and Three release their partners' hands and with right elbows still hooked, walk around each other, clockwise.

8. When the side couples have their backs to their home positions, Ladies One and Two release right elbows. All dancers give left hands to their partners and do a do-paso.

9. Couples Two and Four lead out and perform all the movements described in 1 through 8.

THREE LADIES CHAIN

The gentleman of the active couple is a busy "pivot" man as he turns left continuously while assisting three ladies back and forth across the set in a *three ladies chain.*

The Calls

1. First couple out to the couple on the right
   And circle four hands round.
2. Across the set you chain all three,
   Chain in and out like buzzin' the bee.
   Back and forth you're doin' fine,
   Go home to your own gent in the line.
3. On to the next and circle four,
4. Two ladies chain to the opposite pair,
   Chain right back, you're finished there.
5. On to the last and circle four,
   Go once around and open the door.
   Across the set you chain all three,
   Chain in and out like buzzin' the bee.
   Back and forth you're doin' fine,
   Go home to your own gent in the line.

6. Second couple out, etc. (Repeat 1 through 5.)
7. Third couple out, etc. (Repeat 1 through 5.)
8. Fourth couple out, etc. (Repeat 1 through 5.)

Explanation of Calls

1. Couple One leads out, joins hands with Couple Two, circles four hands once around clockwise, and finishes in the center of the set, facing Couple Two's home position.

2. Ladies One and Two do a ladies chain, with Gentleman One turning *halfway* around with Lady Two, to finish facing Couple Four. At the same time, Gentleman Two turns Lady One around to face the center of the set (Figs. 140, 141). Ladies Two and Four do a ladies chain, with Gentleman One turning *halfway* around with Lady Four, to finish facing Couple Two's home position again. At the same time, Gentleman Four turns Lady Two to face the center of the set (Figs. 142, 143). Lady One then chains with Lady Four (Fig. 144), and the three ladies continue to chain back and forth across the set until they return to their

Fig. 140. Across the set

Fig. 141. you chain all three,

Fig. 142. Chain in and out

Fig. 143. like buzzin'

original partners. During this continuous chaining movement, the center gentleman (Gentleman One) turns halfway to his left each time he chains a new lady, and the end gentlemen (Gentlemen Two and Four) turn the ladies who come to them completely around to face into the center of the set again.

Fig. 144. the bee.

3. Couple One leads on to Couple Three, and they circle four hands once around, clockwise.

4. Ladies One and Three chain across to their opposites, then chain back.

5. Couple One leads on to Couple Four and they circle four hands once around, clockwise. Ladies Four, One and Two do the three ladies chain figure again, as described in 2, until the three ladies return to their original partners.

6. Couple Two leads out and performs all the movements described in 1 through 5.

7. Couple Three leads out as in 6.

8. Couple Four leads out as in 6.

HEADS ADVANCE, SIDES DIVIDE

This change-partner dance employs a series of symmetrical movements which are fun to do and interesting to watch.

The Calls

1. Heads advance, sides divide,
2. Center split, all swing at the side.
   Spin those ladies, watch 'em go
   Twirl around on heel and toe.

3. Heads advance, sides divide,
4. Center split, all swing at the side.
   Swing those gals, they're all so sweet,
   Swing 'em hard and give 'em a treat.

5. Heads advance, sides divide,
6. Center split, all swing at the side.
   Swing 'em boys, and do it right,
   Swing those maids 'til the middle of the night.

7. Heads advance, sides divide,
8. Center split, all swing at the side.
   Swing that darling, swing that maid,
9. Now take your corner and promenade.

10. Heads advance, sides divide, etc. (Repeat 1 through 9.)
11. Heads advance, sides divide, etc. (Repeat 1 through 9.)
12. Heads advance, sides divide, etc. (Repeat 1 through 9.)

Explanation of Calls

1. Couples One and Three walk to the center of the set. At the same time, Couple Two separates and Couple Four separates, with Ladies Two and Four walking to their right and Gentlemen Two and Four walking to their left. Thus, Lady Two meets Gentleman Four at Couple Three's home position and Lady Four meets Gentleman Two at Couple One's home position (Figs. 145–147).

Fig. 145. Heads   Fig. 146. advance,

Fig. 147. sides divide.

2. Couples One and Three are facing each other in the center of the set. Gentlemen One and Three take their opposite ladies as their new partners and walk with them to the nearest home position of the side couples. Thus, Gentleman One walks to Couple Four's home position with Lady Three, and Gentleman Three walks to Couple Two's home position with Lady One. All four gentlemen have now moved one position clockwise in the set and have their original opposite ladies as their new partners (Figs. 148, 149). All gentlemen swing their new partners (Fig. 150), then place them on their right.

3, 4. As in 1 and 2, the head couples advance to the center of the set, while the side couples separate and move into the head couples' home positions to meet new partners. The couples in the center of the set separate and move into the side couples' home positions with their new partners. At the conclusion of these movements, the four gentlemen have moved one position clockwise in the set and all dancers are with

Fig. 148. Center   Fig. 149. split,

Fig. 150. all swing at the side.

their own partners, but are standing in the home position of their original opposite couple. All gentlemen swing their partners, then place them on their right.

5, 6. Head and side couples repeat the movements described in 3 and 4. At the conclusion, each gentleman has moved one position clockwise in the set and is standing with his original opposite lady as his new partner.

7, 8. Head and side couples repeat the movements described in 3 and 4. At the conclusion, all couples are back in their home positions with their original partners.

9. The four gentlemen take their corner ladies as their new partners and promenade them once around the set, back to the gentlemen's home positions.

10, 11, 12. Repeat the movements described in 1 through 9 three times.

CROSSED TRAILS

This square dance, which employs the figure *cross trail thru,* was originated by Frank Frankeberger of Los Angeles, California.

The Calls

1. First and third go forward and back,
2. Forward again let's have a little fun,
   Cross trail thru, go around just one.
3. Go down the center and cross trail thru,
   Go around just one you're still not through.
4. Now pass right through across the set,
   Around just one you're not through yet.
5. Forward again and pass right through,
   Around just one you're almost through.
6. Now cross trail thru in the middle of the land,
7. And turn your corner to a left allemande,
   A right to your own and a right and left grand.
   Hand over hand around the ring,
   Meet your partner and give her a swing.
   Then promenade that pretty little thing.

8. Second and fourth, etc. (Repeat 1 through 7.)

Explanation of Calls

1. Couples One and Three take four steps forward, then four steps back to places.

2. Couples One and Three pass through each other, opposites passing right shoulders. Immediately after passing through each other, each couple does a cross trail thru, with the lady crossing over to her left in front of the gentleman and the gentleman going to his right in back of the lady (Figs. 151, 152).

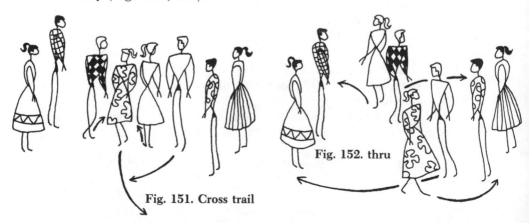

Fig. 152. thru

Fig. 151. Cross trail

After cross trailing thru, the couples separate and each of the four active dancers goes around one person to split the side couples. Thus, Gentleman One walks around Lady Two, and Lady Three walks around Gentleman Two, to split Couple Two; and Gentleman Three walks around Lady Four, and Lady One walks around Gentleman Four, to split Couple Four. Gentleman One and Lady Three are now standing side by side, between Couple Two, with Gentleman One standing to the right of Lady Three; and Gentleman Three and Lady One are standing between Couple Four, with Gentleman Three standing to the right of Lady One (Figs. 153, 154).

Fig. 153. go around

Fig. 154. just one.

3. Couples One and Three (with their opposites as partners), pass through each other and do a cross trail thru, as explained in 2. This time, however, since each active gentleman is on his new partner's right, the cross trail thru is accomplished by the lady crossing over to her right in front of the gentleman, and the gentleman going to his left in back of the lady. After cross trailing thru, each active couple splits a side couple by passing through the couple it is facing. Thus, Gentleman One and Lady Three split Couple Four, and Gentleman Three and Lady One split Couple Two. The four dancers continue to walk around the couples they just split and return to their home positions with their original partners.

4. Couples One and Three pass through each other. The couples separate and each of the four dancers goes around one person to split the side couples. At this point, Gentleman Three and Lady One are standing side by side between Couple Two, and Gentleman One and Lady Three are standing side by side between Couple Four.

5. Couples One and Three (with opposites as partners) pass right through again. They split the opposite couples and each dancer walks around one person and proceeds to the nearest head couple's home position. This leaves Couples One and Three standing with their partners on opposite sides of the set, Couple One standing in Couple Three's home position, and Couple Three standing in Couple One's home position.

6. Couples One and Three pass right through, then do a cross trail thru, as explained in 2. The four dancers continue to move forward toward their corners.

7. All dancers do an allemande left, then a grand right and left. When partners meet on opposite sides of the set, they swing. Partners then promenade back to their home positions.

8. Couples Two and Four lead out and perform all of the movements described in 1 through 7.

SUSIE Q

This square dance, which features changing lines of four, was originated by Jim York of Los Angeles, California.

The Calls

1. First and third bow and swing,
   Lead to the right and form two rings.
2. Circle half and break to a line,
   Four in line you stand.
3. Right and left through two by two,
4. Come right back with a Suzie Q.
   Opposites with a right hand round,
   Partner by the left as she comes down.
   Opposites with a right hand round,
5. Left to your own and wheel around,
   Form new lines and settle down.

6. (Repeat 3 through 5.)
7. (Repeat 3 through 5.)
8. (Repeat 3 through 5.)

9. Second and fourth bow and swing, etc. (Repeat 1 through 8.)

Explanation of Calls

1. Couples One and Three honor their partners, then swing their partners. Couple One leads out to Couple Two; they join hands and circle four hands halfway around, clockwise. At the same time, Couple Three performs the same action with Couple Four.

2. Gentlemen One and Three break the circles of four by freeing their left hands. The two circles open up into two lines of four, each line standing in a side couple's home position and facing into the center of the set.

3. All dancers do a right and left thru by giving right hand to opposites and pulling by. Each gentleman then takes his partner's left hand, places his right hand behind his partner's back and wheels her counterclockwise, to face the center of the set again. The two lines of four have now exchanged places and are facing each other on opposite sides of the set.

4. All dancers turn their opposites with the right hand, all the way around, then their partners with the left hand, all the way around, then their opposites again with the right hand, all the way around.

5. At this point, the lines of four change composition and position as follows: each gentleman takes his partner's left hand in his left hand and places his right hand behind his partner's back; Gentlemen One and Three wheel their partners a one-quarter turn, counterclockwise, while Gentlemen Two and Four wheel their partners a three-quarter turn, counterclockwise. In this manner new lines of four are formed, each couple standing in line with the couple it was facing in the original lines of four, each new line now standing in a head couple's home position, facing the center of the set. Thus, couples One and Four are standing in Couple One's home position, with Couple Four standing to the right of Couple One; and Couples Three and Two are standing in Couple Three's home position, with Couple Two standing to the right of Couple Three.

6. Repeat all the movements described in 3 through 5. At the conclusion, new lines of four are standing in the side couples' home positions.

7. Repeat all the movements described in 3 through 5. At the conclusion, new lines of four are standing in the head couples' home positions.

8. Repeat all movements described in 3 through 5. At the conclusion, the original lines of four are standing in the side couples' home positions. (Although Jim York did not so indicate in his original call, it would be wise at this point to insert a simple break, such as swing partners and promenade, so that partners may return to their home positions before the next call.)

9. Couples Two and Four lead out and repeat all the movements described in 1 through 8.

WAGON WHEEL
Version 2

The only similarity between this square dance, the chorus of which was originated by Lloyd Shaw of Colorado Springs, and Version 1 of "Wagon Wheel" is in the name. Mr. Shaw presented this figure at the Sanford Institute in 1947.

The Calls

1. First couple bow and now you swing,
2. Go down the center and split the ring.
   Lady go East, gent go West,
3. Go past the one you love the best.
   Swing your corners, give 'em a twirl
4. Then promenade that corner girl.

5. Allemande left and a right to your girl,
6. Form a Wagon Wheel and make it whirl.
7. The hub flies out and the rim flies in,
8. It's a right and left, you're goin' again.
9. Now a right hand whirl and another wheel,
   The faster you go the better you feel.
10. The gents sweep out and the ladies sweep in,
11. It's a right and left you're goin' again.
    Find your partner, find your maid,
    There she is, boys, promenade.

12. Second couple bow, etc. (Repeat 1 through 11.)
13. Third couple bow, etc. (Repeat 1 through 11.)
14. Fourth couple bow, etc. (Repeat 1 through 11.)

Explanation of Calls

1. Couple One honors, then swings.
2. Couple One walks across the set and passes through Couple Three, who separate to let them through. The lady turns to her left, the gentleman turns to his right, and both walk around the outside of the set, back to their home positions.
3. Gentleman One and Lady One walk past each other, to their corners. All dancers swing their corners.
4. The gentlemen take their corner ladies as their new partners and promenade once around the set back to the gentlemen's home positions.

Fig. 155. Form a Wagon Wheel

Fig. 156. and make it whirl.

5. All gentlemen allemande left with their corners (original opposite ladies) and join right hands with their partners.

6. Partners walk completely around each other and the gentlemen make a left hand star (Fig. 155). As the gentlemen reach out with their left hands to form the star, they push forward with their right hands to twirl their partners halfway around so that the ladies face in the same direction as the gentlemen. The ladies now hook their left elbow with their partner's right (Fig. 156).

7. The gentlemen break the star by releasing left hands and back out as the ladies walk forward, for one complete turn (Figs. 157–159).

Fig. 157. The hub   **Fig. 158. flies out**

Fig. 159. and the rim flies in,   Fig. 160. It's a right to your own . . .

8. The gentlemen pull back with their right arm, breaking the elbow hook as they do so and twirling their partners to face them. The gentlemen take their partner's right hand and start a grand right and left (Fig. 160). The gentlemen pass by their partners, give their left hand to the next lady, and pass by that lady.

9. The gentlemen give their right hand to the next lady, hold on, walk completely around that lady and make a left hand star. As in 6, the ladies twirl halfway around and hook their left elbow with the gentlemen's right.

10. The gentlemen break the star by releasing left hands and back out as the ladies walk forward, for one complete turn.

11. As in 8, the gentlemen break the elbow hook, face the ladies with whom they had just locked elbows, give right hands to those ladies, and continue the grand right and left. The gentlemen give their left hand to the next lady, then meet their partners with their right hand and promenade back to the gentlemen's home positions.

12. Couple Two leads out and repeats all the movements described in 1 through 11. Gentlemen now have their original opposites as their new partners.

13. Couple Three leads out and repeats all the movements described in 1 through 11. Gentlemen now have their original right-hand ladies as their new partners.

14. Couple Four leads out and repeats all the movements described in 1 through 11. Gentlemen now have their original partners.

CHAIN SIX BITS

This square dance, originated in 1954 by Dan and Madeline Allen of Larkspur, California, employs another figure, *three quarters chain*, in an interesting combination with the movement used in the old standard figure *pass the left-hand dancer under.*

The Calls

1. Head ladies chain three quarters round,
   Head gents promenade one quarter to the right,
   Turn your own between those sides.
2. Forward six and back,
   Right hand over, left hand under,
   Spin the ends and go like thunder.

3. Same girls chain three quarters round,
   Same gents promenade one quarter to the right,
   Turn your own between those two.
4. Forward six and back with you,
   Right hand high and the left hand low,
   Spin the ends and let 'em go.

5. Head ladies chain three quarters round,
   Head gents promenade one quarter to the right,
   Turn your own between those sides.
   Forward six and back,
   Right hand over, left hand under,
   Spin the ends and go like thunder.

6. Same girls chain three quarters round,
   Same gents promenade one quarter to the right,
   Turn your own between those two.
   Forward six and back with you,
   Right hand high and the left hand low,
   Spin the ends and let 'em go.

7. Side ladies chain, etc. (Repeat 1 through 6, substituting "side ladies" for "head ladies" and "side gents" for "head gents.")

Explanation of Calls

1. Ladies One and Three walk forward, join right hands and walk around each other, clockwise, until each lady is standing in front of her right-hand couple. At the same time, Gentlemen One and Three walk one position to their right and meet their partners in front of their right-hand couples. Gentlemen One and Three each take their partner's left hand in their left hand and do a regular courtesy turn between each of the side couples, who separate to give them room to complete this movement (Figs. 161–165). Each head lady remains between the side couple to form a line of three, as each head lady's partner takes one step backward, to stand behind the line of three. Lady One is now standing between Couple Two, and Lady Three is standing between Couple Four (Fig. 166).

Fig. 161. Head ladies chain

Fig. 162. three quarters round. Head gents promenade

Fig. 163. one quarter to the right,

Fig. 164. Turn your own

Fig. 165. between those sides.

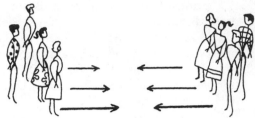

Fig. 166. Forward six . . .

2. The lines of three join hands, take four steps forward, then four steps back to places. Still holding hands, the dancers on either side of Ladies One and Three take a short step forward and face each other. Ladies One and Three raise their right hands to form an arch and the dancers on their left duck under the arch, releasing their hand hold with the center lady and advance in the direction of the nearest head couple's home position. At the same time, the dancers on the right of Ladies One and Three cross in front of them and advance in the direction of the nearest head couple's home position. At the conclusion of these movements, Gentleman Four and Lady Two are standing in Couple One's home position, and Gentleman Two and Lady Four are standing in Couple Three's home position.

3. Ladies One and Three (still standing in side couples' home positions) do a three quarters chain as explained in 1. Lady One finishes at Couple Three's home position and Lady Three finishes at Couple One's home position. Gentlemen One and Three walk one position to their right and meet their partners. They do a courtesy turn between the couples standing in the head couple's home positions. Each head lady remains between these couples to form lines of three, as each head lady's partner takes one step backward, to stand behind the lines of three.

4. The lines of four take three steps forward, then three steps back to places. As in 2, Ladies One and Three raise their right hands and the dancers on either end of the lines cross in front of them and advance to the nearest side couple's home position. At this point, each couple is standing opposite their home positions, except that each head gentleman is standing behind his partner.

5, 6. Repeat all the movements described in 1 through 4. All dancers finish with their original partners in their home positions.

7. Side ladies lead out and perform all the movements described in 1 through 6.

COE STAR

Originated by Harold Neitzel of Cleveland, Ohio, "Coe Star" employs the figure *eight roll away with a half sashay*.

The Calls

1. Ladies to the center and back once more,
2. Gents star right in the center of the floor.
3. Come back by the left, pick up your maid,
   Star promenade, don't be afraid.
4. Eight roll away with a half sashay,
   Girls star left in the same old way.
5. The ladies back right out of the middle,
   And circle eight to the tune of the fiddle.
6. Break and swing with the girl on your right,
   Swing her boys don't take all night.
7. Allemande left, let's have some fun,
8. Go right and left and turn back one,
9. Then promenade with the girl you swung.

10. Ladies to the center, etc. (Repeat 1 through 9.)
11. Ladies to the center, etc. (Repeat 1 through 9.)
12. Ladies to the center, etc. (Repeat 1 through 9.)

Explanation of Calls

1. The four ladies take three steps forward, bow, then walk backward to their places.

2. The four gentlemen walk to the center of the set, form a right hand star and turn the star clockwise.

3. The four gentlemen release right hands, form a left hand star and turn the star counterclockwise. While turning the star in this direction, they return to their partners, place their right arms around their partners' waists to form a Texas star and continue to walk counterclockwise (Fig. 167).

Fig. 167. Gents star promenade.

Fig. 168. Eight roll away

Fig. 169. with a half

Fig. 170. sashay.

Fig. 171. Girls star left in
the same old way.

4. Gentlemen release left hands to break the star. The gentlemen release their ladies and sidestep behind them to the outside of the set as the ladies make a 360-degree turn to their left, moving to the inside of the set to turn the Texas star around counterclockwise (Figs. 168–171).

5. The ladies release left hands to break the star and back away from the center of the set. Ladies are now standing on their partners' left. All dancers join hands, form a circle of eight and turn the circle counterclockwise.

6. All dancers release hands and break the circle of eight. The gentlemen swing the lady on their right.

7. The gentlemen stop swinging and place the ladies they were just swinging (now their new partners) on their right. They allemande left with their corners (original partners).

8. The gentlemen start a grand right and left movement by giving right hands to their new partners, then left hands to the next ladies they meet. They continue to hold left hands and do an allemande left with

those ladies. This movement has the effect of reversing the gentlemen's direction and bringing them back to face their new partners, to whom they now give their right hands.

9. The gentlemen draw their new partners up alongside them in promenade position and promenade around the set back to the gentlemen's home positions. Each gentleman now has his right-hand lady as his new partner.

10. Repeat all the movements described in 1 through 9. At the conclusion, the gentlemen will have their original opposites as their new partners.

11. Repeat all the movements described in 1 through 9. At the conclusion, the gentlemen will have their original corner ladies as their new partners.

12. Repeat all the movements described in 1 through 9. Gentlemen will finish the dance with their original partners.

POPULAR FOLK DANCES: FOR THE STUDENT AND TEACHER

This chapter contains descriptions of twenty-eight international folk dances, presented in order of increasing difficulty. About two thirds of these dances contain the four most frequently used folk dance steps—the two-step, schottische, polka and waltz—which were described in detail in Chapter 4. However, because a certain amount of time-consuming practice is needed to master these steps, the first four dances instead feature simple movements such as walk, slide, heel-and-toe, sidestep and point. These elementary movements can be learned almost as quickly as they are demonstrated, thus providing an immediate sense of accomplishment—an important stimulus for future learning.

After several simple folk dances have been easily learned, the group will be far more receptive to trying the more advanced dances requiring greater application and drill—dances which include not only the two-step, schottische, polka and waltz, but also other delightful steps such as the mazurka and the circassia.

All the steps and dance positions referred to in this chapter appear in the folk dance glossary as well.

260

Certain words appear regularly in the dance descriptions. In order to simplify the instructions, these frequently used words are abbreviated as follows:

L......... left
R......... right
M .... man, man's, men
W .... woman, woman's, women
CW....... clockwise
CCW ..... counterclockwise
fwd....... forward
twd....... toward
bwd...... backward
swd...... sideward
LOD ..... line of direction
ct......... count
cts........ counts
meas...... measure

PATTY CAKE POLKA
(American)

(Folkraft 1145)

Tempo 2/4

Formation: Couples in closed dance position in double circle formation, M with back to center, W facing center.

Steps: Heel-and-toe, slide

First Figure: Heel-and-Toe, Slide

Meas. 1, 2: Starting ML and WR foot, do two heel-and-toe steps. M footwork: place L foot to the L, with the heel on the floor and the toe pointing up (cts. 1 and); keeping weight on R foot, close L foot to R foot, placing L toe on floor next to R instep (cts. 2 and). W uses opposite footwork. Repeat this heel-and-toe movement.

Meas. 3, 4: Couples take four sliding steps to ML and WR (CCW).

Meas. 5–8: Starting MR and WL foot, repeat actions of meas. 1–4, moving in opposite direction (CW).

Second Figure: Clap, Walk Around

Meas. 9: Partners drop hands, M claps WR hand with his R hand three times: clap (ct. 1); clap (ct. and); clap (ct. 2); hold (ct. and).

Meas. 10: M claps WL hand with his L hand three times.

Meas. 11: M claps W both hands with his hands three times.

Meas. 12: Each claps both hands on own knees three times.

Meas. 13, 14: Partners link R elbows and walk around each other, CW in four steps.

Meas. 15, 16: Partners release elbows. W stand still, and M move L one position in circle to stand in front of a new partner.

The caller can assist the dancers by using the following prompt calls:

Meas. 1, 2: Heel and toe, heel and toe,
Meas. 3, 4: Slide, slide, slide, slide.
Meas. 5, 6: Heel and toe, heel and toe,
Meas. 7, 8: Slide, slide, slide, slide.
Meas. 9: Right, right, right,
Meas. 10: Left, left, left,
Meas. 11: Both, both, both,
Meas. 12: Knees, knees, knees,
Meas. 13, 14: Right elbow round, go on to the next,
Meas. 15, 16: And now we start again.

MILITARY SCHOTTISCHE
(American)

(Topic 12TS 245)

Tempo 4/4

Formation: Couples in Varsouvienne position, in double circle formation, facing CCW.

Steps: Point and Sidestep, Walk and Turn

First Figure: Point and Sidestep

Meas. 1: Point L toe fwd. (cts. 1, 2): point L toe to L side (cts. 3, 4).

Meas. 2: Step bwd. on L foot (ct. 1); step swd. to R on R foot (ct. 2); close L foot to R foot (ct. 3); hold (ct. 4).

Meas. 3, 4: Repeat action of meas. 1–2, starting R foot.

Meas. 5–8: Repeat action of meas. 1–4.

Second Figure: Walk and Turn

Meas. 9: Step fwd. L (cts. 1, 2); step fwd. R (cts. 3, 4).

Meas. 10: Half turn in place to R in three steps, to end facing CW, without releasing hands: L (ct. 1); R (ct. 2); L (ct. 3); hold (ct. 4). M now has his partner on his L, and M has his L arm around WL shoulder.

Meas. 11: Walk bwd. CCW: R (cts. 1, 2); L (cts. 3, 4).

Meas. 12: Half turn in place to L in three steps, to end facing CCW, without releasing hands: R (ct. 1); L (ct. 2); R (ct. 3); hold (ct. 4). M now has his partner on his R again.

Meas. 13–16: Repeat action of meas. 9–12.

CSEBOGAR
(Hungarian)

(Folkraft 1196)
Tempo 2/4

Formation: Single circle of couples, W on R of M, all facing center, hands joined.

Steps: Slide, walk, skip, step-draw

First Figure: Slides

Meas. 1–4: Eight sliding steps to L.

Meas. 5–8: Eight sliding steps to R.

Second Figure: Walk, Skip

Meas. 9–12: All walk fwd., raising arms: fwd. L (cts. 1 and); fwd. R (cts. 2 and); fwd. L (cts. 1 and); stamp R (cts. 2 and). All walk bwd., lowering arms: bwd. L (cts. 1 and); bwd. R (cts. 2 and); bwd. L (cts. 1 and); stamp R (cts. 2 and).

Meas. 13–16: Face partners, hook R elbows, and go fwd. and around each other with eight skipping steps.

Third Figure: Step-Draw

Meas. 17–20: Face partners in single circle, M facing CCW, and W facing CW. Hands are joined and extended out to the side. Take four step-draws twd. center. M footwork: step swd. with L (cts. 1 and); close R to L (cts. 2 and). Do three more of these step-draws. Weight is not placed on R on last step-draw. W does opposite footwork. With each step-draw, arms rock up and down.

Meas. 21–24: Four step-draws away from center. Weight is not transferred on last step.

Fourth Figure: Step-Draw, Skip

Meas. 25–28: Partners take two step-draws twd. center, then two step-draws away from center.

Meas. 29–32: Repeat action of meas. 13–16.

PUT YOUR LITTLE FOOT   (Folkraft 1165)
(American)   Tempo 3/4

Formation: Couples in Varsouvienne position, in double circle formation, facing CCW.

Steps: Modified mazurka, three steps and point

First Figure: Modified Mazurka, Three Steps and Point

(This record has an introduction of four measures of music. The first
step of the first figure starts on the third beat of the fourth measure
of introduction.)

Meas. 1, 2: Take two modified mazurka steps: lift L foot in front of R
(ct. 3); slide L foot along floor diagonally fwd. L (ct. 1); close R foot
to L, taking weight on R foot (ct. 2); repeat this sequence.

Meas. 3, 4: Beginning on L foot, W crosses to her L in front of M in three
steps, while M dances the same pattern taking smaller steps to
allow W to finish in a position on his L side. As she crosses, he
reverses the position of his arms, placing his L arm around her L
shoulder: lift L foot in front of R (ct. 3); step diagonally fwd. L on
L foot (ct. 1); cross R foot in front of L (ct. 2); step swd. to L on L
foot (ct. 3); point R toe to floor diagonally fwd. R (ct. 1); hold (ct. 2).

Meas. 5–8: Repeat action of meas. 1–4, starting with R foot and progressing diagonally fwd. to the R.

Second Figure: Three Steps and Point

Meas. 9–16: Repeat the actions in meas. 3–4 four times, starting with
L foot, then R foot, then L foot, then R foot. Each time the action
starts with the L foot, W crosses to her L in front of her partner,
and each time the action starts with the R foot, W crosses to her R
in front of her partner.

HOT PRETZELS
(American)

(RCA Victor 447-0148)

Tempo 2/4

Formation: Couples in Varsouvienne position, in double circle formation, facing CCW.

Steps: Grapevine, walk

First Figure: Grapevine Right and Left

Meas. 1–3: Place L heel fwd. to touch the floor (cts. 1 and); cross L foot behind R foot (ct. 2); step to R with R foot (ct. and); cross L foot in front of R foot (cts. 1 and); place R heel fwd. to touch the floor (cts. 2 and); cross R foot behind L foot (ct. 1); step to L with L foot (ct. and); cross R foot in front of L foot (cts. 2 and).

Meas. 4: Place L heel fwd. to touch the floor (cts. 1 and); close L foot to R foot (ct. 2); step in place with R foot (ct. and).

Second Figure: Swagger

Meas. 5, 6: Take four steps fwd. beginning with the L foot, using a swaggering style: step fwd. with L foot (cts. 1 and); step fwd. with R foot (cts. 2 and); step fwd. with L foot (cts. 1 and); step fwd. with R foot (cts. 2 and).

Meas. 7, 8: Step fwd. on L foot (cts. 1 and); kick R foot fwd. (cts. 2 and); step bwd. on R foot (ct. 1); close L foot to R foot (ct. and); step fwd. on R foot (cts. 2 and).

The melody to which this dance is performed is considerably longer than eight measures. The movements of meas. 1–8 are repeated over and over again as the melodic line changes.

HORA
(Israeli)

(Folkraft 1110)

Tempo 2/4

Formation: Single circle, all facing center, hands joined (or hands may grasp neighbor's elbows or shoulders).

Steps: Step-cross, step-hop

Meas. 1: Step to L with L foot (cts. 1 and); cross R behind L (cts. 2 and).

Meas. 2: Step to L with L foot (cts. 1 and); hop on L and swing R across in front of L (cts. 2 and).

Meas. 3: Step R in place (cts. 1 and); hop on R and swing L across in front of R (cts. 2 and).

Repeat meas. 1–3 until end of record.

OKLAHOMA MIXER
(American)

(Folkraft 1035)

Tempo 2/4

Formation: Couples in Varsouvienne position, in double formation, facing CCW.

Steps: Two-step, heel-and-toe

First Figure: Two-Step and Walk

Meas. 1, 2: Couples take two two-steps fwd. starting with L foot: Step fwd. diagonally to L with L foot (ct. 1); close R foot to L foot (ct. and); step fwd. L foot (cts. 2 and). Repeat this sequence for the second step using opposite feet, moving diagonally fwd. R, beginning with R foot.

Meas. 3, 4: Moving directly fwd., take four walking steps starting with L foot: step fwd. L (cts. 1 and); step fwd. R (cts. 2 and); repeat L, R. For styling, swagger slightly on each step.

Second Figure: Heel-and-Toe Progress

Meas. 5: Place L heel diagonally fwd. L (cts. 1 and); place L toe on floor next to R instep (cts. 2 and).

Meas. 6. Dropping R hands, W crosses to L in front of M with three walking steps: L (ct. 1); R (ct. and); L (cts. 2 and). W finishes on inside of circle at L side of M and facing in CW direction. At the same time, M takes three steps in place: L (ct. 1); R (ct. and), L (cts. 2 and).

Meas. 7: Starting with R foot, both repeat heel-toe pattern in place, as described in meas. 5.

Meas. 8: W takes three steps toward R side of next M in back of present partner: R (ct. 1); L (ct. and); R (cts. 2 and). As she takes these three steps, W turns slightly to L extending R hand to take R hand of new partner and reaching L hand back to assume Varsouvienne position. M takes three steps moving slightly fwd: R (ct. 1); L (ct. and), R (cts. 2 and). As M moves fwd., he extends R hand fwd. to new W and leads W into Varsouvienne position.

TO TUR
(Danish)

(Viking 401)

Tempo 2/4

Formation: Single circle of couples, W on R of M, all facing center, hands joined at shoulder height.

Steps: Walk, two-step

Introduction: Circle Left and Right with Two-Steps

Meas. 1–8: Beginning with L foot all circle CW with eight two-steps.

Meas. 9–16: Beginning with L foot all circle CCW with eight two-steps.

First Figure: Two-step and Walk to the Center and Back

Meas. 17: Release hands and take partner in semi-closed position. Dance twd. center of circle with one two-step, starting ML, WR.

Meas: 18. Continue twd. center of circle with two walking steps, beginning MR, WL.

Meas. 19, 20: Repeat action of meas. 17–18, moving twd. outside of circle, starting MR, WL.

Meas. 21–24: Couples, now in closed position, progress CCW around circle with four two-steps, turning CW with each other as they progress around the circle.

Meas. 25–32: Repeat action of meas. 17–24.

Second Figure: Grand Right and Left

Meas. 33–40: With eight two-steps, starting ML and WR foot, all do a grand R and L around the circle.

Meas. 41–48: Continue the grand R and L with eight more two-steps, and on the last measure take the new partner in semi-closed position. Repeat first and second figures until end of record.

THE TEDDY BEARS' PICNIC (Hoctor 7026)
(English) Tempo 4/4

Formation: Couples in double circle formation with W on outside, facing CCW, inside hands joined.

Steps: Walk, two-step, step-swing

First Figure: Walk and Cross

Meas. 1: Beginning with outside foot (ML, WR), walk fwd. three steps and point. M footwork: step fwd. L (ct. 1); step fwd. R (ct. 2); step fwd. L (ct. 3); touch R toe on floor near instep of L foot (ct. 4). W uses opposite footwork.

Meas. 2: Still facing CCW, partners exchange places in three steps, starting MR foot and WL foot, W crossing in front of M. M footwork: step to R with R foot (ct. 1); cross L foot in front of R foot (ct. 2); step to R with R foot (ct. 3); touch L toe to floor near instep of R foot (ct. 4). W uses opposite footwork.

Meas. 3: Starting ML and WR foot, partners exchange places again with three walking steps, M moving diagonally fwd. to his L, passing in front of W, and W moves diagonally bwd. to her R. M touches R toe to floor near instep of L foot on ct. 4. W uses opposite footwork.

Meas. 4: Starting MR and WL foot, M moves bwd., W fwd., in three steps, to meet and face each other. M footwork: step bwd. on R foot (ct. 1); step bwd. on L foot (ct. 2); step bwd. on R foot (ct. 3); face partner (ct. 4). W uses opposite footwork.

Second Figure: Two-step, Step-Swing, Two-step Turn

Meas. 5: Partners turn away from each other in two two-steps. M turns to L beginning with L foot, W turns to R beginning with R foot.

Meas. 6: Partners face each other, join both hands, and do two step-swings. M footwork: step on L foot (ct. 1); swing R foot across L foot (ct. 2); step on R foot (ct. 3); swing L foot across R foot (ct. 4). W uses opposite footwork.

Meas. 7, 8: In closed position, take four two-steps turning CW and traveling around circle CCW.

JESSIE POLKA   (Folkraft 1256)
(American)   Tempo 2/4

Formation: Any number of dancers, standing side by side, with arms
   around one another's waists, facing CCW.
Steps: Hop, polka

First Figure: Hop and Point

Meas. 1: Hop on ball of R foot and touch L heel fwd. to the floor (cts.
   1 and); jump in place on balls of both feet (cts. 2 and).
Meas. 2: Hop on ball of L foot and touch R toe bwd. to the floor (cts.
   1 and); jump in place on balls of both feet (cts. 2 and).
Meas. 3: Hop on ball of L foot and touch R heel fwd. to the floor (cts.
   1 and); jump in place on balls of both feet (cts. 2 and).
Meas. 4: Hop on ball of R foot and touch L heel fwd. to the floor (cts.
   1 and); hop on ball of R foot and touch L toe to floor, close to R
   instep (cts. 2 and).

Second Figure: Polka Forward

Meas. 5–8: Starting on L foot, take four polka steps moving fwd.

To simplify this dance:
   (a) Omit the hops on cts. "1 and" in meas. 1–4.
   (b) Instead of "Jump in place on balls of both feet" on cts. "2 and,"
substitute "place both feet together."

ROAD TO THE ISLES
(Scottish)

(Folkraft 1095)

Tempo 2/4

Formation: Couples in Varsouvienne position, in double circle formation facing CCW.

Steps: Schottische

First Figure: Point and Cross Step

Meas. 1: Point L toe fwd. slightly to the L (cts. 1, 2).

Meas. 2, 3: Place L foot slightly in back of R foot (ct. 1); step to R with R foot (ct. 2); step fwd. with L foot, placing it in front of R foot (cts. 1, 2).

Meas. 4: Point R toe fwd., slightly to R (cts. 1, 2).

Meas. 5, 6: Place R foot slightly in back of L foot (ct. 1); step to L with L foot (ct. 2); step fwd. with R foot, placing it in front of L foot (cts. 1, 2).

Meas. 7: Point L toe fwd. (cts. 1, 2).

Meas. 8: Point L toe bwd. (cts. 1, 2).

Second Figure: Schottische

Meas. 9, 10: Do a schottische step fwd. beginning with L foot: step fwd. L (ct. 1); step fwd. R (ct. 2); step fwd. L (ct. 1); hop on L foot (ct. 2).

Meas. 11, 12: Do a schottische step fwd. beginning with the R foot: step fwd. R (ct. 1); step fwd. L (ct. 2); step fwd. R (ct. 1); hop on R, doing a half turn to the R, and finish facing in opposite direction (ct. 2). Hands remain joined. ML arm is now around WL shoulder, and W is standing on ML side.

Meas. 13, 14: Do a schottische step fwd. beginning L foot: step fwd. L (ct. 1); step fwd R (ct. 2); step fwd. L (ct. 1); hop on L, doing a half turn to the L, and finish facing in original direction (ct. 2).

Meas. 15, 16: Take three steps in place: Step R (ct. 1); step L (ct. 2); step R (ct. 1); hold (ct. 2).

SEVEN STEPS
(German)

(Folkraft 1163)

Tempo 2/4

Formation: Couples in double circle formation with W on outside, facing CCW, inside hands joined.

Steps: Quick walk, schottische, step-hop

First Figure: Quick Walk

Meas. 1, 2: Seven quick steps fwd. in LOD. M footwork: fwd. L (ct. 1); fwd. R (ct. and); fwd. L (ct. 2); fwd. R (ct. and); fwd. L (ct. 1); fwd. R (ct. and); stamp L, close R foot to L foot. (cts. 2 and). W does opposite footwork.

Meas. 3, 4: M footwork: as in meas. 1–2, starting L, take seven steps bwd., stamping on seventh step and holding. W does opposite footwork.

Second Figure: Schottische, Step-Hops

Meas. 5: In one schottische step, starting ML and WR, M moves away from W, going to his L; and W moves away from M, going to her R.

Meas. 6: Starting MR and WL, each take one schottische step twd. partner.

Meas. 7, 8: M places his hands on W hips, as she places her hands on M shoulders. Turn CW in place in four step-hops. M footwork: step L (ct. 1); hop L (ct. and); step R (ct. 2); hop R (ct. and); step L (ct. 1); hop L (ct. and); step R (ct. 2); hop R (ct. and). W does opposite footwork.

Meas. 9–12: Repeat action of meas. 5–8.

LA RINKA
(English)

(Folkraft 1308)

Tempo 3/4

Formation: Couples in double circle formation, facing CCW, hands joined in skating position.

Steps: Step-close, balance, waltz

First Figure: Step-Close Right and Left

Meas. 1, 2: Step fwd. diagonally R with R foot (cts. 1, 2); close L foot to R foot (ct. 3). Repeat this movement.

Meas. 3, 4: Step fwd. diagonally L with L foot (cts. 1, 2); close R foot to L foot (ct. 3). Repeat this movement.

Meas. 5: Step fwd. diagonally R with R foot (cts. 1, 2); close L foot to R foot (ct. 3).

Meas. 6: Step fwd. diagonally L with L foot (cts. 1, 2); close R foot to L foot (ct. 3).

Meas. 7: Face partner and take one step bwd., away from partner with R foot (cts. 1, 2); close L foot to R foot (ct. 3).

Meas. 8: Partners honor (cts. 1, 2, 3).

Second Figure: Balance, Cross Over

Meas. 9: Holding R hands, partners balance twd. each other with R foot: step fwd. R foot (ct. 1); close L foot to R foot raising heels slightly off floor (ct. 2); lower heels to floor (ct. 3).

Meas. 10: Partners balance bwd., away from each other: step bwd. with L foot (ct. 1); close R foot to L foot raising heels slightly off floor (ct. 2); lower heels to floor (ct. 3).

Meas. 11, 12: Partners change places with two waltz steps, W turning L under their joined R hands.

Meas. 13–16: Repeat actions of meas. 9–12.

Third Figure: Waltz

Meas. 17–24: In closed dance position, take eight waltz steps, turning CW and progressing in LOD.

ST. BERNARD WALTZ
(English)

(National 4528)

Tempo 3/4

Formation: Couples in closed dance position, in double circle formation, M with back to center, W facing center.

Steps: Step-close, waltz, walk

First Figure: Step-Close, Stamp

Meas. 1, 2: Starting with ML foot and WR foot, and traveling CCW, take two step-close steps. M footwork: step to L with L foot (cts. 1, 2); close R foot to L foot (ct. 3); step to L with L foot (cts. 1, 2); close R foot to L foot (ct. 3). W uses opposite footwork.

Meas. 3, 4: M footwork: step to L with L foot (cts. 1, 2); stamp R foot close to L foot (ct. 3); stamp R foot again (ct. 1); hold (cts. 2, 3). W uses opposite footwork.

Meas. 5, 6: M footwork: reversing direction, step to R with R foot (cts. 1, 2); close L foot to R foot (ct. 3); step to R with R foot (cts. 1, 2); close L foot to R foot, without transferring weight to L foot (ct. 3). W uses opposite footwork.

Second Figure: Walk and Waltz

Meas. 7, 8: M footwork: take two walking steps bwd. with L foot (cts. 1, 2, 3); step bwd. with R foot (cts. 1, 2, 3). W uses opposite footwork.

Meas. 9, 10: Reverse direction and take two walking steps fwd. beginning with ML and WR foot.

Meas. 11, 12: With ML hand and WR hands joined and raised, W with two waltz steps makes one complete turn to her R under their raised arms. M takes two waltz steps in place while W is turning.

Meas. 13–16: In closed dance position, partners take four waltz steps turning CW.

LILI MARLENE
(American)

(Mac Gregor 3105)

Tempo 2/4

Formation: Couples in double circle formation with W on outside, facing CCW, inside hands joined.

Steps: Walk, slide, two-step

First Figure: Walk and Slide

Meas. 1, 2: Take four walking steps fwd. starting on outside foot. M footwork: step fwd. with L foot (ct. 1); step fwd. with R foot (ct. 2); step fwd. with L foot (ct. 1); step fwd. with R foot (ct. 2). W uses opposite footwork.

Meas. 3, 4: Partners face each other, join both hands, and take four sliding steps, continuing CCW around the circle.

Meas. 5–8: Repeat actions of meas. 1–4, moving in the opposite direction and starting with the outside feet (MR and WL).

Second Figure: Step-Swing and Walk

Meas. 9–12: Partners face, hold both hands, and do four step-swings. M footwork: step on L foot (ct. 1); swing R foot diagonally across in front of L foot (ct. 2); step on R foot (ct. 1); swing L foot diagonally across in front of R foot (ct. 2). W uses opposite footwork. Repeat these movements for a total of four.

Meas. 13–16: Partners face CCW, join inside hands and take three steps fwd. M footwork: step fwd. with L foot (ct. 1); step fwd. with R foot (ct. 2); step fwd. with L foot (ct. 1); partners drop hands, about-face to face CW, and join inside hands (ct. 2). W uses opposite footwork. Repeat these movements in CW direction, starting with outside feet (MR and WL).

Third Figure: Two-steps and Change Partners

Meas. 17–20: Partners face CCW, join inside hands again, and move fwd. with four two-steps, starting on outside feet (ML and WR).

Meas. 21–24: Partners break away from each other, M turning to his L with four two-steps, and W turning to her R with four two-steps. M makes a wide turn and W turns in a smaller arc, so that when M returns to face the outside of the circle again, he is standing in front of a new partner.

MAYIM, MAYIM
(Israeli)

(Folkraft 1108)

Tempo 2/4

Formation: Single circle, all facing the center, hands joined, arms extended straight downward. No partners required.

Steps: Circassia step, run, hop

First Figure: Circassia Steps

Meas. 1–8: Take a Circassia step going to the L, all starting with R foot, progressing CW around circle: cross R foot in front of L and turn slightly to L (cts. 1 and); step to L with L foot, turning to face center again (cts. 2 and); cross R foot behind L foot and turn slightly to R (cts. 1 and); leap onto L foot, turning to face center again (cts. 2 and). Repeat these movements three more times.

Second Figure: Running Forward and Back, Circle Left

Meas. 9, 10: Starting with R foot, take four running steps to the center. First step is taken with R knee bent and trunk inclined fwd. Body is straightened and arms are raised overhead on the next three steps.

Meas. 11, 12: Starting with R foot, take four running steps bwd. First step is taken with R knee bent. The arms are lowered gradually on the next three steps, and all dancers finish these steps standing erect with arms extending straight downward.

Meas. 13–16: Repeat all movements of meas. 9–12.

Meas. 17, 18: With hands still joined, all dancers face L and take four running steps CW beginning with R foot.

Third Figure: Hop and Tap

Meas. 19–22: Hop on L foot and touch R toe to floor in front of L foot (cts. 1 and); hop on L foot and touch R toe to the R of L foot (cts. 2 and). Repeat these movements three more times.

Meas. 23–26: Hop on R foot and touch L toe to floor in front of R foot, clapping hands in front (cts. 1 and); hop on R foot and touch L toe to the L of R foot clapping hands in front (cts. 2 and). Repeat these movements three more times.

TROPANKA
(Bulgarian)

(Folk Dancer MH 1020)

Tempo 2/4

Formation: Single circle, all facing center, hands joined. No partners
required.

Steps: Running, step-hop

First Figure: Running

Meas. 1, 2: Beginning R foot, take five quick steps CCW: R (ct. 1); L (ct.
and); R (ct. 2); L (ct. and); R (ct. 1); stamp L twice (cts. and 2); hold
(ct. and).

Meas. 3, 4: Repeat action of meas. 1–2 going CW, starting L foot, and
end by stamping R foot twice.

Meas. 5–8: Repeat action of meas. 1–4.

Second Figure: Step-Hop

Meas. 9, 10: All face center. Step on R (ct. 1); hop on R, swing L in front
of R (ct. and); step on L (ct. 2); hop on L swinging R in front of L
(ct. and); step on R (ct. 1); stamp L twice (cts. and 2); hold (ct. and).

Meas. 11, 12: Repeat action of meas. 9–10, starting with L foot.

Meas. 13–16: Repeat action of meas. 9–12.

Third Figure: Step-Hop

Meas. 17, 18: Starting with R foot, take two step-hops fwd. twd. center:
R (ct. 1); hop R (ct. and); L (ct. 2); hop L (ct. and); step R (ct. 1); stamp
L twice (cts. and 2); all hands are raised and all shout "Hey" (ct.
and).

Meas. 19, 20: Repeat action of meas. 17–18, all moving bwd., starting
with L foot and lowering arms.

Meas. 21–25: Repeat action of meas. 17–20.

EIDE RATAS
(Estonian)

(Folkraft 1520)

Tempo 3/4

Formation: Couples in double circle formation with W on outside, facing CCW, in semi-closed position.
Steps: Leap-step-hop, waltz

First Figure: Leap-Step-Hop and Turn

Meas. 1, 2: Leap fwd. onto the outside foot (ML, WR), at the same time bending the body fwd. (ct. 1); step on the inside foot (ct. 2); hop on the inside foot (ct. 3); the body is straightened on cts. 2 and 3. Repeat this leap-step-hop pattern.

Meas. 3, 4: Still in semi-closed position, starting ML and WR foot, couples turn CW once around with six running steps. M footwork: L (ct. 1); R (ct. 2); L (ct. 3); R (ct. 1); L (ct. 2); R (ct. 3).

Meas. 5–8: Repeat action of meas. 1–4.

Meas. 9–16: Repeat action of meas. 1–8.

Second Figure: Waltz Away and Return

Meas. 17: Partners face each other with hands on hips, M with back to center, W facing center. Beginning with ML foot and WR foot, take one waltz step bwd., turning slightly to ML and WR.

Meas. 18: Beginning with MR foot and WL foot, take one waltz step bwd., turning slightly to MR and WL.

Meas. 19, 20: Repeat action of meas. 17–18.

Meas. 21, 22: Partners run fwd., twd. each other, with six running steps.

Meas. 23, 24: Hooking R elbows, partners turn in place CW with six running steps. W ends on inside and M on outside of circle.

Meas. 25–32: Repeat action of meas. 17–24, except that in meas. 23–24, partners hook L elbows, turn CCW, and finish in original position.

This dance can be made progressive by having the M hook L elbows with the W on his R on meas. 23–24.

BOSTON TWO-STEP
(English)

(Folkraft 1158)

Tempo 2/4

Formation: Couples in a double circle formation with W on outside, facing CCW, inside hands joined, outside hands swinging freely.

Steps: Pas de basque, sliding step, two-step

First Figure: Pas de Basque, Walk, Pivot

Meas. 1, 2: Pas de basque on outside foot. M footwork: leap swd. on L foot (ct. 1); step on R foot in front of L foot (ct. and); step in place on L foot (cts. 2 and); W uses opposite footwork. Pas de basque on inside foot (MR, WL).

Meas. 3, 4: Walk three steps fwd. beginning with outside foot, then pivot to face in opposite direction. M footwork: step fwd. on L foot (ct. 1); step fwd. on R foot (ct. and); step fwd. on L foot (ct. 2); release partner's hand, pivot to R on L foot to finish facing CW (ct. and). W uses opposite footwork.

Meas. 5–8: Joining other hands (ML and WR), and starting on other foot (MR and WL), repeat action of meas. 1–4.

Second Figure: Pas de Basque, Sidestep, Two-Step

Meas. 9, 10: Face partner, holding both hands, and take two pas de basque steps beginning ML, WR.

Meas. 11, 12: Take two sidesteps to ML, WR. M footwork: step swd. L (cts. 1 and); place R foot close to L foot (cts. 2 and); step swd. L (cts. 1 and); place R foot close to L (cts. 2 and). W uses opposite footwork.

Meas. 13–16: In closed dance position, take four two-steps, starting ML and WR foot, turning CW and progressing CCW.

NEBESKO KOLO
(Yugoslavian)

(Folkraft 1401)

Tempo 2/4

Formation: Single circle, all facing center, hands joined. No partners required.

Steps: Two-step, pas de basque

First Figure: Two-step

Meas. 1–4: All dancers turn to the R and do a two-step CCW: fwd. R. (ct. 1); place L alongside R (ct. and); fwd. R (cts. 2 and). Do three more two-steps, starting L, then R, then L. On last ct., all turn to face CW.

Meas. 5–8: Take four two-steps CW, starting R foot. All face center on last count.

Second Figure: Rock Step

Meas. 9: Step fwd. R (ct. 1); rock back on L (ct. and); step bwd. on R (ct. 2); step L in place (ct. and).

Meas. 10–12: Repeat action of meas. 9 three times.

Third Figure: Pas de Basque

Meas. 13–16: All do a pas de basque to the R, and then to L. Repeat R, L, and end by quickly stamping R foot in place. R foot is immediately lifted to start dance again.

HARMONICA
(Israeli)

(Worldtone 10030)
Tempo 2/4

Formation: Single circle, all facing center, hands joined, arms straight down. No partners required.

Steps: Grapevine, step-hop, harmonica step, sway

First Figure: Grapevine, Step-Hop

Meas. 1: All dancers move CCW. Cross L in front of R (ct. 1); swd. R (ct. and); cross L behind R (ct. 2) swd. R (ct. and).

Meas. 2: Still moving CCW, step L (ct. 1); hop L (ct. and); step R (ct. 2); hop R (ct. and).

Meas. 3–8: Repeat action of meas. 1–2 three more times.

Second Figure: Harmonica Step, Step-Hop

Meas. 9: All face center and release hands. Cross L in front of R, moving L hip fwd. and clap hands (ct. 1); step R in place (ct. and); step L in place (ct. 2); hop on L (ct. and). (This is one harmonica step.)

Meas. 10: Cross R in front of L, moving R hip fwd. and clap hands (ct. 1); step L in place (ct. and); step R in place (ct. 2); hop R (ct. and).

Meas. 11: Repeat action of meas. 9.

Meas. 12: All do two step-hops fwd. facing CW, starting on R foot.

Meas. 13. Repeat action of meas. 10.

Meas. 14: Repeat action of meas. 9.

Meas. 15: Repeat action of meas. 10.

Meas. 16. All face CCW. Take two step-hops starting on L foot.

Third Figure: Sway, Run

Meas. 17: All face center and place hands on neighbors' shoulders. Step L swd. (sway) (ct. 1); hold (ct. and); step R swd. (sway) (ct. 2); hold (ct. and).

Meas. 18: All face CW. Do not drop hands. Four running steps L (ct. 1); R (ct. and); L (ct. 2); R (ct. and).

Meas. 19–24: Repeat action of meas. 17–18 three more times.

KOROBOUSHKA
(Russian)

(Worldtone 10005)

Tempo 4/4

Formation: Couples in a double circle formation, partners facing and
holding both hands, M with back to center, W facing center.
Steps: Schottische, bokazni, step-swing

First Figure: Schottische, Bokazni

Meas. 1: Partners take three steps away from center of circle. M footwork: step fwd. L (ct. 1); step fwd. R (ct. 2); step fwd. L (ct. 3); hop
in place on L foot (ct. 4). W moves bwd. using opposite footwork.

Meas. 2: Repeat action of meas. 1, moving in the opposite direction,
starting MR and WL foot.

Meas. 3: Repeat action of meas. 1.

Meas. 4: Do the bokazni step. M footwork: hop L foot and tap R toe fwd.
(ct. 1); hop L foot, tap R toe swd. (ct. 2); hop L foot, closing R foot
to L foot (ct. 3); hold (ct. 4). W uses opposite footwork.

Second Figure: Three Steps and Swing, Balance

Meas. 5: Releasing hands, take three steps to own R, moving away from
each other, then swing L foot in front of R: step to R with R foot
(ct. 1); cross L foot in front of R foot (ct. 2); step to R with R foot
(ct. 3); swing L foot in front of R foot (ct. 4). W uses same footwork.

Meas. 6: Repeat action of meas. 5, moving in the opposite direction,
starting ML and WR foot.

Meas. 7: Partners face each other, hold R hands, balance twd. each
other on R foot, then balance back on L foot.

Meas. 8: M and W change places with four walking steps, R, L, R, L, the
W turning to her L under their joined R hands.

Meas. 9: Repeat action of meas. 5.

Meas. 10: Repeat action of meas. 6 but *in place,* to face a new partner.

Meas. 11, 12: Repeat action of meas. 7–8 with the new partner.

MISERLOU
(Greek)

(Worldtone 10001)

Tempo 4/4

Formation: Single circle, all facing the center, hands joined. No partners required.

Steps: Grapevine

First Figure: Step and Point, Grapevine

Meas. 1: Step to R with R foot (cts. 1, 2); point L toe to floor in front of R foot (cts. 3, 4).

Meas. 2: Cross L foot behind R foot (ct. 1); place R foot to R side (ct. 2); cross L foot in front of R foot (ct. 3); pivot on L foot to face diagonally L (ct. 4).

Second Figure: Walking Forward and Backward

Meas. 3, 4: All dancers, facing diagonally to their L, take three steps fwd: step fwd. on R foot (ct. 1); step fwd. on L foot (ct. 2); step fwd. on R foot (ct. 3); rise up on ball of R foot (ct. 4). Repeat this action going bwd., starting with L foot, rising on ball of L foot and facing center on ct. 4.

The melody to which this dance is performed has considerably more than four measures. The action of meas. 1–4 is repeated over and over as the melodic line changes.

GLOWWORM
(American)

(Folkraft 1158)

Tempo 4/4

Formation: Couples in double circle formation, with W on the outside, facing CCW, inside hands joined, ML hand on hip.

Steps: Walk, sashay, grapevine, cut, two-step

First Figure: Walk Forward and Point

Meas. 1: Starting on the outside foot, take three walking steps fwd., then point inside foot fwd. M footwork: step fwd. L (ct. 1); step fwd. R (ct. 2); step fwd. L (ct. 3); point R foot fwd. (ct. 4). W uses opposite footwork.

Meas. 2: Repeat action of meas. 1, starting MR and WL foot.

Second Figure: Grapevine

Meas. 3: Partners face each other and join both hands. M has back to center. Take one grapevine step swd., moving CCW, M beginning L and WR. M footwork: step L foot swd. to L (ct. 1); cross R foot in back of L (ct. 2); step L foot swd. to L (ct. 3); swing R foot across in front of L (ct. 4); W uses opposite footwork.

Meas. 4: Repeat action of meas. 3, moving CW, starting MR and WL foot.

Third Figure: Cross Over

Meas. 5: With MR and WL hands joined (ML hand on hip), change places with three walking steps, M starting L and WR foot. W passes under the joined and raised hands and turns to her L and points L toe diagonally fwd. as she faces partner. M turns to R to face partner at end of three steps and points R foot diagonally fwd.

Meas. 6: Repeat action of meas. 5, returning to place, M starting R and WL foot.

Fourth Figure: Two-step

Meas. 7, 8: Assume closed dance position and take four two-steps progressing CCW in circle and turning CW.

Fifth Figure: Sashay and Cut

Meas. 9: Facing fwd. in LOD, repeat action of meas. 1.

Meas. 10: Partners face each other (M has back to center of circle), join both hands and sashay three times progressing CW, starting MR and WL. Keeping hands joined, they fall back on ML and WR foot, putting the opposite foot diagonally fwd. in CW direction.

Meas. 11, 12: Reversing position of hands, repeat action of meas. 9–10, moving in opposite direction, starting MR and WL foot.

Sixth Figure: Woman Turn and Dip

Meas. 13, 14: M holds WR hand in his L hand. W turns three times to her R with six walking steps, starting on R foot, and turning under her R arm. At the same time, M takes six walking steps fwd., beginning on L foot, as they move CCW. This is done in six cts. Dip in closed position, M back on L, W fwd. on R, at the same time lifting the opposite foot off the floor (ct. 7); hold this position (ct. 8).

Seventh Figure: Two-step and Twirl

Meas. 15, 16: In closed position, take three two-steps, starting MR and WL, turning CW and traveling CCW: first two-step (cts. 1 and 2 and); second two-step (cts. 3 and 4 and); third two-step (cts. 1 and 2 and); M twirls W to her R under her R arm (cts. 3 and 4 and).

COTTON-EYED JOE   (Kik 202)
(American)   Tempo 2/4

Formation: Partners in closed dance position, anywhere in the hall.
Steps: Heel-and-toe polka, polka, chug step

First Figure: Heel-and-Toe Polka

Meas. 1–4: M footwork: hop on R foot and touch L heel to floor (cts. and 1); hop on R foot and touch L toe to floor next to R instep (cts. and 2); take one polka step to L (cts. and 1 and 2). Repeat these movements, hopping on L foot and doing the polka step to the R. W uses opposite footwork.

Second Figure: Break Away

Meas. 5–8: Release hands and break away from partner, turning in a small circle with four polka steps. M turns to his L and W turns to her R. Finish facing partner.

Third Figure: Chug Step

Meas. 9–12: Face partner and take four chug steps going to ML and WR. M footwork: place ball of R foot swd. pushing lightly (ct. and); step swd. to L on L foot (ct. 1); L foot remains close to floor and carries most of the weight except for slight transfer to R foot on the push. Repeat three times (cts. and 2, and 1, and 2). Repeat these four chug steps going in opposite direction, pushing with L foot and traveling to the R. W uses opposite footwork.

Fourth Figure: Polka

Meas. 13–16: In closed dance position, take four polka steps beginning with ML and WR foot, turning CW and traveling in LOD.

VARSOUVIENNE
(Swedish)

(Lloyd Shaw 103/4)

Tempo 3/4

Formation: Partners in Varsouvienne position, standing anywhere in the hall.

Steps: Mazurka, waltz

First Figure: Partners Change Sides Four Times

Meas. 1, 2: W takes three steps to her L and points as M takes three steps to his R and points, to change places. M footwork: cross L foot behind R foot (ct. 1); step to R with R foot (ct. 2); cross L foot in front of R foot (ct. 3); place R foot diagonally fwd. and touch R heel to floor (cts. 1, 2, 3). W footwork: step to L with L foot (ct. 1); cross R foot in front of L foot (ct. 2); step to L with L foot (ct. 3); place R foot diagonally fwd. and R heel to floor (cts. 1, 2, 3). M now has his L arm around WL shoulder.

Meas. 3, 4: Using opposite footwork, M moving to his L and W moving to her R, partners change places again to assume original position.

Meas. 5–8: Repeat actions of meas. 1–4.

Second Figure: Mazurkas and Change Sides

Meas. 9, 10: Starting with L foot, partners take two mazurka steps fwd. Glide fwd. on L foot (ct. 1); close R foot to L foot (ct. 2); hop on R foot, bending L knee outward (ct. 3). Repeat.

Meas. 11, 12: Partners change sides by repeating action of meas. 1–2.

Meas. 13, 14: Starting with R foot, partners take two mazurka steps fwd.

Meas. 15, 16: Partners face each other, taking three short steps, and assume closed dance position: step R (ct. 1); step L (ct. 2); step R (ct. 3); closed dance position (cts. 1, 2, 3).

Third Figure: Waltz

Meas. 17–24: Take six waltz steps turning CW (6 measures), then W twirls R under her R arm (cts. 1, 2, 3), and partners assume original position (cts. 1, 2, 3).

LECH LAMIDBAR
(Israeli)

(IMF 2002)
Tempo 2/4

Formation: Single circle, all facing center, hands joined, arms down. No partners required.

Steps: Leap, step-draw, step-hop, grapevine, balance

First Figure: Leap, Step-Draw

Meas. 1, 2: Leap to R (ct. 1); cross L in front of R, placing weight on L (ct. and); take small step to R on R foot (cts. 2 and). Then two step-draws to L: swd. L (ct. 1); place R next to L (ct. and); swd. L (ct. 2); place R next to L, keeping weight on L (ct. and).

Meas. 3–8: Repeat action of meas. 1–2 three times.

Second Figure: Step-Hop, Grapevine

Meas. 9, 10: Step on R, in place (ct. 1); hop on R and kick L fwd. (ct. and); step on L, in place (ct. 2); hop on L and kick R fwd. (ct. and). Grapevine to L: cross R in front of L (ct. 1); place L to side (ct. and); cross R behind L (ct. 2); place L to side (ct. and).

Meas. 11–16: Repeat action of meas. 9–10 three times.

Third Figure: Balance

Meas. 17, 18: Balance to R, then to L, then fwd., then bwd.

Meas. 19, 20: Repeat action of meas. 17–18.

Fourth Figure: Grapevine

Meas. 19–22: Grapevine to L: cross R in front of L (ct. 1); place L to side (ct. and); cross R behind L (ct. 2); place L to side (ct. and); cross R in front of L (ct. 1); place L to side (ct. and); cross R behind L (ct. 2); hop on R (ct. and). Grapevine to R: cross L in front of R (ct. 1); place R to side (ct. and); cross L behind R (ct. 2); place R to R side (ct. and); cross L in front of R (ct. 1); place R to side (ct. and); cross L in back (ct. 2); hop on L (ct. and).

KOHANOCHKA
(Russian)

(Folkraft 1423)

Tempo 2/4

Formation: Couples in double circle formation with W on outside, facing CCW, inside hands joined, palms of outside hands on chest.

Steps: Polka, Russian polka, balance

First Figure: Russian Polka

Meas. 1, 2: All take two Russian polka steps fwd. starting with outside foot. M footwork: Leap fwd. L (ct. 1); step fwd. R (ct. and); step fwd. L (cts. 2 and). W uses opposite footwork. On this first polka step, the joined hands swing fwd., and the other hands swing bwd. and out. Leap fwd. R (ct. 1); step fwd. L (ct. and); step fwd. R (cts. 2 and). W uses opposite footwork. On this second polka step, the joined hands swing back, and the other hands swing across the chest.

Meas. 3–8: Repeat action of meas. 1–2 three times.

Second Figure: Balance, Russian Polka

Meas. 9, 10: Assume Varsouvienne position facing CCW. Balance fwd. on L and bwd. on R.

Meas. 11, 12: Starting L, take two Russian polka steps fwd., as in meas. 1–2.

Meas. 13–16: Repeat action of meas. 9–12.

Third Figure: Polka

Meas. 17–20: Partners face each other with M back to center of circle. Clap own hands twice: clap (cts. 1 and); clap (cts. 2 and). Both take three polka steps bwd., away from each other. During these three polka steps, M crosses arms in front of his chest, and W places hands on hips.

Meas. 21–24: Both clap twice, then take three polka steps fwd., passing partner's R side.

Meas. 25–28: Both clap twice, then take three polka steps bwd., passing partner's L side.

Meas. 29, 30: Both clap twice, then shake forefingers at each other: clap (cts. 1 and); clap (cts. 2 and); shake forefinger (cts. 1 and); shake forefinger (cts. 2 and).

Meas. 31, 32: Both take two polka steps: M turns to his L as W turns to her R. Partners are now side by side, facing LOD.

Mixers

During the opening minutes of a square or folk dance function, it is usually wise for the leader to call two or three mixers. There is no better way to induce a group of strangers to warm up and relax than to quickly teach a few simple dances in which partners change frequently. The loosening-up effect works as well with beginners as with more advanced dancers.

The music for the mixers on the following pages appears in Chapter 5. Don't worry about using the same record for a mixer and then later for a square dance: the figures for each type of dance are quite different.

TURKEY IN THE STRAW   (Worldtone 10023)

Formation: Couples in a single circle, W on R of M, with hands joined.
Steps: Slide, walk, stamp

First Figure: Slide

Meas. 1–4: All take eight sliding steps moving CW (cts. 1–4).
Meas. 5–8: All take eight sliding steps moving CCW (cts. 1–4).

Second Figure: Walk and Stamp

Meas. 9: All take two steps twd. center: L (cts. 1 and); R (cts. 2 and).
Meas. 10: All stamp three times: L (ct. 1); R (ct. 2); L (cts. 2 and).
Meas. 11: All take two steps bwd: R (cts. 1 and); L (cts. 2 and).
Meas. 12: All stamp three times: R (ct. 1); L (ct. 2); R (cts. 2 and).

Third Figure: Gentlemen Move Right

Meas. 13–16: All release hands. M move to R one position, passing in front of partners, then step bwd. into the circle. M original partner is now standing on his L. All join hands and re-form circle.

PISTOL PACKIN' MAMA   (Old Timer 1103)

Formation: Partners facing CCW in a double circle with W on outside, inside hands joined.
Steps: Walk

First Figure: Forward and Back

Meas. 1, 2: All take four steps fwd: L (cts. 1 and); R (cts. 2 and); L (cts. 1 and); R (cts. 2 and). Release hands.
Meas. 3, 4: Face partners, W facing center, M facing outside of circle. All take four steps bwd., away from partners: L (cts. 1 and); R (cts. 2 and); L (cts. 1 and); R (cts. 2 and).

Second Figure: Meet New Partner

Meas. 5, 6: All half L face. M is now facing a new W in outside circle (the lady on his partner's R), and W is facing a new M in inside circle. New partners move twd. each other: L (cts. 1 and); R (cts. 2 and); L (cts. 1 and); R (cts. 2 and).
Meas. 7, 8: New partners hook R elbows and walk fwd. around each other: L (cts. 1 and); R (cts. 2 and); L (cts. 1 and); R (cts. 2 and).

Third Figure: Promenade

Meas. 9–16: New partners assume promenade position and walk fwd. CCW (cts. 1–8).

RIG A JIG   (Folkraft 1415)

Formation: Couples in a single circle, W on R of M. (Hands are not
    joined.)
Steps: Bumpsy-daisy, swing, promenade

First Figure: Bumpsy-Daisy, Swing

Meas. 1: All clap hands twice (cts. 1 and 2 and).
Meas. 2: All clap hands on own knees twice (cts. 1 and 2 and).
Meas. 3: All touch partners hip to hip twice (cts. 1 and 2 and).
Meas. 4: All face corners (cts. 1 and 2 and).

Second Figure: Swing Corners

Meas. 5, 6: All swing corners.
Meas. 7, 8: Assume promenade position with corners (new partners).

Third Figure: Promenade

Meas. 9–15: Promenade with new partners CCW.
Meas. 16: Re-form single circle, all face center, W on their new part-
    ners' R.

The caller can sing the prompts for this mixer in tune to the music, as
follows:
    Meas. 1: Clap your hands,
    Meas. 2: Clap your knees,
    Meas. 3, 4: Bumpsy-daisy, if you please.
    Meas. 5, 6: Now swing your corner lady round
    Meas. 7, 8: And promenade around the town.
    Meas. 9–15: Promenade around you go, promenade on heel and
        toe, hold on tight and don't let go,
    Meas. 16: Now circle up and don't be slow.

PATTY CAKE POLKA   (Folkraft 1145)

This mixer is a folk dance, described fully on page 262.
The caller can assist the dancers by using the following prompt calls:

Meas. 1, 2: Heel and toe, heel and toe,
Meas. 3, 4: Slide, slide, slide, slide.
Meas. 5, 6: Heel and toe, heel and toe,
Meas. 7, 8: Slide, slide, slide, slide.
Meas. 9: Right, right, right,
Meas. 10: Left, left, left,
Meas. 11: Both, both, both,
Meas. 12: Knees, knees, knees,
Meas. 13, 14: Right elbow round, go on to the next,
Meas. 15, 16: And now we start again.

OH SUSANNAH   (Folkraft 1186)

Formation: Couples in a single circle, W on R of M, all facing center.
Steps: Walk, promenade

First Figure: Walk, Promenade

Meas. 1, 2: W walk four steps fwd. to center: L (cts. 1 and); R (cts. 2 and); L (cts. 1 and); R (cts. 2 and).
Meas. 3, 4: W walk four steps bwd. to places: L (cts. 1 and); R (cts. 2 and); L (cts. 1 and); R (cts. 2 and).
Meas. 5–8: M repeat action of meas. 1–8.

Second Figure: Grand Right and Left

Meas. 9–16: At chorus of song, starting, "Oh, Susannah don't you cry for me," all face partners, give R hand to partners and do a grand R and L, M moving CCW and W moving CW. M counts partner as number one, then stops at the seventh girl he meets and assumes promenade position with her. New couples promenade CCW until end of song, then form single circle once again, all facing center, with W on her new partner's R. The dance may be repeated several times.

IRISH WASHERWOMAN   (Folkraft 1155)

Formation: Couples in a single circle, W on R of M, with hands joined.
Steps: Walk, stamp, swing, promenade

First Figure: Walk, Stamp

Meas. 1, 2: All walk four steps fwd. to center of circle: L (cts. 1 and); R (cts. 2 and); L (cts. 1 and); R (cts. 2 and).
Meas. 3, 4: All stamp L four times (4 cts.).
Meas. 5, 6: All walk bwd. four steps: L (cts. 1 and); R (cts. 2 and); L (cts. 1 and); R (cts. 2 and).

Second Figure: Swing

Meas. 7, 8: Each M swings corner W.
Meas. 9–16: Promenade corners (new partners) CCW around circle. At end of chorus, re-form single circle, all face center, W on their new partners' R.

Repeat as often as desired. The caller may sing the step calls as follows:
  Meas. 1, 2: All join hands and go to the middle
  Meas. 3, 4: And with your big foot keep time to the fiddle.
  Meas. 5, 6: And when you get back remember my call,
  Meas. 7–16: Swing on the corner and promenade all.

8

SENIOR CITIZENS:
HOW DANCES
SHOULD BE REVISED
TO MEET THEIR NEEDS

All too often, dance sessions for senior citizens have to be curtailed because the dancers become tired and frustrated. Tired, because the leader presents dances that are too fast-moving and meant for younger bodies. Frustrated, because the dances call for uncomfortable body movements and an agility which the older folk no longer possess.

How is a program of square and folk dancing geared for senior citizens different from a function in which only younger people participate? Basically the difference lies in the degree of difficulty of the dances which the group can perform successfully. Also, the number of dances offered during a particular time slot must be reduced in order to avoid fatigue. In the typical (non-senior) dance program, square dances are usually offered in "tips" of three. Senior citizens, however, should rarely do more than two square dances at a time before resting. When folk dances are introduced, they should always be taught after a rest period; similarly, a "tip" of two square dances should be taught after a rest period.

The leader must revise those dance movements which older dancers find too difficult or enervating to perform. For example, the square dance buzz swing should be replaced by the Right Elbow Walk Around, in which partners hook right elbows and walk forward one full turn around each other. In the same vein, slides to the left or right should be replaced by walking steps. When dances call for running steps, the leader should cut the time in half, so that the dancers can walk instead. Figures like "wring the dishrag" (see Glossary) should be eliminated in favor of having the dancers simply turning once around in place. In the schottische, dancers can be instructed to hold on the fourth count instead of hopping; similarly, eliminating the hops in a dance like the Jessie Polka will not affect the timing or other movements of the dance. Whenever fast two-steps are indicated, they should be replaced by walking steps. Leaps too, should be avoided, as, for example, the leap on the pas de basque step, which can easily be replaced by a simple step to the dancer's right or left.

There are numerous other instances in which steps should be simplified. Suffice it to say that all dance movements involving running, hopping, sliding, excessive arm extension, and the like should be revised.

As an example, here is how I have revised the steps of the Danish Dance, To Tur (page 268), so that senior citizens can perform it without difficulty. The revisions are in bold type.

Formation: Single circle of couples, W on R of M, all facing center, hands joined at shoulder height.

Meas. 1–8: **Sixteen walking steps moving CW, starting on L foot: step L (cts. 1 and), etc. Do not transfer weight on last ct. but point R toe to R.**

Meas. 9–16: **Repeat action of meas. 1–8, starting on R foot, moving CCW, except on last ct. place feet together.**

Meas. 17, 18: **Partners in closed dance position. Take 2 step-draws twd. center and point toe of outside foot. M footwork: swd. L (cts. 1 and); place R alongside L (cts. 2 and); swd. L (cts. 1 and); touch R toe alongside of L instep (cts. 2 and). W uses opposite footwork.**

Meas. 19, 20: Repeat action of meas. 17–18, moving twd. outside of circle, starting MR, WL.

Meas. 21–24: **Cpls. in semi-closed position, take eight steps CCW, starting ML and WR foot: step L (cts. 1 and), etc.**

Meas. 25–32: Repeat action of meas. 17–24.

Meas. 33–48: **All do a grand R and L around circle. Counting partner as number one, stop at fourteenth person and take new partner in closed dance position.** (If the musical sequence ends before the dancers arrive at person number fourteen, this number may be reduced to ten or twelve.)

Repeat meas. 17–48 until end of record.

In measures 1–16, two-steps have been replaced by walking steps. In measures 17 and 18, the two-step and walk are replaced by two step-draws. All other two-steps are replaced by walking steps.

Now let's analyze how a dance can be revised by comparing the senior citizen version of Csebogar with the original (page 264). The revisions are printed in bold type.

Formation: Single circle of couples, W on R of M, all facing center, hands joined.

Meas. 1–4: **All dancers take eight walking steps moving CW, starting L foot. Do not transfer weight on last ct., but point R toe to R.**

Meas. 5–8: **Repeat action of meas. 1–4, starting R foot, moving CCW. On last ct. place L foot next to R foot. All face center.**

Meas. 9–12: Follow original version, but using opposite footwork, as follows: All walk fwd., raising arms: fwd. **R** (cts. 1 and); fwd. **L** (cts. 2 and; fwd. **R** (cts 1 and); stamp **L** (cts. 2 and). All walk bwd., lowering arms: bwd. **R** (cts. 1 and); bwd. **L** (cts. 2 and); bwd. **R** (cts. 1 and); stamp **L** (cts. 2 and).

Meas. 13–16: **Face partners, hook R elbows and do a REWA in eight steps, starting L foot.**

Meas. 17–20: Face partners in single circle, M facing CCW, and W facing CW. Hands are joined and extended out to the side. Take four step-draws twd. center. M footwork: step swd. with L (cts. 1 and); close R to L (cts. 2 and). Do three more of these step-draws. Weight is not placed on R on last step-draw. W does opposite footwork. With each step-draw, arms rock up and down.

Meas. 21–24: Four step-draws away from center. Weight is not transferred on last step.

Meas. 25–28: Partners take two step-draws twd. center, then two step-draws away from center.

Meas. 29–32: Repeat action of meas. 13–16.

In measures 1–4, the original version calls for eight sliding steps to the left. Since this takes eight beats, I substituted eight walking steps to the left (CW), beginning with the left foot. Note, however, that the simple expedient of using a point rather than a step on the last beat facilitates a smooth reversal of direction because weight is not transferred on the last count. The dancers can now move eight steps to the right beginning with the right foot, ending with the left foot, which is placed alongside the right foot.

Since the right foot is now free, we use footwork which is opposite from that in the original instructions and, in measures 9–12, starting with the right foot, take four steps into the center and four steps back to place.

In measures 13–16, I replaced the skipping steps around partners with eight walking steps starting with the left foot. This is a Right Elbow Walk Around (REWA in the dance description).

I used the original instructions for measures 17–28 because seniors can perform step-draws without difficulty.

In measures 29–32, I again substituted walking steps for skipping steps.

As you become more experienced, you, too, will develop the facility for making revisions in many other folk dances in order to meet the needs of senior citizens.

SQUARE DANCE GLOSSARY

ALL AROUND YOUR LEFT-HAND LADY (Figs. 37–40, page 146) All dancers face their corners and walk forward around each other, keeping right shoulders adjacent. Dancers return to places and face their partners. This figure is frequently followed by *Seesaw Your Partner* (Figs. 41–44, pages 147–148), in which partners walk forward around each other, keeping left shoulders adjacent, then step forward to face their corners.

ALLEMANDE LEFT (Fig. 22, page 96) The gentlemen turn left to face their corners as the ladies turn right to face their corners. Each gentleman takes his corner lady's left hand in his left hand and walks completely around her in a counterclockwise direction, to return to his home position as she returns to her home position.

ALLEMANDE LEFT, ALAMO STYLE All dancers do an allemande left and return to their places, still holding left hands. Then they give their right hands to their partners, forming an unbroken circle with the gentlemen facing into the center and the ladies facing out. All dancers take one step forward, then one step back to places. They release left hands and, as in a right and left grand, join left hands with the next dancer they meet; but they continue to hold right hands. Now the circle has been re-formed, with the gentlemen facing out and the ladies facing in. All dancers take one step forward and back. These right-and-left-and-balance movements are continued until partners meet at the opposite side of the set. Partners then promenade counterclockwise back to their home positions.

ALLEMANDE LEFT, ALLEMANDE THAR All dancers do an allemande left and then start a right and left grand. When the gentlemen reach their original right-hand ladies, they join left hands with them and move into the center to form a right hand star, and all eight dancers turn the star counterclockwise. The gentlemen are moving backward and the ladies are moving forward.

299

BALANCE   Dancers step forward and pause while bringing the other foot forward and touching it to the floor without transferring weight. Dancers step back on the free foot and pause while touching the other foot beside it.

BALANCE (STEP-SWING)   Partners face each other and join right hands. They step on the right foot, then hop on the right foot as they swing the left foot across in front of the right foot. They then step on the left foot, and hop on the left foot as they swing the right foot across in front of the left foot.

BASKET SWING   (Fig. 25, page 111) This movement is performed in the *California breadbasket* formation. All dancers place their right feet slightly in front of their left feet, and pushing with their left feet, as in the buzz swing, circle to the left. They start slowly but gain momentum as they continue to circle.

BOX THE GNAT (Figs. 86–88, page 184)   The lady and gentleman join right hands and walk forward, exchanging positions, the lady making a left face turn under their joined right hands.

BOYS RUN RIGHT (Figs. 98–100, page 193)   This figure starts when a gentleman has his shoulder adjacent to another dancer. The gentleman moves forward in a semicircle to his right around the adjacent dancer, to end in that dancer's starting position. At the same time, the adjacent dancer, who may be facing in any direction, sidesteps into the gentleman's starting position without changing facing direction. The gentleman has reversed his original facing direction.

BUZZ STEP   See *Swing.*

CALIFORNIA BREADBASKET (Figs. 24–25, page 111)   This figure can be performed by two, three or four couples. With two couples, the two ladies join both hands and the two gentlemen join both hands above the ladies' joined hands. The two gentlemen raise their joined hands and lower them behind the ladies' backs. The two ladies then raise their joined hands and lower them behind the gentlemen's backs, thus forming an interlocking California breadbasket.

With three couples, starting from a circle of six, the six dancers release hands and the three ladies join hands to form a circle of three, as the three gentlemen join hands to form a circle of three around the ladies. The three ladies raise their joined hands and bring them down behind the backs of the gentlemen standing alongside of them to form a California breadbasket of six dancers.

With four couples, starting with a circle of eight, the eight dancers perform all the movements described above for three couples.

CALIFORNIA TWIRL (Figs. 69–73, page 173)   Partners are standing side by side, the lady on the gentleman's right. The gentleman's right hand holds the lady's left hand as hands are raised to form an arch. The lady walks forward under their joined hands, making a 180-degree left turn, as the man walks around the lady in a clockwise direction, turning 180 degrees to his right. Dancers have exchanged places and are facing in the opposite direction from which they started.

CHASE RIGHT   This figure starts with two couples standing back to back. Each lady walks to her right in a full 360-degree circle to end in the position of the lady who was diagonally behind her to finish facing in the same direction as when she started the action. Her partner follows her and turns 180 degrees to his right to stand next to her to finish facing out. Partners are now facing in opposite directions.

CIRCLE   All dancers join hands, form a circle of eight, and walk either to the left or right, as indicated by the caller.

CIRCLE TO A LINE (Figs. 89–94, page 190)   This formation starts with facing couples. The couples circle left one half (180 degrees). The lead dancer (the gentleman who started on the inside) releases his left handhold, retains the handhold of the dancer on his right, and becomes the dancer at the left end of the line. The released dancer moves forward to the right end of the line, turning left under the raised right hand of her partner.

CORNER   The gentleman's corner is the lady standing on his left, and the lady's corner is the gentleman standing on her right (see *Set*).

COUPLE   A couple consists of a gentleman and his lady partner. In a square set (see *Set*), the ladies stand to the right of the gentlemen.

COURTESY TURN (Fig. 35, page 141)   This movement starts from a couple formation, with the lady facing the gentleman. The gentleman takes the lady's left hand in his left hand, and places his right hand on the small of the lady's back. Turning together, the couple turns around with the gentleman backing up and the lady walking forward. The couple finishes this movement facing either the center of the set or the center of the formation from which the courtesy turn started.

CROSS TRAIL THRU (Figs. 151–154, page 246)   The two designated couples face each other and pass thru each other, opposites passing right shoulders. Immediately after passing thru, each couple does a cross trail thru, with the lady crossing over to her left in front of the gentleman, and the gentleman going to his right in back of the lady.

DIP AND DIVE (Figs. 32–33, page 136)   This is a continuous figure involving three couples. It starts with two facing couples, one couple with its back to the center of the set. The third couple is on the opposite side of the set. The couple with its back to the center raises its inside hands to form an arch. The facing couple ducks through the arch to the center of the set. The couple in the center now raises its hands to form an arch, and the opposite couple ducks through to the center of the set. As this is happening, the couple that had formed the arch in the center of the set moves forward to the opposite side of the set and turns to face the center, with the lady staying on her partner's right. The new couple in the center now forms an arch, and the dip and dive procedure continues until the three couples return to their original positions.

DO-PASO (Figs. 60–64, page 170)   All dancers do a left forearm 180-degree turn with their partners, then a right forearm 180-degree turn with their corners. The gentlemen then take their partner's left hand in their left hand, place their right arm around their partner's waist, and turn her counterclockwise in place to face the center of the set again *(courtesy turn)*. (If the next figure involves a movement such as a gentlemen's right hand star, the courtesy turn is replaced by a left 180-degree forearm turn, so that the gentlemen's right hands are free to form the right hand star.)

DO-SA-DO   Two designated dancers walk toward each other and pass right shoulders. After passing each other one step, both dancers side-step to their right, passing back to back, then walk backward to their original positions.

EIGHT ROLL AWAY WITH A HALF SASHAY (Figs. 168–170, page 258)   From a couple side-by-side formation, the dancer on the right rolls across a full turn (360 degrees) in front of the dancer on the left, as he sidesteps to the right to exchange places. (In Figs. 168–171, this figure is performed from a Texas star formation. This maneuver is also frequently performed in a circle formation, the ladies rolling left across in front of the gentlemen on their left.)

ELBOW SWING (Fig. 47, page 158)   Dancers link right elbows and dance around each other in a clockwise direction, using the *buzz step* (see *Swing*). Gentleman's right and lady's left feet may be separated from each other somewhat more than in the buzz swing.

FOREARM TURN   Facing dancers join forearms and walk forward around each other the distance specified: half, three quarters, full circle. Each dancer places his hand on the inside of the arm of the person being turned. The fingers and thumb are held in close.

FOUR LADIES CHAIN   See *Ladies Grand Chain*.

GALS ROLL BACK   All couples promenade around the set. Ladies separate from their partners and do a complete full turn to their right, in place, as the next gentlemen move alongside and promenade with them. This is usually done four times until all have original partners.

GRAND RIGHT AND LEFT   See *Right and Left Grand.*

HEAD COUPLES   In a square set (see *Set*), the head couples are couples numbered one and three.

HOME POSITION   This is the station at which the couples stand at the beginning of a square dance. See *Set* for the location of the different home positions.

HONOR   Gentlemen bow by inclining their torso slightly forward, and ladies curtsey by holding their skirt, placing their right toe behind their left foot and taking a half knee bend, inclining their torso slightly forward.

LADIES CHAIN (Figs. 34–35, page 141)   Two couples face each other. The two ladies pass each other's right shoulder, joining right hands briefly as they do so, then continue to walk to the opposite gentlemen. The two gentlemen take their opposite lady's left hands in their left hand, place their right arm around the opposite lady's waist, and turn her around in place, counterclockwise *(courtesy turn).*

LADIES GRAND CHAIN (Figs. 55–58, page 169)   The four ladies step into the center of the set, form a right hand star, and turn the star clockwise until they reach the opposite side of the set and stand in front of their opposite gentlemen. The ladies release right hands. Each gentleman takes his opposite lady's left hand in his left hand and places his right arm around the lady's waist, turning her counterclockwise. Ladies form the right hand star again, and continue to turn the star clockwise until they reach their partners. Each gentleman turns his partner in place, just as he did his opposite lady *(courtesy turn).*

LADIES THREE QUARTERS CHAIN   Two or four ladies walk forward, form a right hand star and turn the star three quarters so that each lady is standing in front of her right-hand couple. Each lady's right-hand gentleman takes her left hand in his left hand, places his right arm around her waist, and turns her around in place counterclockwise to finish facing the center of the set *(courtesy turn).*

LEFT-HAND COUPLE   This is the couple in a set standing one station to the left of a designated couple (see *Set*).

LEFT-HAND LADY (OR GENT)   The gentleman's left-hand lady is the lady standing on his left, or his corner lady. The lady's left-hand gent is the gentleman occupying one station to her left in the *set*.

OCEAN WAVE (Fig. 48, page 161)   This is a formation of three or more dancers holding adjacent hands, each dancer facing in the opposite direction to that of the adjoining dancer.

OPPOSITE COUPLE   This is the couple standing directly opposite a designated couple in a set, as in the case of couple number one and couple number three (see *Set*).

OPPOSITE GENT (OR LADY)   This is the gentleman or lady standing directly opposite a dancer's position, as in the case of gentleman number two and lady number four (see *Set*).

PARTNER   In a square set, partners stand side by side, the ladies to the right of the gentlemen (see *Set*).

PASS THE LEFT-HAND DANCER UNDER (Fig. 31, page 132) This maneuver is usually performed with two lines of three facing each other on opposite sides of a set. In each line of three, a gentleman has one lady standing on his right and one lady on his left. The lines of three have hands joined. The two ladies on either side of the gentlemen take a short step forward and face each other. The gentlemen raise their right hands to form an arch and the ladies on their left duck under the arch and advance in the direction of the set position they are facing. At the same time, the right-hand ladies cross in front of the gentlemen and advance in the direction of the set position they are facing.

   In some instances, the lines of three facing each other have ladies in the center, flanked by a gentleman on their left and lady on their right (Fig. 166, page 256). In this formation, after the center ladies raise their right hand to form the arch, it is the gentlemen who duck under the arch and advance in the direction of the set position they are facing, as the right-hand ladies advance in the opposite direction.

PASS THRU (Figs. 95–97, page 192)   Facing dancers in each of two lines move forward, opposites passing right shoulders. Each line ends in the other's starting position. The dancers do not change facing positions, so that the two lines now have their backs toward each other.

PROMENADE, SKATING POSITION (Fig. 18a, page 74)   Two dancers stand side by side, the lady to the right of the gentleman. The gentleman, with his palms up, holds the lady's left hand in his left hand

and her right hand in his right hand. Thus, their arms are crossed in front of them, with the gentleman's right arm held over the lady's left arm. (Although this version of promenade position is the one recommended by Callerlab, the *Varsouvienne position* is still used rather frequently.)

PROMENADE, VARSOUVIENNE POSITION (Fig. 18b, page 75) Two dancers stand side by side, the lady to the right of the gentleman. The gentleman reaches behind the lady's back and holds her right hand over her right shoulder; he holds her left hand in his left hand, in front.

RIGHT AND LEFT GRAND (Fig. 23, page 97) Partners face each other, join right hands and pull by, passing right shoulders. Each moves forward, around the circle, men moving counterclockwise and ladies moving clockwise. Each gives a left hand to the next, passing left shoulders, a right to the next, a left to the next, until all dancers meet their partners.

RIGHT AND LEFT THRU (Fig. 36, page 142) Two couples face each other and exchange places by passing through the opposite couple. In this movement, the facing dancers step forward, join right hands with the dancers directly ahead (opposites), and pull by. When each couple arrives at the other couple's station, each gentleman takes his partner's left hand in his left hand, places his right arm around her waist, and turns her counterclockwise in place to face his original position *(courtesy turn)*.

RIGHT-HAND COUPLE This is the couple in a set standing one station to the right of a designated couple (see *Set*).

RIGHT-HAND LADY (OR GENT) The gentleman's right-hand lady is the lady occupying one station to his right in the *set*.

RIP 'N' SNORT (Figs. 29–30, page 124) All dancers join hands and form a circle of eight. The designated couple walks across the set and passes under the arch formed by the raised inside hands of the opposite couple. All dancers continue to hold hands. After passing through the arch, the active couple separates, the gentleman going to his left and the lady to her right, leading the other dancers through the arch, and returns to its home position. The couple who formed the arch turns under their own arms to *wring the dishrag* and face the center of the set again.

ROLLAWAY   The designated dancer, or if not specified, the dancer on the right, rolls across a full 360-degree left turn in front of the dancer on the left, as he sidesteps to the right, to exchange places. In circle formation, the ladies roll across in front of the gentlemen.

SASHAY   The sashay is a series of short, quick sliding steps either to the right or to the left. To sashay to the left, step sideward to the left with the left foot, then close the right foot to the left foot, shifting the weight onto the right foot. This movement is usually done four times by an individual, a couple, or several couples.

SEPARATE   A couple separates by turning to stand back to back. Each dancer now walks forward around the outside of the set. The distance walked depends on the next call.

SET (Fig. 10, page 30)   Four couples comprise a set. Each couple stands on the side of an imaginary square whose dimensions are approximately ten feet by ten feet. Each couple faces into the center of the set. Couple One stands with backs to the caller. Couple Two stands to the right of Couple One. Couple Three stands directly opposite Couple One. Couple Four stands to the left of Couple One.

SIDE COUPLES   In a square set, the side couples are Couples Two and Four (see *Set*).

SLIDE THRU (Figs. 101–104, page 194)   Facing dancers *pass thru.* After they have exchanged places, the gentlemen turn right one quarter (90 degrees), and the ladies turn left one quarter.

SPLIT THE RING   The active couple moves forward and passes between the dancers of the opposite couple, who separate slightly to let them pass through. The separated couple then steps together again.

SQUARE THRU (Figs. 74–81, page 176)   Opposite dancers join right hands and pull by. Each dancer turns in one quarter (90 degrees) to face his partner, then joins left hands and pulls by. At this point *square thru one half,* or *two hands square thru* is completed. Dancers turn in once again one quarter (90 degrees), join right hands with opposite dancers and pull by. A *square thru three quarters,* or *three hands square thru,* is now completed. All turn in one quarter (90 degrees), join left hands with partners and pull by, but do *not* turn in. A *full square thru,* or *four hands square thru* is now completed.

In the *square thru* movement dancers give their right hand to their opposite, pull by, do a quarter turn to face their partner, do a left hand pull by, turn a quarter and continue until the figure is completed. When a *five hands square thru* is called, all dancers do turn in at the end of the full square thru, to face their opposites. Opposites then do a right hand pull by, but do not turn in one quarter.

STAR (Fig. 20, page 88)   The star can be done with two or more facing dancers. When moving forward, the inside hands should be joined in a *palm star* position, with the hands touching at about eye level, fingers up, the palm of one dancer's hand resting on the back of the hand of the dancer standing in front of him. When gentlemen only form a star, they use the *packsaddle* position, in which each man grasps the wrist of the man in front of him (Fig. 123, page 229).

STAR THRU (Figs. 66–68, page 173)   With two dancers facing each other, the gentleman's right hand is placed against the lady's left, palms touching, fingers pointed up, to form an arch. Dancers move forward and the lady does a 90-degree left face turn under the arch, as the gentleman does a 90-degree right turn moving behind the lady. They finish side by side, with the lady on the gentleman's right.

SWING (Fig. 17, page 73)   The gentleman takes the lady in the *closed dance position* (see folk dance glossary). Both dancers place the ball of the right foot on the outside and to the right of the other's right foot, and move up alongside one another so that the right hips are almost touching. The *buzz step* is now used to move around each other, clockwise. The ball of the right foot is used as the pivot. The right foot should be raised and lowered rhythmically very close to the pivot point on the floor as the left foot is used to propel the body around in a circle. The toes of the left foot push downward and backward with each step.

TEXAS STAR (Fig. 123, page 229)   This may be either a right or a left hand Texas star. If a left hand Texas star, the gentlemen form a left hand star, place their right arms around the waists of the designated ladies, and turn the Texas star counterclockwise.

THREE LADIES CHAIN (Figs. 140–144, page 241)   This figure involves three couples. It starts with two facing couples, one couple with its back to the center of the set. The third couple is on the opposite side of the set. The two facing couples do a *ladies chain,* with the gentleman who has his back to the center turning halfway around with his new lady to finish facing the opposite couple. The two new facing couples do a *ladies chain,* and again the gentleman in the center of the set turns his new partner halfway around so that he and his new partner are facing in the same direction in which the maneuver was started. This chaining movement is continued until the three ladies return to their original partners.

THREE QUARTERS CHAIN   See *Ladies Three Quarters Chain.*

TURN THRU (Figs. 82–85, page 179)   Facing dancers step forward and join right forearms. They walk halfway around each other, clockwise, release armholds, and step forward, passing each other's right shoulder. They are now facing in the opposite direction from which they started the turn.

U TURN BACK   Each dancer does an in-place 180-degree about-face turn.

WEAVE THE RING   This figure is a *right and left grand* performed without touching hands.

WRING THE DISHRAG (Fig. 30, page 125)   This figure is performed by one couple that has raised its inside hands to form an arch, allowing other dancers to pass under the arch. As the last dancer passes through the arch, the arching couple wrings the dishrag: the gentleman's right hand continues to hold the lady's left hand in the arch position as he turns 360 degrees to his right and she turns 360 degrees to her left.

FOLK DANCE GLOSSARY

BALANCE (tempo 3/4, 2/4, 4/4)   This step may start on either foot and move in any direction. In 3/4 tempo, if starting with R foot, step R foot in any direction (ct. 1); close L foot to R foot while raising heels slightly off the floor (ct. 2); lower heels to the floor (ct. 3). In 4/4 tempo, if starting fwd., step fwd. with L foot (ct. 1); close R foot to L foot while raising heels slightly off the floor (ct. 2); step bwd. with R foot (ct. 3); close L foot to R foot (ct. 4). Another method of doing the balance step in 4/4 tempo is as follows: if going to the L, step to L on L foot (ct. 1); close R foot to L foot (ct. and); step in place on L foot (cts. 2 and); step to R on R foot (ct. 3); close L foot to R foot (ct. and); step in place on R foot (cts. 4 and).

BOKAZNI (tempo 4/4)   This step may be done on either foot. If starting with L foot, hop on L foot and touch R toe fwd. to floor (ct. 1); hop on L foot and touch R toe swd. to floor (ct. 2); hop on L foot, closing R foot to L foot (ct. 3); hold (ct. 4).

CHUG STEP (tempo 2/4)   This is a series of pushing steps done either to the L or to the R. If done to the L, place the ball of the R foot swd. making a slight pushing step (ct. and); step swd. to the L with L foot (ct. 1). Repeat this movement as often as required.

CIRCASSIA STEP (tempo 2/4)   This step may be done either to the L or to the R. If done to the L, cross R foot in front of L foot and turn slightly to L (cts. 1 and); step to the L with L foot, turning to face fwd. again (cts. 2 and); cross R foot behind L foot and turn slightly to R (cts. 1 and); leap to L on L foot, turning to face fwd. again (cts. 2 and).

CLOSED DANCE POSITION   Partners face each other squarely, with M holding his partner an inch or so to his R. M holds his L hand, palm up, at about shoulder level, and W rests her R hand, palm down and fingers relaxed, in ML hand. M holds WR hand lightly but firmly, with his L arm held out in an easy, graceful curve. M open R hand is held just below WL shoulder blade, with his elbow out to the side, a little below shoulder level. WL arm rests easily on M upper arm, and her L hand is held rather firmly behind MR shoulder. At the same time, MR hand should maintain a constant pressure on W back.

CROSS BACK HOLD POSITION   Partners are side by side, both facing in the same direction with W at R of M. M holds WR hand in his R hand behind her back, and W holds ML hand in her L hand behind his back.

CROSS OVER (tempo 2/4, 4/4 or 3/4)   Facing partners hold hands and change places with each other, W turning L under their joined R hands, taking two waltz steps (if done in 3/4 tempo) or four quick walking steps (if done in 2/4 or 4/4 tempo).

CROSS STEP (tempo 2/4)   When doing the cross step to the R, place L foot slightly in back of R foot (ct. 1); step to R with R foot (ct. 2); step fwd. with L foot, placing it in front of R foot (cts. 1, 2).

CUT STEP   This step may be done swd., fwd. or bwd. It is a quick displacement of one foot by the other. To do a cut step swd. to the L, stand with the weight on the L foot, R foot extended to the R side, off the floor. Swing the R foot toward the L foot, leaping onto the R foot and swinging the L foot swd. off the floor.

DIP (tempo 2/4 or 4/4)   This figure is done in *closed dance position*. M steps back on L, W fwd. on R, at the same time lifting the opposite foot off the floor (cts. 1 and); hold this position (cts. 2 and).

GRAND RIGHT AND LEFT   See *Right and Left grand*, page 305.

GRAPEVINE (tempo 2/4 or 4/4)   This step may be done going either to the L or to the R. If done to the L, cross R foot behind L foot (ct. 1); step swd. to the L with L foot (ct. 2); cross R foot in front of L foot (ct. 3); step swd. to the L with L foot (ct. 4). This grapevine step may also be started by crossing R foot in front of L foot.

HARMONICA STEP (tempo 2/4)   This step may start with either foot. If starting with L foot, cross L in front of R, moving L hip fwd. (ct. 1); step R in place (ct. and); step L in place (ct. 2); hop on L (ct. and).

HEEL AND TOE POLKA (tempo 2/4)   This step may be done starting with either foot. If starting with the L foot, touch L heel to the floor diagonally in front of R foot (cts. 1 and); touch the toe of L foot to the floor next to the R instep (cts. 2 and). (If desired, a hop may be taken on the R foot as the L foot is placed fwd., and again as it is brought next to R instep.) Following this, a normal polka step is done, starting with the L foot (see *Polka*).

HOP (tempo 2/4 or 4/4)   A hop is made by springing up in the air and landing on the same foot.

JUMP (tempo 2/4 or 4/4)   A jump is made by springing up from either one or both feet and landing simultaneously on both feet.

LEAP (tempo 2/4 or 4/4)   A leap is made by springing from either foot and landing on the other foot.

LINE OF DIRECTION   When dancers move CCW in a circle, they are moving in the line of direction.

MAZURKA (tempo 3/4)   This step is usually danced diagonally fwd. If moving diagonally fwd. to the L, take a gliding step fwd. with L foot (ct. 1); close R foot to L foot (ct. 2); hop on R foot, bending L knee outward and kicking L heel slightly toward R ankle (ct. 3).

MODIFIED MAZURKA (tempo 3/4)   This step may be done either fwd. diagonally to the L or fwd. diagonally to the R. If done to the L, lift the L foot in front of R foot (ct. 3); slide L foot along floor diagonally fwd. to the L (ct. 1); close R foot to L foot, taking weight on R foot (ct. 2).

PAS DE BASQUE (tempo 3/4, 6/8, 2/4, or 4/4)   This step is done first to the L and then to the R, or vice versa. In 3/4 tempo, if done to the L, leap swd. to the L on L foot (ct. 1); step on R foot in front of L foot (ct. 2); step bwd. in place on L foot (ct. 3). In 2/4 tempo, if done to the L, leap swd. to the L on L foot (ct. 1); step on R foot in front of L foot (ct. and); step bwd. in place on L foot (cts. 2 and).

POLKA (tempo 2/4)   The polka step consists of a quick hop followed by a two-step. To best describe the tempo of the hop, one might say that the number 2 beat of each measure is held just a fraction longer, and the hop is squeezed in just before the next number 1 beat. To do a polka step to the L, take a quick hop on the R foot (ct. and); step swd. to the L foot (ct. 1); close R foot to L foot (ct. and); step swd. to the L with L foot (ct. 2). (See page 54 for a detailed analysis of the polka.)

RIGHT AND LEFT GRAND   See square dance glossary, page 305.

RIGHT ELBOW WALK AROUND   The designated M and W face each other, lock R elbows and walk completely around each other, CW.

ROCK STEP (tempo 2/4)   This step may start with either foot. If starting with R foot, step fwd. R (ct. 1); rock back on L (ct. and); step bwd. on R (ct. 2); step L in place (ct. and).

RUSSIAN POLKA STEP (tempo 2/4)   This step may start with either foot. If starting with L foot, leap fwd. on L foot (ct. 1); step fwd. with R foot (ct. and); step fwd. with L foot (cts. 2 and).

SASHAY (tempo 2/4)   This is a smooth sliding step on the ball of the advancing foot, followed by a quicker closing step with the other foot. The closing step does not take a full half beat; as in the polka, it is squeezed in after the "and" and before the next beat. If done to the L, step swd. to the L with L foot (ct. 1); close R foot to L foot (ct. and); step swd. to the L with L foot (ct. 2); close R foot to L foot (ct. and).

SCHOTTISCHE (tempo 2/4, 4/4)   This step may be danced moving fwd., swd. or in place. If done fwd., step fwd. with L foot (ct. 1); step fwd. with R foot (ct. 2); step fwd. with L foot (ct. 3); hop on L foot (ct. 4). (See page 51 for a detailed analysis of the schottische.)

SEMI-CLOSED DANCE POSITION   Partners assume *closed dance position,* and M faces diagonally to his L and W faces diagonally to her R. Both are now facing in the same direction and may start a dance step going fwd. on the outside foot (ML and WR foot).

SKATING POSITION   Partners stand side by side, both facing in the same direction, W standing at R of M. Hands are joined in front, M holding WR hand in his R hand, and M holding WL hand in his L hand. MR arm is crossed over WL arm.

SLIDE   See *Sashay.*

STAR   See square dance glossary, page 307.

STEP-CLOSE (Tempo 3/4, 2/4)   This step may be taken in any direction. It consists of a step followed by a closing step made by the free foot to the supporting foot. If done to the L in 3/4 tempo, step swd. to L with L foot (cts. 1, 2); close R foot to L foot (ct. 3). If done to the L in 2/4 tempo, step swd. to L with L foot (cts. 1 and); close R foot to L foot (cts. 2 and).

STEP-DRAW Same as *step-close*, except that the closing foot is slid along the floor to the stationary foot.

STEP-HOP (tempo 2/4, 3/4)   This step consists of a step and a hop on the same foot. If done in 2/4 tempo, step on L foot (ct. 1); hop on L foot (ct. and); step on R foot (ct. 2); hop on R foot (ct. and). If done in 3/4 tempo, step on L foot (cts. 1, 2); hop on L foot (ct. 3); step on R foot (cts. 1, 2); hop on R foot (ct. 3).

STEP-SWING (tempo 2/4, 4/4)   This step is done to one side, then to the other side. If started to the L side, step in place on L foot (ct. 1); swing R foot across in front of L foot (ct. 2); step in place on R foot (ct. 3); swing L foot across in front of R foot (ct. 4). Frequently a light hop is taken on the supporting foot as the free foot is swinging across.

TWIRL (tempo 2/4)   This maneuver usually concludes a series of two-steps or polka steps, with partners facing. ML hand holds WR hand. W turns to her R, 360 degrees, under her R arm. W footwork: R (ct. 1); L (ct. and); R (ct. 2); L (ct. and). As the W does the twirl, M does either a two-step or polka step.

TWO-STEP (tempo 2/4)   This step may be done moving in any direction. If done to the L side, step to the L with L foot (ct. 1); close R foot to L foot (ct. and); step to the L with L foot (cts. 2 and). (See page 47 for a detailed analysis of the two-step.)

VARSOUVIENNE POSITION   Partners stand side by side, W to the R of M and slightly in front of M. MR arm is extended across in back of WR shoulder and M holds W raised R hand in his R hand. WL arm is extended across in front of M chest, and M holds WL hand in his L hand, at shoulder height.

WALTZ (tempo 3/4)   This step may be done moving fwd., bwd. or swd. If done going fwd., step fwd. with the L foot (ct. 1); step swd. with the R foot (ct. 2); close L foot to R foot (ct. 3). (See page 56 for a detailed analysis of the waltz step.)

SOURCES OF
SQUARE AND FOLK
DANCE RECORDS

The square and folk dance records referred to in this book may be obtained by writing or calling the following distributors:

Big "O" Record Service
P.O. Box 786
Springfield, VA 22150
    (703) 339-5771

Dance Record Dist./Folkraft
Records
10 Fenwick Street
Newark, NJ 07114
    (201) 243-8700

Fair 'N Square Records
816 Forest Hills Dr. SW
Rochester, MN 55901
    (800) 328-3800

Jim's Record Shop
163 Angelos
Memphis, TN 38104
    (901) 726-9601

Mail Order Master Record Service
10027 N. 19th Avenue
Phoenix, AZ 85021
    (602) 997-5355

Robertson Dance Supplies
3600 33rd Avenue
Sacramento, CA 95824
    (916) 421-1518

Rockin' Rhythms
Listening Post
2248 Casa Vista Drive, Rt. 1
Palm Harbor, FL 33563
    (813) 784-3294

Square Dance Record
Roundup, Inc.
957 Sheridan Blvd.
Denver, CO 80214
    (303) 238-4810

Tape and Record Service
3508 Palm Beach Blvd.
Ft. Myers, FL 33905
    (813) 332-4200

Vernon's Record Shop
106 Parmenter Road
Waltham, MA 02154
    (617) 894-9487

Worldtone Music
230 Seventh Avenue
New York, NY 10011
    (212) 691-1934

BIBLIOGRAPHY

History

Chuhoy, Anatole, and P. W. Manchester, eds. *The Dance Encyclopedia.* New York: Simon and Schuster, 1967.

Crawford, M. C. *Social Life in Old New England.* Boston: Little, Brown & Co., 1914.

Damon, S. Foster. *The History of Square Dancing.* Barre, Mass.: American Antiquarian Society, 1957. (Reprint from proceedings of the American Antiquarian Society, Worcester, Mass.)

Sachs, Curt. *World History of the Dance.* New York: W.W. Norton & Co., 1963.

Sharp, Cecil, and A. P. Oppe. *The Dance: An Historical Survey of Dancing in Europe.* London: Novello and Co., 1924.

Shaw, Dorothy Stott. *The Story of Square Dancing.* Handbook Series. Los Angeles: Sets in Order, 1967.

Shaw, Lloyd. *Cowboy Dances.* Caldwell, Ind.: Caxton Printers, 1939.

Ziner, Feenie. *The Pilgrims and Plymouth Colony.* New York: Harper & Row, 1961.

Square Dancing

Casey, Betty. *The Complete Book of Square Dancing.* Garden City, N.Y.: Doubleday & Co., 1976.

Chase, A. H. *The Singing Caller.* New York: Association Press, 1944.

Durlacher, Ed. *Honor Your Partner.* New York: Devin Adair Co., 1949.

Gowing, Gene. *Square Dancing for Everyone.* New York: Grosset & Dunlap, 1957.

Harris, Jane A. *Dance Awhile!* Minneapolis: Burgess Publishing Co., 1964. (Square dances, folk dances and mixers.)

Hunt, Paul. *Eight Yards of Calico.* New York: Harper & Row, 1952.

Jensen, Clayne R., and Mary Bee Jensen. *Square Dancing.* Provo, Utah: Brigham Young University Press, 1972.

Jones, J. W. *Square Dance.* Glendale, Calif.: Frontier Publishers, 1970.

Kennedy, D. and H. *Square Dances of America.* London: Novello and Co., 1935.

Kirkell, Miriam H. *Partners All, Places All!* New York: E. P. Dutton, 1949.

315

Kraus, Richard. *Square Dances of Today.* New York: A. S. Barnes & Co., 1950.

McNair, R. J. *Square Dance!* Garden City, N.Y.: Garden City Books, 1951.

Maddocks, Durward. *Swing Your Partners.* New York: Stephen Daye Press, 1950.

Mayo, Margot. *The American Square Dance.* New York: Oak Publications, 1964.

Owens, Lee. *Advanced Square Dance Figures of the West and Southwest.* Palo Alto, Calif.: Pacific Books, 1950.

Phillips, Patricia. *Contemporary Square Dance.* Dubuque, Iowa: W. C. Brown Co., 1968.

Putney, Cornelia. *Square Dance, U.S.A.* Dubuque, Iowa: W. C. Brown Co., 1955.

Shaw, Lloyd. *Cowboy Dances.* Caldwell, Ind.: Caxton Printers, 1939.

Folk Dancing

Coles, A. *Old English Country Dance Steps.* London: J. Curwen & Sons, 1909.

Duggin, Anne. *Folk Dances of European Countries.* New York: A. S. Barnes & Co., 1948.

Duggin, Anne. *Folk Dances of Scandinavia.* New York: A. S. Barnes & Co., 1948.

Duggin, Anne. *Folk Dances of the British Isles.* New York: A. S. Barnes & Co., 1948.

Duggin, Anne. *Folk Dances of the United States and Mexico.* New York: A. S. Barnes & Co., 1948.

Fox, Grace. *Folk Dancing.* New York: Ronald Press, 1957.

Hall, J. T. *Dance! Complete Guide to Social, Folk and Square Dancing.* Belmont, Calif.: Wadsworth Publishing Co., 1963.

Harris, Jane A. *Dance Awhile!* Minneapolis: Burgess Publishing Co., 1964. (Square dances, folk dances and mixers.)

Herman, Michael, ed. *Folk Dance Syllabus #1.* New York: Folk Dance House Pub., 1953.

Heaton, Alma. *Recreational Dancing.* Provo, Utah: Brigham Young University Press, 1965.

Playford, John. *The English Dancing Master.* Fascimile reprint of first edition (1651), with introduction by Margaret Dean Smith. New York: Association of Music Publishers, 1957.

Ryan, Grace L. *Dances of Our Pioneers.* New York: A. S. Barnes & Co., 1926.

Sharp, Cecil. *The Country Dance Book.* 6 volumes. London: Novello & Co., 1924.